FULL MOON, HIGH TIDE

TASTES AND TRADITIONS OF THE LOWCOUNTRY

© FULL MOON, HIGH TIDE

First Printing   November 2001   5,000

Copies of FULL MOON, HIGH TIDE may be obtained by
sending $22.95 plus $3.00 shipping to the address below.

Post Office Box 70131
Beaufort, SC 29902

Phone 1-843-470-0078
Fax 1-843-470-0079

Order forms are located in the back of the cookbook.

ISBN: 0-9711057-0-7

Printed in the USA by

WIMMER
C O O K B O O K S
Memphis
1-800-548-2537

Introduction

Beautiful Beaufort by the sea lies in the heart of the Lowcountry. The Lowcountry is the coastal plain stretching from Pawley's Island to the Savannah River. The eight-foot Lowcountry tide is one of the largest along the Eastern coast of America. The tide flows in and out of the marshlands located behind the barrier islands. Beaufort County is composed of sixty-four islands, many of which are connected by causeways and bridges. With the rise and fall of an eight-foot tide, it is no wonder that tide affects the everyday life of those who call the Lowcountry home.

The people of Beaufort have lived off the water, played on the water and made the water a part of their lives for over 300 years. Just as the tides of the Lowcountry are constant and ever-changing, the tastes and traditions of the Lowcountry are constant and ever-changing. This collection of recipes includes everything from traditional recipes passed down through generations, to more contemporary versions of Lowcountry cuisine.

Lowcountry cuisine plays on the incredibly lush bounty of the natural surroundings. The flow of the tide brings crabs, shrimp, fish and oysters; the fertile fields of the sea islands grow tomatoes, cucumbers, melons, corn and onions. Lowcountry cuisine is both innovative and extravagant, uniquely characterized by a combination of past cultures, African, West Indian, Mediterranean, English and French.

In the Lowcountry delicious food and good times go hand in hand. Today we are engaged in such busy lifestyles that time spent with family and friends has become more precious. To make every moment count, entertaining with family and friends may very often include the beauty of the outdoors, such as beach weekends, boating or sandbar picnics, oyster roasts and cookouts. With such a temperate climate in the Lowcountry, this co-dependence of man and nature is a cherished way of life.

Beaufort today is a fantastic melting pot of colorful cultures, where old-fashioned meets New Age. Where tradition and heritage are the solid foundation for the coming tide...

With *Full Moon, High Tide,* **Beaufort Academy** welcomes you within our circle of family and friends. We invite you to share our favorite Lowcountry tastes and traditions, hoping that they will bring as much joy to you as they have to us and our children.

About the Artist:

Alison Crossman was born and raised in Houston, Texas. Her love of painting began early. At the age of five, she took lessons at the Houston Museum of Fine Arts, followed by private lessons taught by various artists over the years. She attended Lake Forest College just outside of Chicago, Illinois, where she majored in both Art History and Studio Art.

Upon graduation Alison moved to New York City, where she put down her paints and enjoyed a successful career as a fashion model in both print and television.

After an eighteen year hiatus, Alison resumed her painting. She specializes in both oil landscapes and still-lifes, and her work is reminiscent of the Dutch School. She has had a one-man show in Beaufort, and her work has also been exhibited at The Prouts Neck Art Show in Maine. Her paintings are in a number of private collections from New Mexico to New England. She resides with her husband and two children (both of whom attend Beaufort Academy) on Spring Island, South Carolina, and summers in Nantucket. Her paintings can be seen in several galleries and boutiques in Beaufort.

Table of Contents

Beaufort Academy Cookbook Committee

Full Moon, High Tide has been lovingly produced by the Beaufort Academy Parents Association to provide families and friends of the school an opportunity to share with others their favorite recipes as well as their love of the South Carolina Lowcountry. All proceeds from the sale of *Full Moon, High Tide* will be used to support the educational mission of Beaufort Academy.

Beaufort Academy is an independent, coeducational, college preparatory day school of 400 students. The campus is located on Lady's Island, just east of Beaufort, South Carolina. Beaufort Academy offers a strong curriculum for children of all religious, racial, social and economic backgrounds who desire to be academically challenged in grades kindergarten through twelve.

Chairmen:

Cindy Collins

Mary Laffitte

Committee Members:

Genine Clark	Robin Koppernaes	Wanda Parks
Alison Crossman	Darryl Laffitte	Maura Rhodin
Janette Danielson	Lauren Laffitte	Beth Runyan
Harlene Deane	Grace Larson	Sharon Sanders
Jeni Feeser	Jane Manos	Sue Shuford
Lolita Huckabee	Erika Marshall	Sandra Turcotte
Kathy Kilgore	Vicki Mix	Martha Lynn Webb
	Kim Olsson	

Full Moon, High Tide Cocktail Fare

Marinated Beef Tenderloin
Horseradish Sauce or Spicy Mustard
Assorted Rolls
Salmon with Dill Sauce
Marinated Seafood and Tortellini Pasta
Mushroom Tarts
Olivada Crostini
Stuffed Cherry Tomatoes
Egg Salad on Endive
Nicole's Beaufort Brie
Gingersnaps, Apple and Pear Slices
Herb Nuts
Butter Crisps
Chocolate Almond Crunch

~

Valentine Dinner Party

Spinach Tart
Ginger Carrot Soup
St. Helena's Salad
Beef Tenderloin with Bordelaise Sauce
Roasted Asparagus and Potatoes
Molten Chocolate Cake with Fudge Sauce

Oyster Roast

Southwest Fiesta Cheesecake and Tortilla Chips
Oysters
Cocktail Sauce
Crackers
Brunswick Stew
Bite-Size Pecan Pies
Cary Cookies

~

Old South Supper

Crab Tarts
Spinach Artichoke Dip
Spinach and Arugula Salad with Champagne Vinaigrette
Herb and Garlic Crusted Beef Tenderloin
Sugar Snap Peas and Carrots
Balsamic Onions
Buffet Potatoes
Old-Fashioned Angel Biscuits
Tidalholm Cheesecake

Celebrate Spring Luncheon

Frosted Bellini

Cheese Straws

Cucumber Soup

Shrimp and Orzo Salad

Goat Cheese and Tomato Tart

Lemon Parfaits

~

Ladies' Afternoon Tea

Lace Cookies

Lemon Pound Cake with Strawberries and Lemon Curd

Melting Moments

Tea-Riffic Truffles

Bakery Petit Fours

Aunt Judy's Cheese Biscuits

Hot Tea with Lemon, Cream and Sugar

Birdie's Nectar Punch

Old Sheldon Picnic

Marinated Shrimp
Grilled Flank Steak
Picnic Potato Salad
Asparagus with Balsamic Vinaigrette
White Chocolate Macadamia Cookies
Auntie M's Brownies

~

Designer House Lunch

LaClaire's Lowcountry Tea
Chilled Tomato Soup with Basil Sorbet
Rosemary Chicken Salad on Mixed Greens
Sugar Snaps and Snow Peas with Lemon Thyme
Parmesan Twists
Berry Baskets

Frogmore Stew

French Bread Pesto
Frogmore Stew
Cornbread Salad
Sweet and Sour Crunch
Lighthouse Bars

~

Bull Point Boater's Picnic

Roasted Red Pepper Dip with Crudités
Parmesan Crusted Chicken
Summer White Corn and Pea Salad
Basil Tomato Couscous Salad
Beaufort's Best Cookie

Summer Supper

Minted Vodka Lemonade
Goat Cheese Crostini with Fresh Herbs
Tomato Basil Grilled Fish
Orzo with Everything
Vidalia Onion Casserole
Asparagus with Shallots and Red Bell Pepper
Focaccia Bread
Summer Peach Trifle

~

Water Festival Picnic

Boiled Peanuts
Southern Pate with Crudités
Battery Creek Shrimp Salad
Boater's Bowtie Pasta Salad
Japanese Cucumber Salad
Watermelon
Decadent Chocolate Cookies

Beach Weekend Supper

Eggplant Tapenade
Cosmopolitans
Grilled Chicken with Soy Lime Sauce
or
Southern Crab Cakes with Lime Sauce
Corn Pie
Spring Island Cornbread
Tomato and Arugula Salad
Lemon Blueberry Pie

~

Plantation Brunch

Bloody Marys
Milk Brandy Punch
Sweet Potato Biscuits with Ham
Cinnamon Roll-Ups
Southern Shrimp and Grits
Smothered Quail
Tomatoes with Mustard and Brown Sugar Dressing
Mushroom and Asparagus Strata
Assorted Melons
Sour Cream Cheese Biscuits

Autumn Supper Club

Shrimp Dijon

Portobello Mushroom Appetizer

Winter Squash Soup

Festive Apple and Blue Cheese Salad

Honey Gingered Pork Tenderloin

Broccoli with Balsamic Vinegar Sauce

Wild Rice with Cranberries

Refrigerator Rolls

Apple Pie with Hard Sauce

~

Lowcountry Holiday Dinner

Shrimp Pâté with Assorted Crackers

Pear Salad with Stilton and Walnuts

Fried Turkey

Cornbread Dressing with Balsamic Gravy

Holiday Cranberry Casserole

Lowcountry Oyster Pie

Sweet Potato Soufflé

Green Beans with Roasted Onions

Almond Butter Pound Cake

Coconut Grove Cake

Peppermint Ice Cream with Thick and Rich Hot Fudge Sauce

APPETIZERS
& BEVERAGES

APPETIZERS & BEVERAGES

People in Beaufort love nothing more than an excuse to share good food and drink with special friends, whether it is a casual cookout or an elegant cocktail affair. With the many islands that compose Beaufort County, chances are you will be on or by the water. Nothing completes the setting more than a full moon glistening on a high tide…somehow the rest of the world seems to drift away.

Artichokes Stuffed with Shrimp–Rémoulade

6	fresh artichokes	¼	cup butter
2	pounds shrimp, peeled and deveined		Rémoulade
1	cup cornbread stuffing mix	6	lemon wedges for garnish

- Trim artichokes, cover with water and boil 30 to 40 minutes or until tender. Remove and chill until ready to serve.

- Cook shrimp in boiling water 2 minutes or until just pink. Divide in half. Chop half of shrimp into chunks, reserve remaining shrimp whole and set aside both.

- Sauté stuffing mix in butter until heated thoroughly. Cool and set aside.

- Combine Rémoulade with chopped shrimp and chill.

- Remove center leaves and spiny texture above artichoke heart. Arrange on salad plate in star fashion. Place ½ cup Rémoulade mixture in center of artichoke heart. Top with whole shrimp generously and sprinkle with cornbread crumbs. Garnish with lemon wedge on side.

Rémoulade

¾	cup mayonnaise	1	teaspoon horseradish
¾	cup sour cream	1	teaspoon dry mustard
1	green onion, minced	1	teaspoon chili powder
1	tablespoon fresh dill, minced	½	teaspoon salt
			Dash of hot sauce

- Combine all ingredients, mixing thoroughly.

Yield: 6 servings

As a first course appetizer or a light summer supper, this Shrimp-Rémoulade sets the stage for a wonderful evening.

Shrimp Dijon

3	pounds large shrimp, peeled and deveined	1	cup olive oil
	Old Bay seasoning	8	tablespoons Dijon mustard
½	cup finely chopped fresh parsley	4	teaspoons crushed red pepper flakes
½	cup finely chopped shallots	2	teaspoons salt
½	cup tarragon vinegar	1	tablespoon fresh lemon juice
½	cup white wine vinegar		Freshly ground black pepper to taste

- Cook shrimp until pink in boiling water seasoned with Old Bay.
- Drain and transfer to a large bowl and set aside.
- Combine parsley and remaining ingredients; pour over warm shrimp, tossing well to coat.
- Cover and chill overnight; drain excess liquid and serve.

Yield: 12 servings

Dijon mustard is a strong and flavorful mustard produced from brown or black mustard seeds. After the seeds' hulls are removed, the seeds are ground, adding to them cloves, cinnamon and other spices and herbs as well as white wine or vinegar. Although the Chinese, Egyptians, Greeks and Romans all grew and consumed mustard, it is the French who claim the mustard capital— Dijon. Beaufort with its wonderful shrimp could easily be "the shrimp capital". What a great combination for this fabulous appetizer! Bon Appétit and Good Eaten' to you!

Easy Baked Shrimp

½	cup olive oil	1	tablespoon honey
2	tablespoons Cajun or Creole seasoning	1	tablespoon soy sauce
2	tablespoons fresh lemon juice		Pinch of cayenne pepper
2	tablespoons chopped fresh parsley	1	pound large shrimp, peeled and deveined
			Lemon wedges, for garnish

- Combine olive oil and next 6 ingredients in small bowl; transfer to 9x13-inch baking dish. Add shrimp, tossing to coat. Chill 1 hour.
- Preheat oven to 450°. Bake for 10 minutes, stirring occasionally. Garnish with lemon wedges.

Yield: 6 to 8 servings

Marinated Shrimp

3	pounds cooked, peeled and deveined shrimp	2	cups cider vinegar
1	(16-ounce) can large mushrooms	1	tablespoon sugar
1	(14-ounce) can artichoke hearts	1	tablespoon dry mustard
1	large onion, sliced into rings	1	tablespoon dill
1	pint cherry tomatoes	1	teaspoon garlic powder
		1	teaspoon salt
		1	teaspoon black pepper
		1½	cups cooking oil

- Combine shrimp and next 4 ingredients in large bowl and set aside.
- Mix vinegar and remaining ingredients; pour over shrimp mixture, tossing to coat.
- Cover and chill.

Yield: 16 to 20 servings

Beaufort, South Carolina, is home to pristine waterways, historic homes and undoubtedly the best seafood on the East coast! Shrimping is a way of life on the local waters from early spring until winter. From dawn 'til dusk, the familiar sight of a working shrimp boat can be seen on the horizon. Boats unload their catch daily, and it is likely that when you dine at area restaurants that advertise "catch of the day", they mean it literally!

Shrimp Delights

1	sheet frozen puff pastry, thawed	¾	cup mayonnaise
1	pound cooked, peeled and deveined shrimp	1	cup shredded sharp Cheddar cheese
2	tablespoons chopped bell pepper	⅛	teaspoon Worcestershire sauce
¾	cup chopped celery		Tabasco sauce to taste
2	tablespoons minced onion		Salt and pepper to taste
			Fresh Parmesan cheese

- Unfold pastry sheet and cut into 2-inch squares. Place on baking sheet.
- Bake at 350° for 10 minutes or until lightly browned.
- Remove top half of the pastry squares and discard.
- Combine shrimp and next 7 ingredients, mixing thoroughly. Season with salt and pepper.
- Place 1 tablespoon shrimp mixture on each pastry square. Sprinkle with Parmesan cheese.
- Place on baking sheet. Broil 3 to 4 minutes or until cheese just begins to melt. Serve warm.

Yield: 36 appetizers

Shrimp may be substituted with crabmeat.

Beaufort Academy is located on one of the larger islands in Beaufort County. This popular island has the beautiful name "Lady's Island". It is believed to have been named in 1762 for Lady Elizabeth Blake, wife of Royal Governor Joseph Blake of South Carolina.

Grilled Shrimp Kabobs

2	pounds large shrimp, peeled and deveined	1	garlic clove, minced
½	cup lemon juice	½	teaspoon salt
½	cup olive oil	½	teaspoon black pepper
¼	cup soy sauce	2	tablespoons finely chopped shallots
3	tablespoons fresh parsley, chopped		

- Place shrimp in shallow baking dish.
- Combine lemon juice and next 7 ingredients in small bowl, mixing well; pour marinade over shrimp, turning to coat. Chill 1 hour.
- Thread 2 to 3 shrimp on skewer. Grill 3 to 4 minutes on each side, basting with remaining marinade.
- Serve hot or cold.

Yield: 3 dozen

Shrimp Pâté

1	tablespoon butter	1	(3-ounce) package cream cheese, softened
1	tablespoon olive oil	1	tablespoon lemon juice
1½	pounds medium shrimp, peeled and deveined	1	teaspoon Worcestershire sauce
1	garlic clove, minced		Dash of hot sauce
	Salt and pepper to taste		Fresh basil, for garnish
	Old Bay seasoning		

- Melt butter and oil in skillet; add shrimp and garlic. Season with salt, pepper and Old Bay. Cook until shrimp are pink and remove from heat.
- Blend shrimp, skillet juices and remaining ingredients in a blender or food processor.
- Shape into a ball and chill several hours. Garnish with basil and serve with assorted crackers.

Yield: 10 to 12 servings

House Guests' Favorite Crab

1	(8-ounce) package cream cheese, softened	½	pound fresh crabmeat
1	cup seafood cocktail sauce		Juice of 1 lemon
	Dash of Worcestershire sauce		Dash of lemon pepper
			Assorted crackers

- Place cream cheese on serving plate; flatten to desired size.
- Combine cocktail sauce and Worcestershire sauce. Pour over cream cheese. Top with crabmeat and sprinkle with lemon juice and lemon pepper. Serve with assorted crackers.

Yield: 8 to 10 servings

Marinated Seafood and Tortellini Antipasto

Antipasto

1	pound cooked, peeled shrimp	1	(14-ounce) can artichoke hearts, drained and halved
8	ounces provolone cheese, cubed	2	(9-ounce) packages cheese tortellini, cooked al dente and drained
6	ounces Genoa salami, cubed		
1	red bell pepper, seeded and diced	1	cup small fresh mushrooms, sliced
1	yellow bell pepper, seeded and diced		

- Combine shrimp and next 7 ingredients in large bowl and set aside.

Marinade

¼	cup white wine vinegar	2¼	teaspoons sugar
¾	cup olive oil	1	teaspoon salt
⅔	cup plus 2 tablespoons lemon juice	¼	teaspoon Greek seasoning
2	tablespoons plus 2 teaspoons Dijon mustard	¼	teaspoon black pepper
			Dash of cayenne pepper
		2½	tablespoons fresh thyme

- Mix vinegar and remaining ingredients; pour over shrimp, tossing well to coat.
- Cover and chill 4 hours before serving.

Yield: 18 to 20 servings

Substitute 1½ teaspoons dried thyme for fresh thyme.

You can be a "house guest" in Beaufort even if you know no one who lives here! There are many beautiful Bed and Breakfast Inns. Most are in lovely restored homes found in the main historic district. Each offers its unique touch to make a visit to Beaufort special.

For those who don't want to fry, try this alternative:

8 ounces fresh crabmeat

¼ cup crumbled feta cheese

1 green onion, chopped

1 tablespoon Dijon mustard

4 ounces cream cheese, softened

1 tablespoon white wine

Salt and pepper to taste

24 (3x3) wonton wrappers

• Preheat oven to 350°.

• Combine crabmeat, feta and green onion. Add Dijon, cream cheese and wine. Season with salt and pepper.

• Spray miniature muffin pans with nonstick cooking spray. Place 1 wonton wrapper in each cup and gently press down.

• Place 1 tablespoon crab mixture in each cup.

• Fold in sides or twist to seal.

• Bake for 12 to 15 minutes or until lightly brown. Serve immediately.

Yield: 24 wontons

Sean's Crab Wontons

1	(7½-ounce) can crabmeat, drained	1	(12-ounce) package wonton wrappers
1	(8-ounce) package cream cheese, softened	½	cup milk
			Cooking oil

• Place 1 teaspoon crabmeat and ½ teaspoon cream cheese in middle of wonton wrapper; brush edges with milk to seal.

• Fold wrapper over to form triangle; press down edges to seal tightly. Fold two opposite corners toward middle.

• Fry in hot oil until crisp; remove with slotted spoon and drain before serving.

Yield: 24 servings

Substitute 8 ounces fresh lump crabmeat for one (7½-ounce) can of crabmeat. Serve with duck sauce or Chinese mustard.

Lady's Island Crab Dip

1	pound fresh blue crabmeat	½	teaspoon lemon pepper
1	tablespoon horseradish	2	dashes of Tabasco Sauce
2	tablespoons capers, rinsed and drained	1	teaspoon Worcestershire sauce
2	cups mayonnaise		Dash of Old Bay seasoning
1	teaspoon lemon zest		
½	teaspoon garlic powder		

• Combine crabmeat and remaining ingredients, blending well. Pour crab mixture into prepared dish.

• Bake at 350° for 20 to 30 minutes. Serve warm with assorted crackers.

Yield: 3 cups

Crab dip may also be served in a chafing dish for a buffet.

Tasty Crab Tarts

1	(7½-ounce) can crabmeat, drained	1	(5-ounce) can water chestnuts, finely chopped
1	shallot, finely chopped		
1	cup shredded Swiss cheese	½	teaspoon curry powder
1	teaspoon lemon juice	2	packages frozen 1-inch phyllo shells
⅓	cup mayonnaise		

- Combine crabmeat and next 6 ingredients, mixing well.
- Spoon rounded teaspoonful crab mixture into each shell.
- Bake at 400° for 10 to 12 minutes.

Yield: 30 tarts

Canned crabmeat may be substituted with ½ pound fresh crabmeat.

Salmon with Dill Sauce

Salmon

2½-3	pounds whole salmon fillet, skinned	⅛-¼	cup chopped fresh dill
¼	cup mayonnaise	¼	cup small capers, rinsed and drained
¼	cup milk		Dill sprigs and grape tomatoes, for garnish
¼	cup sherry		
¼	cup Parmesan cheese		

- Coat salmon with mayonnaise and set aside. Combine milk and sherry in 9x13-inch glass casserole dish; place salmon fillet in dish.
- Sprinkle fillet with Parmesan, dill and capers. Bake at 350° for 20-30 minutes.
- Place fish on serving platter. Garnish with dill sprigs and grape tomatoes.

Dill Sauce

1	(16-ounce) container sour cream	½-1	teaspoon horseradish
½	cup chopped fresh dill	½	teaspoon garlic salt
		½	teaspoon seasoning salt

- Combine sour cream and remaining ingredients, mixing well. Serve sauce chilled or at room temperature on the side.

Yield: 24 servings

Two of our Beaufort Academy students are quite the entrepreneurs! They operate a company called Crabco (Children Raised Around Beaufort County). JaneAnn and Lucius Laffitte offer a boxed crab trapping kit that includes all you need to catch crabs, minus a net and bait! These students, ages 7 and 10, have some good advice for catching a crab or two...

"The smellier the bait, the better! I use chicken necks, but let them sit out for a while to get real smelly. That way, the crab can smell the bait on your line, and then you scoop him up."

Lucius Laffitte

"wear shoes when you crab, just in case the crab gets loose and tries to claw your toes!"

JaneAnn Laffitte

Grilled Salmon Quesadillas
with Cucumber Salsa

CUCUMBER SALSA

3 cucumbers, chopped

1 garlic clove, minced

1 jalapeño pepper, seeded and chopped

½ red onion, chopped

½ yellow bell pepper, seeded and chopped

2 tablespoons chopped fresh cilantro

2 teaspoons red wine vinegar

1 teaspoon olive oil

½ teaspoon sugar

¼ teaspoon salt

⅛ teaspoon freshly ground black pepper

• Combine cucumber with remaining ingredients, tossing well. Cover and chill.

Salsa may be prepared ahead and chilled.

~

Dotted along the rivers in Beaufort are the buoys of crab traps. These traps are used by commercial crabbers who make their livelihood by catching crabs. Crab traps are also found hanging from many family docks.

Grilled Salmon Quesadillas

1	(2-pound) salmon fillet	2	jalapeño peppers, seeded and thinly sliced
8	(6-inch) flour tortillas		Cucumber Salsa
1	cup shredded Monterey Jack cheese		Fresh cilantro sprigs, for garnish
½	cup crumbled goat cheese		

- Grill salmon with lid closed over medium (350° to 400°) coals 5 minutes; turn salmon and grill additional 5 minutes. Cool and flake fish with fork. Spoon salmon evenly over 4 tortillas; top with cheeses, jalapeño slices and cover with another tortilla.

- Cook tortillas in large nonstick skillet or grill pan over high heat for 1 minute on each side or until tortilla is lightly browned and cheese melts.

- Cut each tortilla into fourths and top with Cucumber Salsa and fresh cilantro sprigs.

Yield: 4 servings

Crab Quesadillas

1½	cups shredded jalapeño blend Monterey Jack cheese	8	ounces crabmeat
2	ounces cream cheese, softened	1	cup seeded, chopped plum tomatoes
¼	cup chopped fresh cilantro	½	cup chopped green onions
2	tablespoons orange juice	8	(8-inch) flour tortillas
2	teaspoons lemon zest		Salt and pepper to taste
			Cooking oil

- Combine cheeses, cilantro, juice and zest in medium bowl and set aside.

- Combine crab, tomatoes and onions in large bowl, blending well. Spread cheese mixture on half of each tortilla. Top evenly with crab mixture. Season with salt and pepper. Fold in half, pressing gently to seal.

- Heat small amount of cooking oil in large skillet over medium heat. Cook until cheese melts and tortillas are golden brown.

- Cut into wedges and serve.

Yield: 4 servings

Serve with green salsa.

Pinky's Oysters

Rock salt
Oyster shells, cleaned
12 select oysters
Salt and pepper to taste

¼ cup butter, melted
2 tablespoons Worcestershire
    sauce

- Preheat oven to 400°.
- Layer baking sheet with rock salt and top with oyster shells. Place seasoned oysters on shells.
- Combine butter and Worcestershire sauce. Top oysters with butter mixture.
- Bake until edges of oysters begin to curl. Serve immediately.

Yield: 12 oysters

Oh, de oyster, fresh out de crick,

Jus' wash 'um off and take yuh pick.

Den roast 'um wid a croaker sack,

Taste so good, dat yuh go right back!

Printed with the kind permission of Vida Miller

Beef Tenderloin with Horseradish Sauce

Beef
1 garlic clove, minced
2 tablespoons butter, softened
1 tablespoon soy sauce
1½ tablespoons black pepper

1 tablespoon fresh rosemary, chopped
1 (3- to 4-pound) trimmed beef tenderloin

- Preheat oven to 500°.
- Combine garlic and next 4 ingredients, forming a thick paste.
- Rub paste on all sides of tenderloin and marinate 1 to 2 hours.
- Place beef in roasting pan and put in oven. Reduce heat to 400° immediately. Cook 40 minutes or until meat thermometer registers 140° for rare.
- Slice and serve chilled or at room temperature.

Horseradish Sauce
1 cup mayonnaise
1½ cups sour cream
¼ cup horseradish

¼ cup drained capers
    Freshly ground black
    pepper taste

- Combine mayonnaise and remaining ingredients and chill.
- Serve on the side of tenderloin.

Yield: 10 to 12 servings

Never put mushrooms in plastic; it will only cause them to lose their firmness. Always store them dry and in paper bags, allowing them to breathe.

Portobello Mushroom Appetizer

1   (8-ounce) package portobello mushrooms, sliced
1   large Vidalia onion, chopped

½   cup butter
      Garlic to taste
1   package phyllo pastry

- Sauté mushrooms and onion in melted butter and garlic and set aside.
- Follow package directions for phyllo pastry, using 4 sheets brushed with melted butter. Cut into 4-inch squares.
- Place each square into muffin pan cup. Fill with mushroom mixture; fold in edges. Bake at 400° for 20 minutes.

Yield: 12 servings

Brie and Portobello Mushroom En Croûte

1   (5-ounce) wheel of Brie
1   sheet frozen puff pastry, thawed
1   tablespoon grained Dijon mustard

1   cup chopped portobello mushrooms
1   egg
1   tablespoon water

- Preheat oven to 375°.
- Shave rind of Brie with sharp knife and discard.
- Unfold puff pastry and trim to a 13 to 14-inch circle.
- Place Brie in center of puff pastry. Spread Dijon over cheese; top with mushrooms.
- Combine egg and water in small bowl and beat lightly. Brush edges of pastry with egg mixture; fold over top of cheese to seal. Brush top with egg mixture.
- Place pastry on baking sheet. Bake at 375° for 25 minutes. Allow to rest 15 minutes before serving.

Yield: 20 servings

Mushroom and Thyme Turnovers

Dough

1	(8-ounce) package cream cheese, softened	½	cup butter, softened
		1½	cups all-purpose flour

Mushroom Filling

3	tablespoons butter	½	teaspoon thyme
1	large onion, finely chopped	2	tablespoons flour
½	pound fresh mushrooms, chopped	¼	cup sour cream
		2	tablespoons soy sauce
1	garlic clove, minced		Salt and pepper to taste
		1	egg, beaten

- Beat cream cheese and ½ cup butter. Add flour, stirring until smooth. Shape dough into ball and cover with plastic wrap. Chill 1 hour.

- Melt 3 tablespoons butter in skillet. Sauté onion, mushrooms and garlic over low heat until tender, stirring frequently.

- Remove from heat and stir in thyme, flour, sour cream and soy sauce; season with salt and pepper.

- Roll pastry to one-fourth inch thickness on lightly floured surface. Cut with 3-inch round cookie cutter.

- Place ½ teaspoon Mushroom Filling in center of each circle. Fold in half and seal edges with water, pressing together tightly with fork; brush with egg. Bake at 450° for 15 to 20 minutes.

Yield: about 4 dozen turnovers

May be frozen prior to baking.

Time moves like a wind rushing by my face,

But it can be as still as the Beaufort River in the early morning.

Time can be thrown away like the trash on Friday,

Or you can hold it next to you like your baby brother.

Time can be as ancient as the old oak by my bedroom window,

Or modern like the battery-powered cars.

Time can be lost like a sock in the dryer,

Or found like your favorite teddy bear.

Time is a river of leaping fish.

Time is a dance of fast-moving music.

Time is an arrow of things waiting to be hit.

Time is a canvas waiting to be painted.

Louisa Williams,
Grade 5

In a hurry? Phyllo pre-baked tart shells can be bought in the freezer section of your local grocery.

Mushrooms Tarts

3	tablespoons chopped shallots	¼	teaspoon salt
¼	cup butter	⅛	teaspoon cayenne pepper
8	ounces fresh mushrooms, finely chopped		Dash of freshly ground black pepper
2	tablespoons all-purpose flour	2	tablespoons Parmesan cheese
1	cup heavy cream	1	tablespoon fresh parsley, chopped
2	tablespoons fresh chives, chopped	30	phyllo pastry shells Parmesan cheese, for garnish
½	teaspoon lemon juice		

- Sauté shallots in butter over medium heat in medium saucepan 4 minutes. Stir in mushrooms, cooking uncovered for 15 minutes or until most of liquid has evaporated.

- Slowly stir in flour; add cream, stirring until thick and bubbly. Cook additional 1 minute and remove from heat.

- Stir in chives and next 6 ingredients.

- Pour into pastry shells; sprinkle with Parmesan. Bake uncovered at 350° for 15 minutes.

Yield: 30 tarts

Feta Pastry Puffs

4	eggs, beaten	1	pound feta cheese, crumbled
1	(8-ounce) package cream cheese, softened	3	packages mini phyllo dough shells, frozen

- Combine eggs and cream cheese, blending well; fold in feta. Place 1 teaspoon cheese mixture into each phyllo shell. Bake at 350° for 15 to 20 minutes.

Yield: 45 pastry puffs

Caramelized Onion, Apple and Brie Tartlet

8	cups very thinly sliced sweet onion	1	sheet frozen puff pastry, thawed
2	tablespoons olive oil	1	medium peeled, cored and thinly sliced Granny Smith apple
1	tablespoon fresh thyme, minced		
	Salt and pepper to taste	2	(6-ounce) wedges chilled Brie

- Sauté onion in olive oil over medium heat 20 to 30 minutes or until deep golden brown, stirring occasionally. Add thyme, salt and pepper and set aside.

- Roll pastry sheet to 12-inch square. Cut pastry into thirty-six (2-inch) squares. Spray baking sheet with cooking spray. Place pastry squares on baking sheet, allowing space between each square.

- Place 2 teaspoons onion mixture on each square; top with 2 apple slices. Bake at 350° for 20 minutes or until golden brown.

- Remove and discard rind from Brie; cut into ¼-inch slices. Top each baked square with cheese slice and continue to cook at 350° for 3 minutes or until cheese melts. Serve warm.

Yield: 18 servings

Nicole's Beaufort Brie

1	(16-ounce) wheel of Brie	¼	cup pecans, whole or chopped
¼	cup brown sugar		

- Remove and discard rind of Brie; allow Brie to come to room temperature. Place on oven-proof plate.

- Cover Brie with brown sugar.

- Broil for 3 to 5 minutes, making sure cheese melts but brown sugar does not burn; remove from broiler.

- Top with pecans; broil for additional 2 minutes. Serve with apple and pear slices and gingersnaps.

Yield: about 20 servings

At room temperature ripe Brie cheese should feel soft to the touch, especially in the center. To hasten the ripening process, allow to stand at room temperature overnight.

Chicken and Artichoke Tarts

1	(15-ounce) package refrigerated pie crusts	3	tablespoons mayonnaise
2	cups diced, cooked chicken	3	tablespoons sour cream
⅔	cup coarsely chopped pecans, toasted	3	green onions, very finely chopped
1	(14-ounce) can artichoke hearts, drained and chopped	1	garlic clove, minced
		½	teaspoon salt
		½	teaspoon black pepper
		¼	teaspoon cayenne pepper

- Cut pie crusts into 2½-inch rounds with a cookie cutter. Press rounds into prepared 1-inch miniature muffin pans. Bake at 425° for 5 to 6 minutes or until golden brown. Allow to cool.

- Combine chicken and remaining ingredients; spoon evenly into tart shells.

Yield: 4 dozen

Substitute phyllo pastry shells for pie crust shells.

Chicken salad is also good alone.

Pimiento Cheese Spread

Southerners eat five times more pimientos than any other part of the country. Have a homemade pimiento cheese sandwich, and you will fall in love with this easy and delicious luncheon treat.

1	pound extra sharp Cheddar cheese, shredded	¾	cup mayonnaise
		¼	teaspoon salt
2	(4-ounce) jars chopped pimiento, drained	½	teaspoon pepper
			Dash of garlic powder
			Pinch of sugar

- Combine cheese and remaining ingredients in food processor; pulse until well mixed.

Yield: 2 cups

Spread may be mixed with fork for more texture.

Penn Center Shrimp Paste Sandwiches

5	pounds boiled shrimp, peeled and deveined	1	tablespoon Worcestershire sauce
1	large bell pepper		Dash of Tabasco Sauce
1	large onion		Dash of lemon pepper
2	cups mayonnaise		Dash of salt
	Juice of 1 lemon	20	slices thin white sandwich bread, crusts removed

- Process shrimp, bell pepper and onion in food processor. Stir in mayonnaise and next 5 ingredients. Cover and chill overnight.

- Spread mixture on bread and cover with another bread slice. Cut into 4 triangles.

Yield: 40 servings

Shrimp Paste may be served on crackers or used for stuffing tomatoes.

On St. Helena Island stand the seventeen buildings of the Penn Center, established in 1862 as the first school for newly freed slaves. This is a national landmark because of its historic role beginning with emancipation, through the Civil Rights movement, to the present in African-American history. It is an active community center, preserving the unique past and enriching the culture of the Lowcountry.

Southern Pâté

1	(8-ounce) package cream cheese, softened	3	pounds sharp Cheddar cheese, shredded
1½	cups mayonnaise	3	(4-ounce) jars diced pimiento, drained
4	tablespoons grated onion	1	(2-ounce) jar diced pimiento, drained
2	teaspoons cayenne pepper		

- Combine cream cheese, mayonnaise, onion and cayenne, mixing well. Stir in Cheddar and pimiento. Chill overnight and serve at room temperature with crackers, celery sticks or lavosh.

Yield: 5 cups

Southern Pâté serves a crowd or makes a great hostess gift.

Beaufort's rich soil, accessibility to water and warm climate make it an ideal region for the vast tomato farms located here. One of our favorite summer treats is a fresh tomato sandwich.

~

Garlic peeling can be a chore. Soak garlic in warm water before peeling and the skins will slide right off. Also, the microwave can be a help in the peeling process. Place a whole head of garlic on a microwave-safe dish. Microwave approximately two minutes, rotating once. Allow the garlic to cool for one minute more— an easy peel!

Beaufort's Finest Tomato Sandwiches

1	loaf thin white sandwich bread	2-3	Beaufort tomatoes, peeled and sliced
¼	cup butter Mayonnaise		Salt and pepper to taste

- Cut bread slices into 3-inch rounds with a biscuit cutter; spread thin layer of butter on each round. Top with thin layer of mayonnaise; add tomato slice. Salt and pepper to taste. Top with additional bread round.

Yield: 10 servings

Sandwiches may be served open-faced.

Marinated Goat Cheese

1½	cups extra virgin olive oil	6	(4-ounce) rounds goat cheese
4	bay leaves	3	garlic cloves, slivered
1	tablespoon mixed peppercorns	3	tablespoons fresh basil, very finely chopped
1½	tablespoons dried thyme	1	tablespoon pink peppercorns

- Heat oil, bay leaves, mixed peppercorns and thyme in skillet. Remove from heat and pour over cheese.
- Top with remaining ingredients. Cover and chill overnight. Bring to room temperature before serving.

Yield: 24 servings

Serve with crackers or French bread.

Old South Sandwiches

2	(8-ounce) packages cream cheese, softened	20	slices thin white sandwich bread
½	cup mayonnaise		Cucumbers, sliced
½	cup sour cream		Fresh basil, chopped
1	(1-ounce) package dry ranch dressing mix		Roma tomatoes, sliced
			Fresh dill, chopped

- Combine cream cheese, mayonnaise, sour cream and dressing mix; set aside.

- Cut bread slices into 1-inch rounds with a cookie cutter; spread cream cheese mixture on each round. Top with tomato and sprinkle with basil, or top with cucumber and sprinkle with dill. Cover with plastic wrap and chill until ready to serve.

Yield: 80 sandwiches

French Bread Pesto

1	loaf French bread	½	cup pesto sauce
1	(8-ounce) package cream cheese, softened	2	tomatoes, chopped
1	teaspoon garlic powder	½	cup Parmesan cheese

- Split loaf lengthwise and set aside. Combine cream cheese and garlic powder; spread on each loaf. Spread pesto sauce over cream cheese.

- Top with tomatoes and Parmesan. Bake at 350° for 10 minutes.

Yield: 8 servings

In Beaufort many people "entertain" on their docks overlooking tranquil tidal creeks with names such as Rock Springs, Combahee and Whale Branch. A simple appetizer such as French Bread Pesto comes in handy, as you may have unexpected guests come by boat! This quick and easy appetizer served with a cold beer, glass of wine or iced tea will leave your visiting sailor and crew satisfied and complimentary of your Southern hospitality!

Crostini translated means "little toasts". Slices of bread are brushed with olive oil and toasted on both sides.

Goat Cheese Crostini with Fresh Herbs

1	baguette, cut into ¼-inch slices	¼	cup chopped fresh basil
	Olive oil	¼	cup chopped fresh parsley
8	ounces goat cheese, crumbled	¼	cup finely chopped oil-packed sun-dried tomatoes, drained
¼	cup chopped fresh rosemary		

- Preheat oven to 350°.

- Brush baguettes with olive oil and toast on baking sheet for 10 minutes; turn over and bake additional 5 minutes or until crisp.

- Sprinkle cheese on baguette; top with herbs and sun-dried tomatoes.

- Bake for 5 minutes.

Yield: 12 servings

Spinach–Artichoke Dip

1	(10-ounce) package frozen chopped spinach, thawed and drained	1	(5.5-ounce) jar prepared garlic cheese spread
1	(14-ounce) can artichoke hearts, drained and chopped	1	cup sour cream
		1	cup Parmesan cheese
		½	cup mayonnaise
1	(2-ounce) jar chopped pimiento, drained	6	slices cooked bacon, crumbled

- Combine spinach and remaining ingredients in large bowl, mixing well.

- Transfer to baking dish. Bake at 350° for 30 minutes. Serve with crackers or toasted sliced baguettes.

Yield: 4 cups

Dip may also be served by placing 1 heaping teaspoon spinach mixture into baked pastry shells. Bake at 350° for 11 to 12 minutes.

Olivada Crostini

	French bread	2	teaspoons fresh parsley
	Fresh Parmesan cheese	½	teaspoon sugar
1	garlic clove	⅓	cup olivada or black olive paste
¼	teaspoon salt		Salt and black pepper to taste
2	(28-ounce) cans diced Italian tomatoes, drained		Parsley, for garnish
¼	cup olive oil		

- Cut bread into thin rounds. Arrange in a single layer on baking sheet and toast in oven until golden. Turn over and sprinkle with Parmesan; toast another 2 minutes.
- Mash garlic clove with salt and set aside.
- Combine tomatoes with oil, parsley, sugar and garlic paste. Toss well and season with salt and pepper.
- Spread Parmesan toast with olivada. Top with tomato mixture. Garnish with parsley.

Yield: 12 servings

PISTACHIO OLIVADA

¾ cup peeled pistachios

3 tablespoons fresh lemon juice

2 tablespoons minced garlic

2 teaspoons freshly ground black pepper

1 cup pitted black olives

1 cup pitted green olives

1 bunch cilantro, stemmed

⅓ cup olive oil

Red bell pepper, thinly sliced, for garnish

Chopped pistachios, for garnish

- Combine pistachios and next 5 ingredients in food processor until smooth. Add cilantro and process for 30 seconds. Add olive oil to form a paste.

- Transfer to serving bowl; garnish with red pepper and chopped pistachios. Serve with toasted baguette slices.

Yield: 1½ to 2 cups

Eggplant Tapenade

1½	pounds eggplant, peeled and chopped	⅓	cup red wine vinegar
1	(28-ounce) can diced tomatoes, drained	2	tablespoons sugar
3	cups chopped onions	2	tablespoons capers, rinsed and drained
2	cups chopped bell pepper	2	tablespoons tomato paste
2	garlic cloves, minced	2	teaspoons dried basil
½	cup olive oil	1	teaspoon salt
½	cup fresh parsley, chopped	½	teaspoon black pepper
½	cup black olives, pitted and halved	½	cup pine nuts

- Sauté eggplant and next 4 ingredients in olive oil 20 minutes or until tender. Add parsley and next 8 ingredients. Simmer 5 to 10 minutes.
- Transfer to serving dish.
- Toast pine nuts and sprinkle over top. Serve warm or chilled with pita chips.

Yield: 12 servings

Sun-dried tomatoes add a zesty flavor to appetizers, salads, sauces and pastas. They are a nice staple to have on hand for unexpected guests.

Sun-Dried Tomato and Mushroom Dip

1½	pounds shiitake mushrooms, chopped	4	(3-ounce) packages cream cheese, softened
3	tablespoons butter	8	ounces sour cream
12	sun-dried tomatoes, chopped	8	ounces shredded mozzarella cheese
1½	cups mayonnaise	8	ounces shredded Swiss cheese

- Sauté mushrooms in butter and set aside.
- Boil sun-dried tomatoes until soft; drain and set aside.
- Combine mayonnaise, cream cheese and sour cream. Add mushrooms, tomatoes and remaining ingredients. Pour into greased casserole.
- Tent casserole with aluminum foil. Bake at 350° for 1 hour, 15 minutes.

Yield: 12 to 15 servings

Serve in a hollowed bread round with crackers.

Sun-Dried Tomato Dip

¼	cup oil-packed sun-dried tomatoes, drained	7	dashes of Tabasco sauce
1	(8-ounce) package cream cheese, softened	¾	teaspoon freshly ground black pepper
½	cup mayonnaise	2	green onions, very thinly sliced
½	cup sour cream		

- Puree tomatoes and next 5 ingredients in food processor. Add green onions; pulse 3 times. Serve at room temperature. Serve with crackers or vegetables.

Yield: 2 cups

Roasted Red Pepper Dip

1 (7-ounce) jar roasted red peppers
1 (4-ounce) package oil-packed sun-dried tomatoes, drained
2 garlic cloves
2 teaspoons cumin
1-2 pickled jalapeños, coarsely chopped
¼ cup chopped fresh cilantro
1 bunch green onions, bulbs only, chopped
2 (3-ounce) packages cream cheese, softened
½ teaspoon salt

- Puree red peppers and remaining ingredients in food processor until smooth. Serve with tortilla chips.

Yield: 1 cup

Perk up a turkey sandwich by using Roasted Red Pepper Dip instead of mayonnaise, and serve it on a rolled tortilla.

~

Peanut–Sesame Dip

½ cup sesame oil
½ cup peanut oil
1 tablespoon chili oil
1 egg yolk
¼ cup soy sauce
1 teaspoon minced garlic
¼ cup creamy peanut butter, room temperature

- Whisk oils into egg yolk; add remaining ingredients, mixing well. Cover loosely and chill 2 hours.

Yield: 1¾ cups

Dip may be prepared a day in advance. Serve with steamed asparagus, snow peas or grilled shrimp.

"The food that reminds me most of Beaufort has to be boiled peanuts. They are wet, soft and salty. They would be the food I would miss the most if I ever had to move away from Beaufort."

Robert Jennings,
Grade 9
Beaufort Academy
student

Traveling on the roads of the Lowcountry, visitors often notice beautiful "sweetgrass" baskets being sold at rustic roadside stands. These special baskets are crafted of palmetto palm strips woven over sweetgrass and pine needles. Baskets made in the days of the rice plantations were called "fanner baskets" and were made specifically for cleaning rice. Now the sweetgrass baskets come in all sizes and shapes and are beautiful, practical additions to any home, still crafted with love and hard work, truly earning the title "handmade".

Sweet Grass Egg Salad on Endive

1	tablespoon Dijon mustard	¼	cup chopped celery
6	tablespoons mayonnaise	¼	cup chopped fresh basil
8	hard-boiled eggs, peeled and quartered		Belgian endive spears
¼	cup chopped onion	1	ounce black caviar, rinsed and drained

- Combine Dijon with next 5 ingredients in food processor. Cover and chill until ready to serve.

- Separate endive spears and fill with egg salad. Top with caviar.

Yield: 6 to 8 servings

Chinese-Style Chicken in Lettuce Cups

¾	pound ground chicken	1	teaspoon sugar
¼	cup fresh basil	1	teaspoon garlic chili sauce
2	tablespoons soy sauce	1	tablespoon sesame oil
2	tablespoons lime juice		Boston lettuce leaves
2	garlic cloves, minced	1-2	green onions, chopped
1	large jalapeño, seeded and chopped	¼	cup roasted peanuts, chopped

- Combine chicken and next 7 ingredients in medium bowl, stirring to blend well.

- Heat oil in heavy skillet over high heat. Add chicken mixture and sauté until chicken is thoroughly cooked. Allow to cool.

- Place heaping teaspoon in lettuce leaf. Garnish with onion and peanuts.

Yield: 10 to 12 servings

Hot pepper sauce may be substituted for garlic chili sauce.

Beaufort Snow Peas and Shrimp Cocktail

3	pounds cooked shrimp, peeled and deveined	1	garlic clove, minced
2	pounds snow peas, cooked	½	cup olive oil
¾	cup dry white wine	½	cup cooking oil
1	tablespoon sugar	1	teaspoon dill
3	tablespoons shallots, minced	1	teaspoon dried parsley

- Wrap 1 snow pea around each shrimp, securing with toothpick, and set aside.
- Combine wine with remaining ingredients; pour over shrimp. Chill overnight.
- Drain before serving.

Yield: 30 servings

Beaufort County was established in 1785 and named for Henry Somerset II, Duke of Beaufort, one of the Lords Proprietors of Carolina.

~

Stuffed Cherry Tomatoes

6	dozen cherry tomatoes, halved	2	green onions, minced
	Salt to taste	2	tablespoons fresh dill, minced
2	(8-ounce) packages cream cheese, softened	1	teaspoon lemon juice

- Scoop pulp from each tomato half; arrange on baking sheet. Sprinkle with salt and set aside for 30 to 45 minutes.
- Combine cream cheese and remaining ingredients with mixer until smooth.
- Pipe cream cheese mixture into tomato halves using pastry bag with decorative tip.

Yield: 24 servings

A cool refreshing treat for those hot Lowcountry nights.

*In the late 1700s
the Hext Morris House
on "the Point" was the
plantation home of
Elizabeth Hext. It was
separated from the town
of Beaufort by water
and called Black's
Island. After Elizabeth
Hext married William
Sams, it became known
as Sams Point. Today
Beaufort Academy
sits on Sams
Point Road.*

Savory Artichoke Cheesecake

¼	cup dry Italian breadcrumbs	1	can artichoke hearts, drained and chopped
2	(8-ounce) packages cream cheese, softened	1	red bell pepper, seeded and chopped
4	ounces crumbled feta cheese	½	cup sliced green onions
1	cup sour cream	1	garlic clove, chopped
3	eggs	1	teaspoon dried tarragon leaves, crushed
		½	teaspoon basil

- Preheat oven to 375°. Grease bottom and sides of 9-inch springform pan. Press breadcrumbs in bottom and up sides of pan.
- Beat cream cheese at medium speed with an electric mixer until creamy. Add feta, sour cream and eggs, beating until smooth. Add artichokes and remaining ingredients and blend.
- Spoon mixture into prepared pan and spread evenly.
- Bake for 35 minutes or until set. Cool on wire rack to room temperature. Chill 3 hours and remove from springform pan, carefully pressing remaining breadcrumbs into sides of cheesecake.

Yield: 24 servings

Tortellini Delights

1	package pesto tortellini	1	cup marinara sauce, divided
1	package mozzarella tortellini	1	cup pesto, divided
3-4	tablespoons balsamic vinegar	¾	cup freshly grated Parmesan cheese
		1	pint grape tomatoes

- Prepare tortellini according to directions, rinsing under cold water; drain.
- Toss pasta with vinegar, ½ cup marinara sauce and ½ cup pesto. Chill 2 hours.
- Toss with remaining marinara sauce and pesto; add Parmesan.
- Spear tomato then tortellini with toothpick and serve.

Yield: 24 servings

Fiesta Cheesecake

1½ cups very finely crushed tortilla chips
¼ cup butter, softened
2 (8-ounce) packages cream cheese, softened
1 (3-ounce) package cream cheese, softened
2 eggs
2½ cups shredded Monterey Jack cheese
1 (4-ounce) can chopped green chiles, drained
¼ teaspoon cayenne pepper
2 bunches fresh cilantro, chopped
8 ounces sour cream
½ cup chopped bell pepper
½ cup chopped red bell pepper
½ cup chopped yellow bell pepper
½ cup chopped green onions
1 tomato, seeded and chopped
2 tablespoons chopped black olives

- Combine crushed tortilla chips and butter; press into bottom of prepared 9-inch springform pan. Bake at 325° for 15 minutes; cool.

- Beat cream cheese until fluffy. Add eggs one at a time, mixing well after each addition. Add cheese, chiles and cayenne pepper, stirring well. Pour into pan. Bake at 325° for 30 minutes. Cool 10 minutes.

- Cover serving plate with bed of cilantro. Place pan on serving plate; run knife along edge of pan to loosen sides. Cool completely.

- Spread sour cream over top of cheesecake; cover and chill.

- Arrange peppers, onions, tomatoes and olives on cheesecake. Serve with tortilla chips.

Yield: 25 servings

In 1525 Pedro de Quexos, a young Spaniard, sailed north from Florida and entered what is now known as St. Helena Sound. He saw a large beautifully wooded island, and in the name of Spain, christened it "Punta de Santa Elena" to honor Saint Elena. St. Helena Island is one of the largest South Carolina Sea Islands. One hundred fifty years later, the island became a network of cotton plantations.

The Beaufort Water Festival is an annual July celebration centered around the Beaufort River and the historic downtown waterfront. The Water Festival offers art, music, food, entertainment and endless types of aquatic fun! The 46th Annual Water Festival celebrated ten days of "Sandbar Summers and Ever Changing Tides".

Water Festival Nachos

2   (8-ounce) packages tortilla chips
½   pound thinly sliced Prosciutto
1   cup sliced banana peppers
1   cup sliced green onions
1   cup seeded, chopped tomatoes

3   cups shredded Monterey Jack cheese, divided
1   cup crumbled blue cheese, divided
    Green onion stems, for garnish

- Preheat oven to 350°.
- Line 2 baking sheets with foil and spray with cooking spray. Spread one bag of chips over each pan.
- Coarsely chop Prosciutto and layer over chips. Sprinkle with peppers, green onions and tomatoes.
- Top each nacho pan with 1½ cups Monterey Jack and ½ cup blue cheese.
- Bake for 20 minutes.
- Transfer nachos to serving plates using large spatula. Garnish with fanned green onion stems.

Yield: 10 servings

Mango Chutney Torta

1 cup cottage cheese
2 (8-ounce) packages cream
   cheese, softened
1 teaspoon curry
1 (9-ounce) jar mango
   chutney, divided
1 cup dry roasted peanuts,
   finely chopped and
   divided

1 cup green onion, finely
   chopped and divided
1 cup golden raisins, finely
   chopped and divided
   Additional peanuts, onion
   and raisins, for garnish

- Process cottage cheese, cream cheese and curry until very smooth.

- Combine 2 tablespoons chutney, ½ cup peanuts, ½ cup onion and ½ cup raisins to half of cheese mixture. Process until smooth and set aside. Repeat process with remaining cheese mixture and set aside.

- Line an 8½x4½-inch loaf pan with plastic wrap, allowing edges to extend over sides of pan. Spoon first half of cheese mixture into pan; spread ¼ cup chutney over it. Top with second half of cheese mixture.

- Cover and chill 8 hours; invert on serving plate. Garnish with peanuts, onion and raisins.

Yield: 25 servings

Chutney is a spicy condiment containing fruit, vinegar, sugar and spices. Chutney, whether sweet or hot, can often be found on Southern sideboards.

STYLE NOTES FOR ENTERTAINING

- *Choose a theme color.*

- *Bring the season to the table.*

- *Don't forget little details to make each guest feel special.*

- *Set the table the night before.*

- *Use cherished heirlooms to add tradition, history and beauty to the table.*

- *Create new traditions for your family and friends to enjoy.*

Herb Roasted Nuts

5	cups mixed nuts	2	tablespoons unsalted butter
1	teaspoon extra virgin olive oil	¼	cup coarsely chopped fresh rosemary
2	small shallots, thinly sliced into rings	¼	teaspoon cayenne pepper
3	garlic cloves, thinly sliced lengthwise	1	tablespoon firmly packed dark brown sugar
		1	tablespoon kosher salt

- Preheat oven to 350°. Toast nuts 8 to 12 minutes. Transfer to large bowl and set aside.

- Heat olive oil in small skillet over medium heat. Add shallot and garlic, frying about 3 to 5 minutes or until golden. Drain and set aside.

- Melt butter and pour over nuts. Add rosemary, cayenne, sugar and salt, tossing well to coat. Add garlic and shallot. Serve warm.

Yield: 5 cups

Nuts may be reheated at 300° for 10 minutes.

Sugar and Spice Nuts

1	cup sugar	¼	cup water
2	teaspoons cinnamon	2	cups pecan halves
½	teaspoon salt		

- Cook sugar, cinnamon, salt and water until it spins a thread (about 5 minutes from the time it begins to boil).

- Stir in pecans quickly; pour mixture onto prepared platter. Cool and break into pieces.

Yield: 2 cups

LaClaire's Lowcountry Tea

2	lemons	2	quarts water	
1½	cups sugar	10	regular tea bags or 6 large	
6	fresh mint sprigs		tea bags	

- Squeeze lemon and reserve rind. Bring lemon juice, rind, sugar, mint and water to a rolling boil over high heat.
- Add tea bags and continue boiling until sugar dissolves.
- Remove from heat. Allow to steep 10 minutes.
- Remove tea bags, rind and mint.
- Add enough water and ice to make 1 gallon.

Yield: 1 gallon

After an extended trip away from the South, nothing welcomes you home more than a tall glass of cold, sweet tea! Welcome home!

~

Homemade Lemonade

6	lemons, scrubbed to remove oil and wax	6	cups water
1	cup sugar		Fresh mint sprigs, for garnish

- Cut lemon in half. Place in heat resistant pitcher. Add sugar and set aside.
- Bring water to a boil.
- Pour over lemon and sugar, stirring until sugar dissolves.
- Cool about 40 minutes or until lemons are cool.
- Squeeze lemon juice in pitcher and discard rinds.
- Chill until cold. Garnish with mint sprigs.

Yield: 8 glasses

Summer days in Beaufort can be hot and muggy. A tall glass of iced cold lemonade makes a cool refreshing treat... Also, you can make "tea lemonade" by mixing equal amounts of lemonade and sweetened tea.

Yummy, different, and very easy—my kind of drink! A "birdie" in the hand is worth... a second glass!

~

These popular blends take just seconds to prepare. Kids will love the creamy taste and the opportunity to whirl something in the blender!

Birdie's Nectar Punch

2   (12-ounce) cans apricot nectar
1   (6-ounce) can frozen lemonade, thawed
1½ cups water
1   (12-ounce) bottle club soda, chilled

- Combine nectar, lemonade and water.
- Add club soda just before serving. Serve over ice.

Yield: 5 quarts

Smoothies

Strawberry Smoothie

1   (8-ounce) container vanilla yogurt
1   (10-ounce) package frozen sliced strawberries, thawed
1   banana, sliced
⅓   cup orange juice
1   tablespoon honey

- Blend ingredients in blender until smooth, stopping once to scrape down sides. Serve immediately.

Yield: 3¼ cups

Berry Special Smoothie

2   cups vanilla ice cream, softened
1   cup fresh strawberries, hulled
½   cup fresh blueberries
½   cup fresh raspberries
2   tablespoons sugar
½   cup cranberry juice
1   tablespoon lemon juice
    Mint sprigs for garnish

- Blend ice cream and next 6 ingredients in blender. Add ice cubes and process until smooth, stopping once to scrape down sides. Garnish with mint sprigs.

Yield: 4 cups

Reunion Refresher

1	(12-ounce) can frozen orange juice concentrate, thawed	2	family-size tea bags	
1	(12-ounce) can frozen lemonade concentrate, thawed	1	quart boiling water	
		1¼	cups sugar	
		1	(46-ounce) can pineapple juice	
			Mint sprigs for garnish	

- Prepare orange juice and lemonade according to package directions and set aside.
- Steep tea bags in boiling water 30 minutes. Remove tea bag and discard.
- Add sugar, stirring until sugar dissolves.
- Dilute with additional water to make 1 gallon.
- Add orange juice and lemonade. Stir in pineapple juice.
- Chill until cool. Serve over ice and garnish with mint sprigs.

Yield: 2¼ gallons

Each year Beaufort Academy has a class reunion. Alumni are drawn together for an exciting soccer game and an evening of entertainment, including dancing, fellowship and, of course, a "reunion refresher"!

~

Cath's Champagne

1	(750-milliliter) bottle sparkling white grape juice, chilled	3	ounces undiluted frozen lemonade
16	ounces white grape juice, chilled	1	(10-ounce) package frozen raspberries or strawberries
2	liters ginger ale, chilled		

- Pour grape juices, ginger ale and lemonade in punch bowl. Stir in berries gently, mixing well.

Yield: 1 gallon

Substitute sparkling white grape juice with champagne.

Make an ice ring with either raspberries or strawberries frozen in ginger ale.

No Lowcountry yard or garden is complete without mint. Southerners are famous for their mint tea and mint juleps. You will also find this herb in sauces and desserts, as well as garnishes.

~

The Fall Festival sponsored by the Historic Beaufort Foundation celebrates the rich history of homes, plantation and gardens of the area. The festival includes candlelight, garden and kitchen tours.

Woodstock Plantation Mint Julep

6	cups water	Shaved ice
4½	cups sugar	Kentucky Bourbon
20-30	large mint leaves	

- Boil water, sugar and mint leaves in large pot 10 minutes. Allow to cool and pour into 3 large canning jars. Seal and chill at least 30 days.
- Pour 1½ ounces syrup and 3 ounces bourbon in a silver julep cup. Add shaved ice and a sprig of mint.

Yield: 24 servings

Raspberry Spritzers

| 1 | (10-ounce) package frozen raspberries | 1 | (12-ounce) can frozen pink lemonade concentrate, thawed |
| 1 | (12-ounce) can frozen cranberry juice concentrate, thawed | 2 | (2-liter) bottles ginger ale, chilled |

- Process raspberries in blender until smooth.
- Combine raspberry puree, juice and lemonade in 1½-gallon container.
- Stir in ginger ale just before serving.

Yield: 5 quarts

Minted Vodka Lemonade

1	cup packed, chopped fresh mint leaves	1½	cups vodka
⅔	cup sugar	½	cup water
1	cup fresh lemon juice		Mint sprigs, for garnish

- Combine chopped mint and sugar in large bowl or pitcher.
- Stir in juice, vodka and water. Cover and chill at least 30 minutes and up to 2 hours.
- Strain mixture into pitcher. Pour over ice and garnish with mint sprigs.

Yield: 6 servings

Frosted Bellinis

1	bottle of champagne
2	(11.5-ounce) cans peach nectar
½	cup peach Schnapps

- Combine champagne, nectar and schnapps in large pitcher. Stir until well blended.
- Serve immediately over crushed ice.

Yield: 12 servings

Frosted Bellinis are a welcoming opener for a spring luncheon.

~

Summertime Martini

3	cups vodka
2½	cups champagne
½	cup sweet-and-sour mix
2	tablespoons Chambord
6	tablespoons fresh lime juice

- Combine vodka and remaining ingredients. Strain into martini glasses.

Yield: 12 servings

Sugar rims of martini glasses.

For the ladies at the party, try the colorful and tasty Cosmopolitan Martini!

2 splashes cranberry juice

Juice of 1 lime

1 tablespoon Cointreau

6 ounces vodka

• Shake! Shake! Shake and strain into two martini glasses garnished with lime slices.

Mango Margarita

1	cup peeled, chopped mango
1½	cups ice cubes
6	tablespoons gold tequila
6	tablespoons confectioners' sugar
3	tablespoons triple sec or orange liqueur
2	tablespoons fresh lime juice

- Puree mango and remaining ingredients in blender until smooth. Serve cold.

Yield: 4 servings

Brandy Milk Punch

2	cups milk	1	teaspoon vanilla
2	cups half-and-half	2	cups crushed ice
1	cup brandy		Ground nutmeg
½	cup white corn syrup		

- Whisk together milk and next 5 ingredients in large bowl.
- Pour through wire mesh strainer into chilled glasses.
- Sprinkle with nutmeg.

Yield: 8 cups

Brandy Milk Punch is a new version of the old Southern, frothy, egg and milk concoction, syllabub, which has become all but a memory.

~

Christmas Eve Eggnog

6	eggs, separated	1	pint whiskey
¾	cup sugar, divided	1	ounce rum
½	pint cream	½	gallon vanilla ice cream
½	pint half-and-half		

- Beat egg yolks with ½ cup sugar and set aside.
- Beat egg whites and ¼ cup sugar with clean, dry beaters until stiff.
- Fold in yolks. Stir in cream, half-and-half, whiskey and rum and chill.
- Add ice cream just before serving and stir.

Yield: 5 pints

Eggnog—thick, rich and generously spiked with bourbon—makes a once a year appearance during the holidays.

BREADS
& BRUNCH

BREAD & BRUNCH

Breakfast on a Lowcountry porch…hot coffee, fresh juice, biscuits hot out of the oven, the aroma of eggs, bacon and buttered grits…could there be a better place short of Heaven to start the day?

The menu may vary—from coffee cake made from a recipe passed down through generations to mushroom strata—as well as the time, be it an early morning breakfast or a brunch. But the pursuit of good meals and good times is as endless as the tides that cover the Lowcountry.

Refrigerator Rolls

1	cup sugar	2	eggs, beaten
1	cup shortening	½	teaspoon salt
1	cup water	6	cups sifted all-purpose
2	(.25-ounce) packages active		flour
	dry yeast	¼	cup butter
1	cup lukewarm water		

- Preheat oven to 400°.
- Bring sugar, shortening and water to a boil. Cool to lukewarm (about 1 hour).
- Dissolve yeast in 1 cup lukewarm water. Add to sugar mixture.
- Add eggs, salt and flour, mixing with wooden spoon until consistency of batter. Cover tightly and chill.
- Roll out dough on floured surface, adding flour to stiffen if needed.
- Cut with biscuit cutter 2 hours prior to baking. Place small pat of butter on roll; fold over and pinch edges together.
- Place on greased baking sheet and cover with dishcloth. Allow to rise 2 hours.
- Bake for 8 to 10 minutes until golden brown.

Yield: 5 to 6 dozen

Aunt Judy's Cheese Biscuits

1	cup butter, softened	¼	teaspoons salt
½	pound shredded sharp	¼	teaspoon dry mustard
	Cheddar cheese	¼	teaspoon cayenne pepper
2	cups all-purpose flour		

- Preheat oven to 425°.
- Cream butter, then add cheese. Mix well and set aside.
- Sift together flour, salt, mustard and pepper. Add to butter mixture.
- Roll dough to ¼-inch thickness on floured wax paper. Cut with miniature cookie cutter.
- Place on baking sheet and bake for 8 to 10 minutes.

Yield: 3 to 4 dozen biscuits

Old-Fashioned Angel Biscuits

1	(.25-ounce) package active dry yeast	3	tablespoons baking powder
2	tablespoons warm water	3	tablespoons sugar
5	cups flour	1	cup shortening
2	teaspoons salt	2	cups buttermilk
1	teaspoon baking soda		

- Preheat oven to 400°.
- Dissolve yeast in warm water and set aside.
- Sift together flour and next 4 ingredients in bowl; cut in shortening until crumbly. Add yeast mixture and buttermilk, stirring until blended.
- Knead dough gently on lightly floured surface. Roll out to ½-inch thickness and cut with biscuit cutter.
- Place on ungreased baking sheet. Bake for 10 minutes or until lightly golden. Serve with Honey Butter.

Yield: 4 to 5 dozen

Dough may be stored in a very airtight container in the refrigerator to be used as needed for up to a week.

Honey Butter

¼	cup honey	½	cup butter, softened

- Combine honey and butter in small bowl, stirring until well blended.

If anyone asks you for "beaten biscuits", beware! It involves much elbow grease. An old saying about beaten biscuits goes, "200 hundred strokes for home folks, 500 strokes for company". The results might have been "satiny" smooth tops and flaky insides, but it was elbow grease that got them there!

Sour Cream Cheese Biscuits

2	cups sifted self-rising flour	1	cup sour cream
1	cup butter, melted	1	cup shredded sharp Cheddar cheese

- Preheat oven to 450°.
- Combine flour, butter and sour cream, mixing well. Fold in cheese, stirring gently.
- Spoon into prepared miniature muffin pans. Bake for 10 to 15 minutes.

Yield: 2 dozen biscuits

Rosemary Biscuits

1 (3-ounce) package cream cheese	½ cup milk
1¾ cups biscuit baking mix	2 teaspoons chopped fresh rosemary

- Preheat oven to 400°.
- Cut cream cheese into baking mix until crumbly. Add milk and rosemary, stirring until just moistened.
- Knead dough gently 4 or 5 times on lightly floured surface. Roll out to ¾-inch thickness and cut diagonally into 1-inch diamonds.
- Place on lightly greased baking sheet. Bake for 10 minutes.

Yield: 2 dozen biscuits

Fresh rosemary may be substituted with dried rosemary.

ROSMARINU OFFICINALIS: **ROSEMARY**

The Romans gave this lovely herb its name based on its love for seaside air, "dew of the sea". Its fragrant leaves have been linked to love, remembrances and cheerfulness— a nice addition to any meal.

Sweet Potato Biscuits

¾ cup cooked sweet potatoes, lightly mashed	1¼ cups all-purpose flour
⅔ cup milk	1 tablespoon sugar
¼ cup butter, melted	4 teaspoons baking powder
	½ teaspoon salt

- Preheat oven to 450°.
- Combine potatoes, milk and butter in large mixing bowl.
- Sift together flour, sugar, baking powder and salt into potato mixture, mixing to form a soft dough.
- Knead dough until smooth on lightly floured surface. Roll out to ½-inch thickness and cut with 2-inch biscuit cutter.
- Place on lightly greased baking sheet. Bake for 8 to 10 minutes.

Yield: 3 dozen

Makes a nice variation to popular ham biscuits.

These quick and easy muffins are for those who have better things to do than stay in the kitchen all day!

~

In the greater Beaufort area, there are over a dozen outstanding public, resort and private golf courses. These lovely, natural settings offer challenges golfers will long remember.

Butter–Me–Nots

2	cups self-rising flour, sifted	1	(8-ounce) container sour
1	cup butter, melted		cream

- Preheat oven to 350°.
- Combine ingredients, mixing well.
- Spoon into miniature muffin pans. Bake for 20 to 30 minutes.

Yield: 2 dozen biscuits

Biscuits may be frozen.

Pleasant Point Dilly Bread

1	(.25-ounce) package active dry yeast	1	tablespoon dried minced onion
¼	cup lukewarm water	2	teaspoons dill seed
1	cup cottage cheese	¼	teaspoon baking soda
1	tablespoon butter	1	teaspoon salt
2	tablespoons sugar	1	egg
		2¼	cups all-purpose flour

- Preheat oven to 350°.
- Add yeast to water and set aside.
- Heat cottage cheese and butter to lukewarm and set aside.
- Combine sugar and next 5 ingredients in large bowl. Add yeast mixture, then cottage cheese mixture, mixing well.
- Add flour one cup at a time, beating well until soft dough begins to form.
- Cover and place in warm draft-free area. Allow to rise until double in size (about 1 hour).
- Punch down dough and lightly knead. Place in well-greased loaf pan.
- Allow to rise until double in size (about 1 hour).
- Bake for 30 minutes or until golden brown.

Yield: 1 loaf

Bread may be stored in plastic wrap after cooling. Makes a great summer sandwich.

Focaccia Bread

3½ cups unbleached all-purpose flour
1⅓ cups lukewarm water
1 teaspoon salt
1 (.25-ounce) package active dry yeast
2 tablespoons olive oil
8 ounces Gorgonzola cheese, crumbled
Chopped rosemary

- Preheat oven to 400°.

- Make a well in center of flour. Add water to well. Sprinkle salt around well edges. Add yeast to well. Allow to stand 5 minutes.

- Add oil to well and begin to blend in with flour.

- Shape into ball and knead 6 to 10 minutes until smooth and elastic.

- Place in bowl and cover with cloth. Allow to rise 1 to 1½ hours.

- Punch dough down and allow to rest.

- Divide dough evenly in half and roll out to ¼-inch thickness.

- Place on lightly greased baking sheets and cover with plastic wrap. Allow to rise 30 minutes.

- Sprinkle with cheese and rosemary. Bake for 12 to 15 minutes or until crisp.

Yield: about 32 slices

Bread may also be topped with pesto, black olives or sun-dried tomato spread.

While Focaccia Bread is a wonderful addition to a meal, it also makes excellent sandwiches and incredible stuffing for poultry dishes.

CARAMELIZED ONIONS

8 white onions, thinly sliced

1 (10½-ounce) can chicken broth

2 tablespoons balsamic vinegar

8 ounces Gorgonzola cheese, crumbled

- Place onions and broth with enough water to cover in large Dutch oven.

- Simmer uncovered 2 hours, stirring occasionally.

- Remove from heat and add vinegar.

- Spread on uncooked focaccia bread.

- Sprinkle with Gorgonzola cheese and bake as directed.

When making Caramelized Onion topping, omit cheese and rosemary from Focaccia Bread recipe.

Southern food historians say the term "hushpuppies" came from cooks who tended to outdoor fires for fried fish. They sometimes threw spoonfuls of cornmeal mush into the boiling fat and tossed the puffed pastries to barking dogs with an admonition of "Hush, puppies!"

Tomato–Green Onion Hushpuppies

1	cup yellow cornmeal	1	egg, beaten
½	cup all-purpose flour	¼	cup milk
1½	teaspoons baking powder	1	tomato, seeded and finely chopped
1	teaspoon salt	3	green onions, finely chopped
1	teaspoon sugar		Cooking oil for frying
¼	teaspoon garlic powder		
¼	teaspoon black pepper		

- Combine cornmeal and next 6 ingredients in large bowl, making a well in center of mixture, and set aside.
- Combine egg and milk; add to cornmeal mixture, stirring to moisten. Add tomato and onions and lightly mix.
- Pour oil to 3-inch depth in heavy skillet or Dutch oven and heat to 375°.
- Drop batter by rounded teaspoonfuls into oil. Fry 3 minutes or until golden brown and drain.

Yield: 3 dozen

Tasty Parmesan Twists

1	cup all-purpose flour	1	cup fresh Parmesan cheese
½	teaspoon dried Italian seasoning	½	cup sour cream
⅔	cup butter, softened	½	cup butter, melted

- Preheat oven to 350°.
- Combine flour and seasoning in medium bowl and set aside.
- Cream softened butter; add cheese and sour cream, blending until smooth.
- Add flour mixture to butter mixture, blending until smooth.
- Roll half of dough into a 12x7-inch rectangle on lightly floured surface. Cut into 6x1-inch strips. Twist each strip 2 to 3 times. Place on greased baking sheet. Repeat with remaining dough.
- Brush dough with melted butter. Bake for 10 to 12 minutes or until light golden brown.

Yield: 2 dozen

Fripp Island Herb Bread

⅓ cup oil-packed sun-dried tomatoes, drained
2½ cups all-purpose flour
2 teaspoons baking powder
1¼ teaspoons salt
½ teaspoon baking soda
1 cup shredded Provolone cheese
½ cup chopped green onions
2 tablespoons fresh minced parsley
2 tablespoons fresh minced rosemary
½ teaspoon freshly ground black pepper
2 tablespoons reserved oil from tomatoes
2 tablespoons shortening
2 tablespoons sugar
2 garlic cloves, minced
2 eggs, beaten
1¼ cups buttermilk

- Preheat oven to 350°.

- Pat tomatoes dry and cut in julienne strips; set aside.

- Combine flour, baking powder, salt and baking soda in large bowl. Add tomatoes, cheese and next 4 ingredients and set aside.

- Whisk together reserved oil, shortening and sugar in small bowl until smooth. Add garlic, eggs and buttermilk, mixing until well blended.

- Add oil mixture to flour mixture, stirring to incorporate flour.

- Pour into 2 prepared loaf pans. Bake for 45 minutes or until tester comes out clean.

- Turn out on wire rack to cool.

Yield: 2 loaves

Serve with dipping oil and Parmesan cheese.

A day at the beach
Brings happiness
to my heart,
Sunlight to my soul.

Kate Godley, Grade 8
Beaufort Academy
student

Cornmeal is sometimes referred to as "the staff of life" since it is as prevalent in Southern dishes as wheat and corn are elsewhere in the country.

Fork–Eating Cornbread

1	large onion, chopped	1	(7-ounce) package corn muffin mix
½	cup butter		
1½	cups shredded Cheddar cheese, divided	10	drops hot sauce
		½	cup milk
1	cup sour cream	1	egg
		1	cup cream-style corn

- Preheat oven to 325°.

- Sauté onion in butter until golden and cool slightly. Add 1 cup cheese and sour cream, stirring well, and set aside.

- Combine corn muffin mix and remaining ingredients in bowl, mixing well. Transfer to casserole.

- Drop onion mixture by spoonfuls into center of corn muffin mix, being careful not to stir.

- Top with remaining ½ cup cheese. Bake uncovered for 30 to 35 minutes or until golden. Allow to cool 15 minutes before serving.

Yield: 8 to 10 servings

Spring Island Cornbread

1	cup butter, melted	4	rounded tablespoons yellow cornmeal
1	cup milk		
2	cups biscuit baking mix	½	teaspoons baking soda
¾	cup sugar		

- Preheat oven to 350°.

- Beat together butter and milk until well blended and set aside.

- Combine baking mix and remaining ingredients in large bowl, making a well in center of mixture.

- Pour butter mixture into well, stirring well to moisten.

- Pour into greased 9-inch square baking pan. Bake uncovered for 30 to 40 minutes or until golden.

Yield: 8 servings

Zucchini Bread

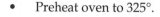

3	cups all-purpose flour	1	cup cooking oil
2	teaspoons baking soda	2	teaspoons vanilla
1	teaspoon salt	1	(8-ounce) can crushed pineapple, drained
½	teaspoon baking powder		
1½	teaspoons cinnamon	2	cups shredded zucchini
3	eggs	¾	cup walnuts
2	cups sugar		

- Preheat oven to 350°.
- Sift together flour and next 4 ingredients and set aside.
- Beat eggs and next 4 ingredients, mixing well. Add to flour mixture, then fold in zucchini and walnuts.
- Pour into greased and floured loaf pans. Bake for 1 hour.

Yield: 2 loaves

Don't throw overripe bananas away. They are excellent in breads, pancakes, muffins or smoothies.

Banana Bread

2	cups bananas, mashed	2	teaspoons cinnamon
3	eggs, beaten	½	teaspoon baking powder
2	cups sugar	2	teaspoons baking soda
1	cup cooking oil	2	teaspoons vanilla
2	cups all-purpose flour	1	cup chopped pecans
1	teaspoon salt		

- Preheat oven to 325°.
- Combine bananas, eggs, sugar and oil in large bowl. Mix well and set aside.
- Combine flour and next 4 ingredients in medium bowl, blending thoroughly. Add to banana mixture, mixing well.
- Stir in vanilla and pecans. Pour into 2 prepared loaf pans. Bake for 1 hour to 1 hour, 15 minutes.
- Cool 10 minutes before turning out.

Yield: 2 loaves

Lemon Bread

1	cup sugar	1½	cups all-purpose flour
½	cup cooking oil	1	teaspoon baking powder
	Zest of 1 lemon	½	teaspoon salt
2	eggs	½	cup milk

To obtain greatest yield from a lemon, microwave for 15 to 20 seconds.

- Preheat oven to 325°.
- Cream together sugar and oil. Add zest and eggs and set aside.
- Combine flour, baking powder and salt. Add to sugar mixture alternately with milk.
- Pour into well-greased loaf pan. Bake for 1 hour.
- Spoon Lemon Topping over bread immediately upon removal from oven. Allow to cool 15 to 30 minutes before removing from pan.

Yield: 1 loaf

Lemon Topping

¼	cup sugar	Juice of 1 lemon

- Combine sugar and juice, stirring until sugar dissolves.

~

Apple Bread

2	cups sugar	1	teaspoon cinnamon
1	cup cooking oil	1	teaspoon nutmeg
3	eggs	2	teaspoons vanilla
3	cups all-purpose flour	3	cups chopped apples
1	teaspoon salt	1	cup chopped nuts
1	teaspoon baking soda		Sugar

"My favorite thing about cooking is the dishwater. The sound of the water churning—it is almost as if you could hear the plates and cups singing, just waiting for me to put them back up in the cabinets."

Anne Chambers,
Grade 5
Beaufort Academy
student

- Preheat oven to 325°.
- Beat sugar, oil and eggs, mixing well, and set aside.
- Combine flour and next 4 ingredients in large bowl. Add vanilla, apples and nuts. Add sugar mixture, mixing well.
- Pour into 2 greased and floured loaf pans. Sprinkle tops with sugar. Bake for 1 hour.

Yield: 2 loaves

Batter may be made into muffins. Bake for 20 to 25 minutes.

Rhubarb Muffins

1¼   cups brown sugar, firmly
     packed
½   cup cooking oil
1   egg
2   teaspoons vanilla
1   cup plain yogurt

2   cups frozen chopped
     rhubarb
2½   cups all-purpose flour
1   teaspoon baking soda
1   teaspoon baking powder
½   teaspoon salt
     Cinnamon Topping

- Preheat oven to 400°.

- Combine sugar and next 4 ingredients in large bowl, beating well. Stir in rhubarb and set aside.

- Stir together flour, baking soda, baking powder and salt until thoroughly blended. Add to rhubarb mixture, stirring until just blended.

- Spoon batter into greased muffin cups, filling two-thirds full. Drizzle Cinnamon Topping into cups, pressing lightly into batter. Bake for 20 to 25 minutes.

Yield: 20 muffins

Cinnamon Topping
1   tablespoon butter, melted
⅓   cup brown sugar

1   teaspoon cinnamon

- Combine ingredients, mixing thoroughly.

Rhubarb is a deadly poisonous plant when referring to the leaves, but the root is where its value lies for cooking. Believed to have originated in northern China, the plant grows primarily in cold weather spots, such as Poland and Russia, but it has made its way to the Northern climates of this country.

Orange Blossoms

3	eggs	½	cup water
1⅓	cups sugar	½	teaspoon vanilla
½	teaspoon salt	½	cup butter, melted and
1½	cups all-purpose flour		divided
1½	teaspoons baking powder		Orange Topping

- Preheat oven to 400°.

- Beat eggs until very light. Add sugar, mixing well. Add salt, flour and baking powder alternately with water and vanilla.

- Add ¼ cup melted butter, mixing well.

- Place ½ teaspoon remaining butter in bottom of each miniature muffin cup. Pour batter into miniature muffin pans.

- Bake for 12 minutes or until lightly browned.

- Dip in Orange Topping while still hot and place on wax paper.

Yield: 5 dozen miniature muffins

Orange Blossoms may be frozen.

Orange Topping

1	(16-ounce) box confectioners' sugar	Juice and zest of 2 oranges
1	cup plus 1 tablespoon confectioners' sugar	Juice and zest of 2 lemons

- Combine sugar, juices and zests in double boiler, mixing well until sugar dissolves.

Cranberry Nut Orange Bread

2 cups all-purpose flour
1 cup sugar
1½ teaspoons baking powder
½ teaspoon baking soda
½ teaspoon salt
¼ cup shortening
¾ cup orange juice

1 teaspoon orange zest
1 egg, beaten
½ cup pecans or walnuts, chopped
1½ cups fresh cranberries, halved

- Preheat oven to 350°.

- Sift together flour and next 4 ingredients into large bowl. Cut in shortening and set aside.

- Combine orange juice, zest and egg in small bowl, mixing well. Pour into flour mixture, stirring to moisten. Fold in nuts and cranberries.

- Pour into greased 9x5x3-inch loaf pan. Bake for 1 hour.

Yield: 1 loaf or 1 dozen muffins

Batter may be made into muffins. Fill prepared muffin cups two-thirds full. Combine ⅔ cup sugar and 2 teaspoons cinnamon and sprinkle on muffins before baking. Bake at 350° for 15 minutes or until tester comes out clean.

Best Muffins

3	cups all-purpose flour
1	tablespoon baking powder
½	teaspoon baking soda
½	teaspoon salt
10	tablespoons unsalted butter, softened
1	cup minus 1 tablespoon sugar
2	eggs
1½	cups plain lowfat yogurt

- Preheat oven to 375°.
- Spray muffin pan with nonstick cooking spray.
- Combine flour, baking powder, baking soda and salt and set aside.
- Beat butter and sugar on medium high speed with electric mixer until light and fluffy.
- Add eggs one at a time, beating well after each addition.
- Beat in half of flour mixture and half of yogurt, mixing well. Repeat.
- Pour evenly into muffin pans. Bake for 25 minutes or until golden.
- Cool 5 minutes on wire rack and serve warm.

Yield: 12 muffins

Variations:

CINNAMON COATED MUFFINS

Combine ½ cup sugar and 2 teaspoons cinnamon. Dip warm muffins in melted butter, then in sugar mixture.

POPPYSEED MUFFINS

Add 3 tablespoons poppyseeds to flour mixture and 1 tablespoon lemon zest to butter and sugar mixture. Heat ¼ cup sugar and ¼ cup lemon juice until sugar dissolves and a light syrup forms. Brush over warm muffins.

Overnight Coffee Cake

2	cups all-purpose flour	1	teaspoon ground cinnamon	
1	cup sugar			
½	cup firmly packed brown sugar	1	cup buttermilk	
1	teaspoon baking soda	½	cup plus 2⅔ tablespoons butter, melted	
1	teaspoon baking powder	2	eggs	
½	teaspoon salt		Brown Sugar Topping	

- Combine flour and next 6 ingredients in large bowl. Add buttermilk, butter and eggs, beating with electric mixer on low speed until moist. Beat at medium speed 3 minutes or until well blended.

- Spoon batter into greased and floured 9x13-inch pan. Sprinkle Brown Sugar Topping over batter.

- Cover and chill 8 to 12 hours.

- Preheat oven to 350°.

- Bake uncovered for 30 to 35 minutes or until tester comes out clean. Serve warm.

Yield: 12 to 15 servings

Brown Sugar Topping

½	cup firmly packed brown sugar	½	cup chopped pecans
		1	teaspoon cinnamon

- Combine ingredients together in small bowl, mixing well.

Coffee cake may be baked immediately.

Kayaking has become a very popular way to explore tidal marshes, rivers and barrier islands. Early morning "yakers" may be seen along our waterways.

Mrs. Heaton's Cherry Coffee Cake

1	cup butter, softened	1	teaspoon baking powder
1	cup sugar	1	teaspoon baking soda
2	eggs	1	(16-ounce) can cherry pie
1	(8-ounce) carton sour cream		filling
1	teaspoon vanilla		Nut Topping
2	cups all-purpose flour		

- Preheat oven to 375°.
- Cream butter and sugar. Add eggs, sour cream and vanilla, mixing well, and set aside.
- Combine flour, baking powder and baking soda. Fold into butter mixture.
- Pour half of batter into greased 9x13-inch baking pan. Spread pie filling over batter. Pour remaining batter over filling. Spread Nut Topping over batter. Bake for 45 minutes.

Yield: 12 to 15 servings

Nut Topping

½	cup chopped nuts	3	tablespoons butter,
¼	cup all-purpose flour		softened
¼	cup sugar		

- Combine ingredients, mixing well.

Almond Crusted Coffee Cake

1	cup butter, melted	2	tablespoons almond extract
1½	cups sugar	⅛	teaspoon salt
1¾	cups all-purpose flour	1	(2½-ounce) package sliced
2	eggs		almonds

- Preheat oven to 350°.
- Spray a 10-inch pie pan with nonstick cooking spray.
- Combine butter and next 5 ingredients, stirring well.
- Spread in pie pan and sprinkle with almonds.
- Bake for 35 to 40 minutes until edges are lightly browned, being careful not to overbake. Cool before serving.

Yield: 6 to 8 servings

Blueberry Almond Coffee Cake

1   cup all-purpose flour
½   cup sugar
¾   teaspoon baking powder
½   teaspoon salt
¼   teaspoon baking soda
1   cup fresh blueberries,
       divided
⅔   cup buttermilk

2   tablespoons butter, melted
1   egg
1   teaspoon vanilla
½   teaspoon almond extract
¼   cup sliced almonds
2   tablespoons brown sugar
½   teaspoon cinnamon

*A delicious,
no-fuss breakfast
for guests.*

- Preheat oven to 350°.

- Combine flour and next 4 ingredients in large bowl, blending well. Add ⅔ cup blueberries, tossing well, and set aside.

- Whisk together buttermilk and next 4 ingredients in small bowl. Add to flour mixture, stirring gently until moist.

- Pour into prepared 8 or 9-inch round cake pan. Sprinkle with remaining ⅓ cup blueberries, almonds, brown sugar and cinnamon.

- Bake for 35 minutes. Allow to cool 5 minutes before serving.

Yield: 6 to 8 servings

Cinnamon Roll-Ups

1   loaf thinly sliced bread,
       crusts removed
1   (8-ounce) package cream
       cheese, softened
1   egg yolk

½   teaspoon vanilla
1   cup plus 2 tablespoons
       sugar
½   cup butter, melted
1½   teaspoons cinnamon

- Preheat oven to 400°.

- Roll bread flat and set aside.

- Combine cream cheese, yolk, vanilla and 2 tablespoons sugar, mixing well. Spread mixture on bread and roll tightly.

- Combine 1 cup sugar and cinnamon, blending well. Dip bread in butter, then cinnamon mixture.

- Arrange on baking sheet and freeze. Cut into bite-size pieces. Store in zip-top plastic bags in freezer.

- Bake for 8 to 10 minutes or until lightly brown.

Yield: 50 pieces

French Toast Bake

The city of Beaufort sits on Port Royal Island. When French captain Jean Ribaut arrived in 1562, he exclaimed that he would find "no faurer or fytter place than Porte Royall".

1	(16-ounce) loaf French or Italian bread	4	teaspoons sugar
		¾	teaspoon salt
8	eggs	1	tablespoon vanilla
3	cups milk	2	tablespoons butter, cubed

- Preheat oven to 350°.

- Cut bread into 1-inch thick slices and arrange in single layer on the bottom of prepared 13x9x2-inch baking pan.

- Beat eggs and next 4 ingredients in large bowl, mixing well. Pour over bread.

- Cover and chill 4 to 36 hours.

- Dot bread with butter. Bake uncovered for 45 to 50 minutes. Allow to set 5 minutes before serving.

Yield: 8 servings

Serve with maple syrup, fruit or confectioners' sugar.

Nellie's Hotcakes

1	egg	1	tablespoon baking powder
1	cup milk	1	tablespoon sugar
2	tablespoons cooking oil	½	teaspoon salt
1¼	cups sifted all-purpose flour		

- Beat egg, milk and oil together in bowl and set aside.

- Sift together flour and remaining ingredients. Add to egg mixture, mixing well.

- Drop by spoonfuls into greased electric skillet or griddle at 400°. Brown each side.

- Serve warm with syrup and sour cream.

Yield: 8 hotcakes

Baked Blueberry French Toast

1	(12-ounce) loaf sourdough bread, crusts removed	4	eggs
1	(8-ounce) package cream cheese, cubed	2	cups milk
1	pint blueberries, rinsed and drained	1½	teaspoons cinnamon
1	tablespoon sugar	3	tablespoons confectioners' sugar, sifted
			Blueberry Syrup

- Preheat oven to 375°.

- Cut bread into cubes and place half in prepared 9x13-inch baking pan. Top with cream cheese. Place blueberries over cream cheese. Sprinkle sugar on top of blueberries. Top with remaining bread cubes.

- Combine eggs, milk and cinnamon in small bowl, mixing well. Pour over bread.

- Bake for 35 to 45 minutes or until puffed and set. Sprinkle with confectioners' sugar and serve with Blueberry Syrup.

Yield: 6 to 8 servings

Blueberry Syrup

1	cup sugar	2	cups fresh or frozen blueberries
2	tablespoons cornstarch		
1	cup water	2	tablespoons butter

- Heat sugar, cornstarch and water in small saucepan over medium high heat, stirring occasionally. Cook 5 minutes or until thickened.

- Stir in blueberries gently, simmering 10 minutes or until berries have burst. Add butter, stirring gently.

Most Southerners forgo traditional breakfasts these days, but we all enjoy the indulgent treat of waffles. Cooked on a specially made honey-combed surface, they are a Lowcountry weekend and holiday favorite.

~

"I love Christmas morning when we have waffles, strawberries and as much whipped cream as we want!"

Emily Collins, Grade 4
Beaufort Academy
student

Madelaine's Favorite Buttermilk Waffles

2	cups all-purpose flour	2	egg yolks, beaten
¼	teaspoon baking soda	1¾	cups buttermilk
1½	teaspoons baking powder	6	tablespoons butter, melted
1	tablespoon sugar	2	egg whites
½	teaspoon salt		

- Sift together flour and next 4 ingredients. Beat in yolks; add buttermilk and butter, mixing well.

- Beat egg whites until stiff, but not dry. Fold into batter.

- Cook in preheated waffle iron following manufacturer's instructions.

Yield: 6 servings

Thanksgiving Waffles

1	cup all-purpose flour	½	cup mashed pumpkin or yams
½	teaspoon salt	3	eggs, beaten
2	teaspoons baking powder	1½	cups milk
2	tablespoons sugar	2	tablespoons butter, melted
⅛	teaspoon cinnamon		
⅛	teaspoon nutmeg		

- Sift together flour and next 5 ingredients and set aside.

- Combine pumpkin, eggs, milk and butter, mixing well. Add to flour mixture, stirring until moist.

- Cook in preheated waffle iron following manufacturer's instructions

Yield: 6 servings

Serve with melted butter and syrup or cinnamon and sugar.

Sea Island Strata

1	9-inch unbaked pie shell	1	cup half-and-half
1	small red bell pepper, seeded and chopped	1	teaspoon salt
½	cup sweet onion, chopped	½	teaspoon black pepper
2	garlic cloves, minced	⅓	cup fresh Parmesan cheese
2	tablespoons olive oil	2	cups shredded Monterey Jack cheese
2	tablespoons fresh basil, chopped	3	plum tomatoes, thinly sliced
4	eggs		

- Place pie shell in 9-inch tart pan. Prick shell with fork.

- Bake at 425° for 10 minutes.

- Sauté red bell pepper, onion and garlic in olive oil until tender (about 5 minutes). Stir in basil and set aside.

- Whisk together eggs, half-and-half, salt and pepper in large bowl. Add sautéed vegetables and cheeses to egg mixture.

- Pour into crust and top with tomato slices. Bake at 375° for 45 to 50 minutes or until center is set. Cool 5 minutes before serving.

Yield: 6 to 8 servings

The Sea Islands are a series of islands near the Atlantic Ocean. Port Royal, St. Helena, Lady's, Hunting and Fripp are just a few of the beautiful Sea Islands in Beaufort County.

Chili Rellenos Casserole

2	(4.5-ounce) cans chopped green chiles	⅓	cup milk
½	pound shredded Monterey Jack cheese	4	eggs, beaten
		¼	cup all-purpose flour
8	ounces shredded Cheddar cheese	¼	cup baking powder
		1	(12-ounce) jar salsa

- Preheat oven to 350°.

- Layer half of chiles in prepared 8-inch square baking pan. Sprinkle Monterey Jack over chiles. Arrange remaining chiles over Monterey Jack. Sprinkle Cheddar cheese over chiles and set aside.

- Combine milk, eggs, flour and baking powder, mixing well. Pour over chiles.

- Bake for 45 minutes.

- Serve salsa over casserole.

Yield: 6 servings

Mushroom and Asparagus Strata

1	pound thin asparagus spears	2	tablespoons fresh dill, minced
1	tablespoon olive oil	6	slices French bread
4	cups fresh mushrooms, sliced	6	eggs
2	garlic cloves, minced	2¼	cups half-and-half
¼	teaspoon salt	¼	cup shredded Romano or Parmesan cheese
¼	teaspoon black pepper		Fresh dill sprigs, for garnish
2	cups shredded Swiss cheese		

- Preheat oven to 325°.

- Cut asparagus into 3-inch pieces. Bring 1 inch of water to a boil in skillet. Add asparagus and cook 1 minute. Drain and rinse immediately with cold water. Set aside.

- Heat oil in large skillet and sauté mushrooms and garlic about 5 minutes or until liquid has reduced. Season with salt and pepper and set aside.

- Combine Swiss cheese and dill in small mixing bowl and set aside.

- Cut bread into 4x1x1-inch sticks. Arrange half of bread on lightly greased rectangular baking pan.

- Layer half of mushroom mixture, half of cheese mixture and half of asparagus. Repeat layers and top with remaining bread.

- Beat together eggs and half-and-half in small bowl, mixing well. Pour over layers and press with back of spoon, making sure bread is thoroughly moistened.

- Sprinkle with Romano cheese. Bake uncovered for 45 minutes or until center is set. Cool 10 minutes before serving. Garnish with dill.

Yield: 6 to 8 servings

Fresh dill may be substituted with 1 teaspoon dried dill.

Zucchini–Ham Frittata

3	tablespoons olive oil	6	eggs, beaten
¾	cup red bell pepper, seeded and chopped	¼	cup half-and-half
¾	cup yellow or white onion, chopped	1	(8-ounce) package cream cheese, cubed
1½	cups fresh mushrooms, sliced	1½	cups shredded Cheddar cheese
1½	cups zucchini, chopped	1	teaspoon salt
1	garlic clove, minced	¼	teaspoon black pepper
1	cup cooked ham, cubed	2	cups fresh French bread cubes

- Preheat oven to 350°.

- Heat oil in skillet over low to medium heat. Sauté peppers, onions, mushrooms and zucchini about 10 minutes or until crisp tender. Add garlic during last 2 to 3 minutes of cooking.

- Stir in ham and allow mixture to cool slightly.

- Beat eggs with half-and-half in large mixing bowl.

- Stir in vegetable mixture and remaining ingredients.

- Pour into well-greased 10-inch springform pan. Bake for 1 hour or until center is set. Allow to cool 10 minutes before cutting.

Yield: 8 servings

Stratas and frittatas also make excellent light suppers that can be prepared ahead.

Hunting Island Grits

1	pound bacon	1	(28-ounce) can diced tomatoes, drained
2	bell peppers, seeded and chopped	1½	cups white grits
2	medium onions, chopped	1½	cups shredded Cheddar cheese
1½	cups ham, ground		Salt and pepper to taste

- Cook bacon in skillet, reserving the drippings. Drain bacon, crumble and set aside.
- Sauté peppers and onions in reserved drippings until tender. Add ham and sauté 15 minutes, stirring well.
- Add tomatoes and simmer 30 minutes.
- Cook grits according to package directions. Add to ham mixture, stirring well. Salt and pepper to taste.
- Pour into casserole and top with bacon and Cheddar. Place under broiler until cheese melts.

Yield: 12 servings

If you really want a treat, forego the regular store varieties of grits and look for specialty stone-ground brands in gourmet cooking shops or specialized grocery aisles.

~

Sausage Bake

4	cups biscuit baking mix	¾	cup Parmesan cheese
1	cup milk	1-1½	cups shredded Swiss cheese
1	cup mayonnaise		
3	pounds hot sausage	2	eggs, beaten
1	cup chopped onion		

- Preheat oven to 350°.
- Combine baking mix, milk and mayonnaise, mixing well to form dough. Place half of dough in greased 9x13-inch baking pan. Set aside remaining dough.
- Cook sausage with onion. Drain well and cool slightly. Add cheeses and eggs. Spoon over dough in baking pan and set aside.
- Form biscuit mounds with remaining dough and place atop sausage mixture. Bake for 30 minutes.

Yield: 12 servings

Sausage Bake may be frozen.

"These we have loved—lazy summer days; lying out on the beach; ice cold lemonade; skiing in the river; watermelons; smoothies at the Cabana Club; vacationing; summer."

Caroline Webb
Caroline Brown
Chris Scholl
Suzanne Staak
Beaufort Academy
students,
Grades 11 & 12

Sausage–Hash Brown Mini Frittatas

8 ounces turkey sausage, casings removed
1 medium onion, chopped
2 cups frozen hash brown potatoes, thawed
4½ ounces shredded Cheddar cheese
3 tablespoons flour
6 eggs, lightly beaten
1 cup reduced-calorie creamy ranch dressing
½ cup skim milk

Few things make us feel as pampered as a leisurely breakfast with homemade treats.

- Preheat oven to 325°. Spray 24 muffin cups with nonstick cooking spray.

- Cook sausage and onion in large skillet. Transfer to colander and drain, then to large bowl.

- Add potatoes and cheese, mixing well. Stir in flour and set aside.

- Combine eggs, dressing and milk, mixing well. Add to sausage mixture, tossing well.

- Spoon evenly into muffin cups. Bake for 15 to 20 minutes or until set and golden.

Yield: 12 servings

Serve topped with fresh salsa.

Fruit Pizza

1	package commercial sugar cookie dough
1	(8-ounce) package cream cheese, softened
½	cup confectioners' sugar

	Fresh fruit
1¾	cups white grape juice
⅓	cup sugar
2	tablespoons cornstarch

- Slice cookie dough and arrange on 16-inch pizza or rectangular pan, pressing cookies together.
- Bake according to package directions, careful not to overbake. Allow to cool.
- Combine cream cheese and confectioners' sugar, mixing well. Spread over dough.
- Slice fruit and arrange on cream cheese mixture.
- Cook juice, sugar and cornstarch in small saucepan over medium heat until thickened. Allow to cool and spread over fruit.

Yield: 8 servings

Use any assortment of fresh fruit, such as strawberries, kiwi, blueberries, peaches or bananas.

Part of the Lowcountry's economic history is based on the rise and fall of truck farming, particularly tomatoes and cucumbers, which were once grown on hundreds of acres in the Sea Islands. Farmers, not corporations, produced what Americans consumed and brought the produce to market by trucks.

SOUPS & SALADS

SOUPS & SALADS

During the summer it is a familiar sight to see a fleet of boats high and dry in the middle of the river on a sandbar. There is no finer way to spend a sunny day in the Lowcountry with family and friends than at low tide on exposed sandbars. Sandbar Sundays involve the young and old packing picnics, volleyball nets, chairs, floats and goodness knows what else to spend a few hours until the high tide comes along and tells them it is time to go home.

Cream of Artichoke Soup

6	tablespoons unsalted butter	¼	teaspoon freshly ground black pepper
½	cup finely chopped onion	¼	teaspoon dried thyme
½	cup finely chopped celery	1	(15-ounce) can whole artichoke hearts, drained and chopped
6	tablespoons all-purpose flour		
6	cups chicken broth	2	cups heavy cream
¼	cup fresh lemon juice		Lemon slices
1	teaspoon salt		Fresh thyme

- Melt butter in large saucepan over medium heat. Add onion and celery, and sauté until tender. Add flour, stirring to coat vegetables. Add chicken broth and lemon juice, stirring 3 to 5 minutes or until thickened.
- Season with salt, pepper and thyme; add artichokes.
- Reduce heat and simmer 30 minutes.
- Remove from heat, puree in food processor or blender and return to saucepan.
- Add cream and slowly reheat, being careful not to boil.
- Spoon into bowls and garnish with lemon slices and fresh thyme.

Yield: 8 servings

Artichokes are considered one of the most beautiful vegetables. They are actually immature thistles, and if left on the stem, they would blossom into gorgeous flowers. Because of their delicate taste, we take them from the stem and serve them hundreds of different ways.

Carrot and Ginger Soup

Ginger is a versatile spice with a distinct bite and aroma. It is available in several different forms. Dried ground ginger is often found in cakes, cookies, pies, rice and marinades. Crystallized and preserved ginger may be found in cakes and cookies. Fresh ginger may be used in marinades for vegetables, fish, poultry and other meats.

6	tablespoons unsalted butter	2	tablespoons fresh lemon juice
1	large onion, chopped		Pinch of curry powder
¼	cup peeled, chopped fresh ginger		Salt to taste
3	cloves garlic, minced		Freshly ground pepper to taste
7	cups chicken broth		Sour cream
1	cup dry white wine		Fresh parsley sprigs
2	pounds carrots, peeled and chopped into ½-inch cubes		

- Melt butter in large stockpot over medium heat. Add onion, ginger and garlic. Sauté 15 minutes or until tender. Add chicken broth, wine and carrots and bring to a boil.

- Reduce heat and simmer, uncovered 30 to 45 minutes or until carrots are tender.

- Remove from heat and puree in food processor or blender.

- Stir in lemon juice. Season with salt, pepper and curry powder.

- Spoon into individual bowls and serve hot. Garnish with sour cream and sprig of parsley.

Yield: 6 servings

Soup may be made ahead and frozen.

Szechuan Carrot Soup

1 medium onion, chopped
1 garlic clove, minced
1 teaspoon olive oil
1 pound carrots, peeled and chopped
1 (1-inch) piece fresh ginger, peeled and sliced
⅛ teaspoon crushed red pepper flakes
3 cups chicken or vegetable broth
1½ tablespoons soy sauce
1 tablespoon creamy peanut butter
1 cup whole milk
Chopped green onions or chives for garnish

- Sauté onions and garlic in oil in saucepan over medium high heat until onion is tender. Add carrots, ginger, red pepper flakes and broth. Simmer covered about 20 minutes or until carrots are tender.

- Remove from heat and puree in blender or food processor.

- Return soup to saucepan and stir in soy sauce, peanut butter and milk.

- Simmer until thoroughly heated. Garnish with green onions or chives before serving.

Yield: 6 to 8 servings

Winter Squash Soup

2 tablespoons olive oil
2 celery stalks, chopped
1 medium onion, chopped
12 baby carrots, peeled and chopped
1 pound butternut squash, peeled and chopped
½ pound white potatoes, peeled and chopped
⅛ teaspoon red pepper flakes
2 teaspoons salt
3½ cups boiling water or chicken broth

- Heat olive oil in heavy skillet over low heat. Add celery, onion and carrots and cook until tender, being careful not to brown. Add squash, potatoes, salt and pepper.

- Stir in boiling water or broth and simmer covered about 15 to 20 minutes or until vegetables are tender.

- Remove soup from heat. Puree in blender or food processor until smooth. Add additional boiling water or broth until desired consistency is reached. Serve warm .

Yield: 6 cups

Old Point Primavera

1	cup peas	2	cups chicken broth, divided
1	large onion, sliced	1	teaspoon salt
1	carrot, peeled and sliced		Freshly ground black
1	celery stalk, sliced		pepper
1	medium potato, peeled and sliced	¾	teaspoon curry powder
		1	cup light cream

- Boil peas and next 4 ingredients in 1 cup broth in medium saucepan. Add salt, pepper and curry powder.
- Reduce heat, cover and simmer about 15 minutes.
- Remove from heat. Puree in blender or food processor until smooth.
- Return soup to saucepan. Add cream and remaining broth. Simmer until thoroughly heated. Serve warm or chilled.

Yield: 3 to 4 servings

Broccoli and Spinach Soup

¼	cup unsalted butter	2	ripe plum tomatoes, coarsely chopped
1	large onion, chopped		
2	leeks, rinsed and thinly sliced	¼	cup chopped fresh parsley
1	carrot, peeled and chopped	1	(10-ounce) bag of fresh spinach
6	garlic cloves, minced		Salt and pepper to taste
8	cups chicken broth	¼	cup fresh lemon juice
2	(2-pound) heads broccoli, chopped		

- Melt butter in stockpot over low heat and cook onion, leeks, carrot and garlic 10 minutes. Add broth, broccoli, tomatoes and parsley. Bring to a boil.
- Reduce heat and simmer covered about 25 minutes. Stir in spinach and season with salt and pepper.
- Remove from heat and cool slightly. Puree in blender or food processor.
- Return to stockpot and simmer until thoroughly heated. Stir in lemon juice and serve.

Yield: 8 servings

Soup may be prepared ahead and frozen.

Baked Potato Soup

2-3	tablespoons olive oil
1	medium onion, chopped
⅔	cup all-purpose flour
6	cups chicken broth
5	large russet potatoes, baked, peeled and thinly sliced
2	cups half-and-half
¼	cup chopped fresh parsley
1½	teaspoons minced garlic
1½	teaspoons dried basil
1	teaspoon salt
1	teaspoon freshly ground black pepper
½	teaspoon hot pepper sauce
¼	cup chopped green onions
1	cup shredded Cheddar cheese
	Cooked, crumbled bacon for garnish
	Shredded Cheddar cheese for garnish
	Sour cream for garnish
	Minced fresh parsley for garnish

- Heat olive oil in large saucepan over medium high heat. Cook onion until transparent.

- Add flour, stirring until mixture just begins to turn golden.

- Whisk in chicken broth until liquid thickens. Add potatoes. Stir in half-and-half and next 6 ingredients. Reduce heat and simmer about 10 minutes, being careful not to boil.

- Add green onions and 1 cup Cheddar cheese, heating until cheese melts.

- Ladle into bowls and garnish with bacon, Cheddar cheese, sour cream and parsley.

Yield: 6 to 8 servings

The simpler the soup, the more elaborate the garnish. The garnish should only supplement the soup's own flavor.

Try some of these:

- *Freshly chopped herbs*

- *Shredded cheese*

- *Dollop of caviar*

- *Slice of lemon*

- *Dash of sherry*

- *Chopped hard-boiled egg*

- *Dollop of sour cream*

Cream of Vidalia Onion Soup

A bowl of soup is the ultimate comfort food. It's what we feed our families when they are sick and what we crave on cold, rainy days. Just add your favorite crusty bread and a leafy salad, and you've got the makings of the perfect supper when nothing else seems appealing.

¼	pound bacon, cooked and crumbled
4	Vidalia onions, sliced
2	garlic cloves, minced
½	cup unsalted butter
2	cups dry white wine
4	cups chicken broth
1	bay leaf
1	tablespoon minced fresh thyme
1	cup half-and-half
1	cup sour cream
3	tablespoons fresh lemon juice
½	teaspoon salt
¼	teaspoon white pepper
	Dash of hot pepper sauce
	Green onions, minced
	Dash of nutmeg

- Cook bacon in large skillet over medium high heat until crisp, reserving 2 tablespoons bacon drippings. Drain on paper towels, crumble and set aside.

- Sauté onions and garlic in butter and 2 tablespoons bacon drippings in large saucepan over medium heat until onions are lightly caramelized.

- Add wine, broth, bay leaf and thyme. Cover and simmer 30 minutes.

- Remove from heat and discard bay leaf. Puree in blender or food processor until smooth. Add half-and-half and next 5 ingredients.

- Serve warm garnished with bacon, green onions and dash of nutmeg.

Yield: 8 servings

Apple Soup with Roquefort Croutons

6 tablespoons unsalted butter, divided
3 large Red Delicious apples, peeled, cored and sliced
3 large Granny Smith apples, peeled, cored and sliced
1 cup chopped onion
1 teaspoon minced garlic
5 cups chicken broth
1½ cups heavy cream
¼ cup apple brandy

Salt to taste
Freshly ground white pepper to taste
½ Red Delicious apple, cut into 12 slices
½ Granny Smith apple, cut into 12 slices
1 tablespoon fresh lemon juice
2 tablespoons snipped fresh chives
Roquefort Croutons

- Melt ¼ cup butter in heavy saucepan. Add apples, onion and garlic. Cook 5 minutes, stirring occasionally. Reduce heat, add broth and simmer about 25 minutes or until apples are tender.

- Remove from heat. Puree apple mixture in blender or food processor. Return puree to saucepan and add cream and apple brandy. Bring to a simmer. Season with salt and pepper.

- Allow to cool; cover and chill.

- Toss apple slices with lemon juice in medium bowl.

- Melt remaining 2 tablespoons butter in skillet over medium high heat. Sauté apples until golden and set aside.

- Bring soup to a simmer over medium heat. Ladle into bowls and top with 2 red apple slices and 2 green apple slices. Sprinkle with chives and serve with Roquefort Croutons.

Yield: 6 servings

Roquefort Croutons

4 bacon slices
18 baguette slices, cut ¼-inch thickness
4 ounces Roquefort cheese, crumbled
¼ cup unsalted butter, softened

- Preheat oven to 350°. Place rack in center of oven.

- Cook bacon in skillet until crisp. Drain on paper towels. Crumble and set aside.

- Arrange baguette slices on baking sheet and bake 10 minutes or until golden.

- Process cheese and butter in food processor until smooth. Spread on baguette slices.

- Preheat broiler. Place baguettes under broiler 2 minutes or until cheese melts. Sprinkle with crumbled bacon.

Yield: 18 slices

Butter and cheese mixture may be prepared up to 4 hours ahead, covered and kept at room temperature.

Seafood Gumbo

*Oh, de crab,
he taste so fine.*

*Yuh catch 'um wid
a neck an' a line.*

*Bile de water
'til 'e good 'n hot,*

*Den eat de crab
straite from de pot!*

Printed with the
kind permission of
Vida Miller

⅓	cup cooking oil	1	teaspoon dried basil
1	yellow onion, chopped	1	teaspoon dried oregano
1	red bell pepper, chopped	1	teaspoon dried thyme
2	garlic cloves, minced	1	teaspoon hot pepper sauce
3	tablespoons all-purpose flour		Salt to taste
			Freshly ground black pepper to taste
4	cups chicken broth	1	pound smoked sausage, sliced
1	(28-ounce) can diced tomatoes with juice	1	pound medium shrimp, peeled and deveined
1	pound cooked lump crabmeat	4	cups steamed long grain white rice
½	pound fresh or frozen okra		
2	bay leaves		

- Heat oil in large saucepan over medium heat and sauté onions and red bell pepper until tender. Add garlic and reduce heat to low. Stir in flour and cook 5 minutes or until flour turns slightly brown.

- Stir in chicken broth slowly. Add tomatoes and next 9 ingredients. Bring to a boil. Reduce heat, cover and simmer 1 hour.

- Boil sausage in second pan then drain. Add warm sausage to gumbo.

- Stir in shrimp and simmer 5 minutes or until shrimp are pink and cooked through.

- Mound rice in soup bowls. Ladle gumbo over rice and serve.

Yield: 8 servings

She-Crab Soup

¼ cup unsalted butter
3 tablespoons minced sweet onion
4 tablespoons all-purpose flour
4 cups half-and-half
Salt and pepper to taste

2 teaspoons Worcestershire sauce
½ teaspoon paprika
Dash of Old Bay seasoning
1 pound lump crabmeat
2 hard-boiled eggs, finely chopped
Sherry to taste

- Melt butter in Dutch oven over medium high heat. Sauté onion about 8 to 10 minutes or until tender. Add flour and stir until flour begins to turn golden.

- Reduce heat and whisk in half-and-half. Continue whisking 3 to 5 minutes or until slightly thickened.

- Season with salt and pepper. Add Worcestershire, paprika and Old Bay. Fold in crab and eggs, heating on low about 15 to 20 minutes.

- Ladle into bowls and sprinkle with sherry to taste.

Yield: 8 servings

In the Lowcountry crabs come two ways— shes and jimmies. They can be identified very simply using the landmarks of Washington, D.C. Each crab has a distinctive shell on its back. The she crab shell looks like the Capitol building, and the jimmy (male) shell looks like the Washington Monument.

Shrimp Bisque

2 (14½-ounce) cans diced tomatoes, drained
2 (10¼-ounce) cans beef broth
1 cup chopped celery with leaves
2 medium carrots, shredded
2 teaspoons chopped fresh parsley
4 garlic cloves, peeled

6 black peppercorns
1 bay leaf
2 teaspoons salt
3 tablespoons uncooked white rice
Pinch of dried thyme
1½ pounds shrimp, peeled, deveined and cooked
2 cups half-and-half
Sherry

- Combine tomatoes and next 11 ingredients in large saucepan and simmer 1 hour.

- Remove and discard bay leaf. Remove soup from heat. Puree in blender or food processor until smooth.

- Return to saucepan. Add shrimp and half-and-half, simmering until thoroughly heated.

- Ladle into bowls and sprinkle with sherry.

Yield: 4 servings

Factory Creek Oyster Bisque

1	tablespoon olive oil	36	ounces select oysters, drained
¾	cup finely chopped carrots	¼	cup chili sauce
¾	cup chopped celery	1	tablespoon Worcestershire sauce
¾	cup chopped red bell pepper	1	teaspoon paprika
2	cups evaporated milk or half-and-half		Dash of cayenne pepper
3	tablespoons all-purpose flour		

- Heat oil in medium Dutch oven over medium high heat. Sauté carrots, celery and red bell pepper about 5 minutes or until tender. Set aside.

- Whisk together milk and flour in small bowl. Add to vegetables.

- Reduce heat and simmer 3 to 5 minutes or until thickened, stirring constantly.

- Fold in oysters and simmer about 2 minutes or until edges curl. Stir in chili sauce, Worcestershire sauce, paprika and cayenne. Serve hot.

Yield: 6 servings

For a richer bisque, do not drain oysters.

"The oyster canning and packing industry, once prominent in Beaufort, has all but disappeared. One can hardly believe Factory Creek's history as an oyster canning factory with mountains of shucked oysters lining the banks. Oyster scows brought tons of raw oysters to the cannery for processing. The sound of steam whistles signaled 'shuckers' to report to work. The smell of steaming oysters permeated the air."

Charles Webb, III
Beaufort Academy
alumnae and parent

Shrimp and Corn Chowder

2 tablespoons kosher salt
6 cups fresh or frozen corn
  kernels
¼ cup unsalted butter
2 large sweet onions, finely
  chopped
½ cup all-purpose flour
1 teaspoon freshly ground
  black pepper

½ teaspoon turmeric or Old
  Bay seasoning
10 cups chicken broth
1½ pounds potatoes, peeled
  and chopped
1 cup half-and-half
½ pound shredded sharp
  Cheddar cheese
1½ pounds shrimp, peeled
  and deveined

- Bring medium saucepan of salted water to a boil. Add corn and cook over high heat about 3 minutes. Drain, rinse under cold water and set aside.

- Melt butter in medium Dutch oven over medium high heat and sauté onions 10 minutes or until tender. Stir in flour, pepper and turmeric and continue stirring 3 minutes.

- Add chicken broth and potatoes. Bring to a boil and cook 15 to 20 minutes or until potatoes are tender.

- Stir in corn, half-and-half, cheese and shrimp. Cook 3 additional minutes or until shrimp are pink. Serve hot.

Yield: 6 servings

SHORT CUT SEAFOOD SOUP

1 (10¾-ounce) can cream of potato soup

1 (10¾-ounce) can cream of shrimp soup

1 (10¾-ounce) can cream of mushroom soup

1 (10¾-ounce) can tomato soup

1 small onion, finely chopped

Butter for sautéing

4 cups half-and-half

1 pound shrimp, peeled and deveined (slightly cooked)

1 pound scallops (slightly cooked)

1 pound crabmeat, cooked

⅓ cup dry sherry

Fresh parsley for garnish

- Sauté onion in butter in skillet over medium high heat and set aside.

- Combine soups in large saucepan and heat, stirring occasionally. Add onions, half-and-half and seafood, stirring gently. Add sherry to soup in saucepan or serving bowls. Garnish with parsley and serve.

Yield: 10 to 12 servings

To eliminate grease, drop a lettuce leaf on top of the soup. You may have to repeat the process until all of the grease is absorbed.

~

Brunswick Stew

2	whole fryer chickens, cut up	1	cup chopped onion
2	celery stalks, cut into 1-inch pieces	2	(28-ounce) cans diced tomatoes, undrained
1	small onion, quartered	2	medium potatoes, peeled and chopped
7	cups water, divided	2	tablespoons unsalted butter
2	(10-ounce) packages frozen baby lima beans	1	tablespoon salt
2	(10-ounce) packages frozen whole kernel corn	1½	teaspoons cayenne pepper

- Combine chicken, celery, onion and 5 cups water in large stockpot. Bring to a boil, cover and simmer 1 hour.

- Remove chicken, celery and onion from broth. Allow chicken to cool and debone. Discard skin, bones, celery and onion. Skim fat from broth and return chicken to stockpot.

- Add lima beans and next 7 ingredients. Simmer uncovered 4 hours, adding remaining 2 cups water if needed.

Yield: 8 servings

Gullah Soup

The Gullah Festival each May honors the African-American rituals of daily life. It celebrates the Gullah language in story telling and gospel singing. The Gullah culture is celebrated through taste sensations, arts, dance traditions and crafts, such as the famous handmade sweet grass baskets.

1	large sweet onion, coarsely chopped	1	(15-ounce) can dark red kidney beans, drained
1	pound Italian sausage, casings removed and crumbled	4-5	(15-ounce) cans chicken broth
1	(28-ounce) can diced tomatoes	1	head escarole, coarsely chopped

- Sauté onions with sausage in large stockpot over medium high heat until sausage is brown. Drain sausage and return to stockpot. Stir in tomatoes, beans, broth and escarole.

- Reduce heat and simmer 45 minutes. Serve with crusty bread.

Yield: 6 servings

Soup is better if prepared one day ahead.

Spicy Corn and Cheese Chowder

5   large potatoes, unpeeled and diced
5   cups chicken broth
3   bay leaves
1   tablespoon unsalted butter
1   cup chopped green onions
1   teaspoon cumin or cumin seed
4   cups fresh or frozen corn kernels
2   tablespoons all-purpose flour

1   cup heavy cream
1½   cups shredded sharp Cheddar or Monterey Jack cheese
1   cup shredded Monterey Jack cheese with peppers
Salt and pepper to taste
1   tablespoon minced fresh chives
1   tablespoon minced fresh parsley

- Combine potatoes, broth and bay leaves in medium stockpot and bring to a boil.

- Reduce heat, cover and simmer until potatoes are tender.

- Melt butter in skillet over medium high heat and sauté green onions with cumin until tender. Add green onions and corn to soup.

- Combine flour and cream in small bowl, blending thoroughly, and slowly whisk into soup.

- Add cheese ¼ cup at a time and stir until cheese melts. Season with salt and pepper. Stir in chives and parsley.

Yield: 6 to 8 servings

Serve hot with rolls.

In the Lowcountry the agricultural staples of colonial times were cattle and corn in the high land, rice in the swampy areas, and indigo in the sea islands.

Chicken or Duck Gumbo

"Gumbo" is the West African word for okra. Despite the fact that Louisiana claims gumbo, okra first entered South Carolina with the slave trade long before Louisiana was settled by the Europeans.

Okra, when cooked, yields a natural thickening agent that works well in stews and gumbos. Okra is also delicious steamed, fried and pickled.

3	chicken or duck breasts, skinned, boned and cut into 2-inch pieces
	Salt and pepper to taste
	Cayenne pepper to taste
½	cup cooking oil
	All-purpose flour
2	medium onions, chopped
1	cup chopped celery
1	large bell pepper, chopped
1	bunch green onions, chopped
2	garlic cloves, minced
2	quarts hot water

1	bay leaf
1	tablespoon Worcestershire sauce
	Pinch of dried thyme
	Hot pepper sauce to taste
2	(10-ounce) packages frozen sliced okra, thawed
2	(10-ounce) packages frozen corn, thawed
⅓	cup tomato paste
1	pound smoked sausage, cut into ¼-inch slices
6	cups cooked rice
¼	cup minced fresh parsley

- Season chicken or duck breasts with salt, pepper and cayenne. Brown breasts in oil in 6-quart Dutch oven. Remove breasts and keep warm. Discard all but ⅓ cup oil.

- Reduce heat to low and stir in enough flour to achieve a dark roux. Add onions and next 4 ingredients, stirring into roux. Add hot water and next 7 ingredients. Season with salt and pepper, stirring well.

- Add breasts and sausage. Simmer over low heat 2 hours, stirring occasionally. Add water if needed. Serve in individual bowls over rice and sprinkle with parsley.

Yield: 8 servings

Old-Fashioned Chicken Noodle Soup

1	(5-pound) chicken	½	cup fresh parsley, chopped
3	quarts water	2	bay leaves
1	tablespoon salt	2	teaspoons dried thyme
1	large onion, chopped	2	teaspoons lemon pepper seasoning
6	celery stalks with leaves, chopped	8	ounces thin egg noodles
6-8	carrots, peeled and sliced		

- Combine chicken and next 9 ingredients in large stockpot. Bring to a boil. Reduce heat and simmer 2 hours, 30 minutes to 3 hours or until chicken is tender.

- Remove chicken from soup and cool. Debone chicken and discard skin and bones. Return chicken to soup.

- Bring to a boil and add noodles. Cook noodles al dente and serve.

Yield: 6 to 8 servings

Women from most times and countries have started boiling chicken for soup at the first sign of illness. In every land and climate, chicken soup is considered an excellent remedy for fevers, colds, hangovers, queasy appetites, bad tempers and chills.

Taco Soup

1½	pounds ground beef	2	(15-ounce) cans crushed tomatoes, undrained
1	medium onion, chopped	2	(1.25-ounce) packages taco seasoning
1	(15-ounce) can corn, undrained		Shredded sharp Cheddar cheese
1	(15-ounce) can pinto beans, undrained		Fried tortilla strips
1	(15-ounce) can kidney beans, undrained		

- Brown beef with onions in large skillet over medium high heat and drain. Return to skillet and add corn, beans and tomatoes. Stir in taco seasoning and simmer 20 to 30 minutes.

- Serve topped with tortilla strips and cheese.

Yield: 4 servings

White Bean Chili

6	cups chicken broth	4	cups cooked, chopped chicken breast
1	pound dried large white beans	2	cups shredded colby or Monterey Jack cheese for garnish
2	garlic cloves, minced		
2	large onions, chopped and divided		Salsa for garnish
1	tablespoon olive oil		Minced parsley for garnish
2	(4-ounce) cans chopped green chiles		Guacamole for garnish
			Sour cream for garnish
2	teaspoons ground cumin		Sliced green onions for garnish
1½	teaspoons dried oregano		
¼	teaspoon ground cloves		Tortilla chips for garnish
¼	teaspoon cayenne		

- Combine broth, beans, garlic and half of onions in large heavy Dutch oven. Cover and bring to a boil.

- Reduce heat and simmer 3 to 4 hours or until beans are soft. Additional broth may be added if needed.

- Sauté remaining onions in olive oil in heavy skillet over medium high heat. Add chiles and next 4 ingredients, stirring well. Add onion mixture and chicken to bean mixture. Simmer 1 hour.

- Garnish with cheese and remaining ingredients.

Yield: 8 to 10 servings

Chilled Tomato Soup with Basil Sorbet

2	tablespoons unsalted butter			Dash of hot pepper sauce
1	large onion, chopped		3	cups chicken broth
2	carrots, peeled and shredded		1	bouquet garni
3	pounds fresh tomatoes, peeled and chopped		1	cup half-and-half
½	teaspoon salt		½	cup heavy cream
¼	teaspoon freshly ground black pepper		1	tomato, seeded and minced

Basil Sorbet
Fresh basil leaves, minced

- Melt butter in Dutch oven over medium high heat and sauté onion and carrot about 8 minutes or until tender. Add tomatoes and next 5 ingredients.

- Reduce heat and simmer 45 minutes.

- Remove from heat, discard bouquet garni and cool. Puree in blender or food processor in batches until smooth.

- Combine puree, half-and-half and cream in large bowl. Chill thoroughly.

- Serve topped with minced tomato, heaping tablespoon of Basil Sorbet and basil leaves.

Yield: 6 servings

Basil Sorbet

½	cup sugar		¼	cup finely chopped fresh parsley
1½	cups water			Zest and juice of 1 lemon
1½	cups finely chopped fresh basil			

- Combine sugar and water in microwavable bowl. Microwave until sugar dissolves. Cool completely.

- Add basil, parsley, lemon zest and juice, blending well, and freeze.

Yield: 1½ cups

Cucumber Soup

½	cup unsalted butter	¼	teaspoon white pepper
2	medium Vidalia onions, chopped	½	cup heavy cream
2	leeks, chopped (bulbs only)	1	teaspoon minced fresh dill
		1	teaspoon fresh lemon juice
2	cucumbers, peeled, seeded and chopped	1	cucumber, peeled, seeded and chopped
2	(14-ounce) cans chicken broth		Sour cream
½	teaspoon salt		Fresh borage blossoms or salad burnet

- Melt butter in Dutch oven over medium high heat and sauté onions, leeks and 2 cucumbers 8 to 10 minutes or until tender.

- Add chicken broth, reduce heat and simmer at least 1 hour.

- Remove from heat. Puree in blender or food processor. Pour soup into large bowl and stir in salt and next 5 ingredients.

- Chill thoroughly. Garnish with sour cream and borage blossoms or salad burnet before serving.

Yield: 6 servings

Summer Strawberry Soup

There is nothing quite as refreshing on a warm summer evening as a chilled soup made from fresh berries. The humidity will drop a point with every spoonful!

1	quart fresh strawberries, stemmed and hulled	⅛	teaspoon cinnamon
		½	cup sugar
1	teaspoon lemon zest	1	tablespoon fresh lemon juice
1	cup fresh orange juice		
1½	tablespoons instant tapioca	2	cantaloupes, halved
			Lemon slices for garnish
1	cup buttermilk		Strawberries for garnish
⅛	teaspoon allspice		

- Blend 1 quart strawberries, lemon zest and orange juice in blender until smooth. Pour through mesh strainer into saucepan and set aside.

- Combine tapioca with strawberry puree in bowl, mixing well. Add buttermilk and next 4 ingredients, blending well. Cover and chill.

- Scoop out cantaloupe centers and scallop edges. Spoon soup into cantaloupes and garnish with lemon slices and strawberries.

Yield: 4 servings

Berry Special Soup

1	cup fresh blueberries	1	tablespoon chopped fresh mint
1	cup fresh raspberries		
4	cups hulled fresh strawberries	2	tablespoons sugar
½	cup port	1	tablespoon white wine vinegar
1	teaspoon minced fresh ginger	4	tablespoons orange juice
¼	cup light cream		Fresh mint springs

- Process blueberries in food processor until smooth. Strain through double layer of cheesecloth into small bowl and set aside.

- Process raspberries and strawberries in food processor until smooth. Repeat straining procedure and set aside.

- Bring port and ginger to a boil in heavy saucepan. Reduce heat and simmer 5 minutes. Add cream and return to a boil. Cook 1 minute, stirring constantly. Remove from heat and set aside.

- Process strained berries, chopped mint, sugar and vinegar in food processor until blended. Add orange juice and cream mixture and process again.

- Pour into bowl, cover and chill thoroughly. Garnish with mint sprigs and serve.

Yield: 6 to 8 servings

"I have lived many places, and food always tastes best to me in Beaufort. It must be the water and the love of the people in town."

Holly Healy Jahn
Beaufort Academy
alumnae

Boater's Bowtie Pasta Salad

1	pound bowtie pasta	1	yellow bell pepper, chopped
1	(6½-ounce) jar marinated artichoke hearts	1	pint grape tomatoes
2	garlic cloves, minced	½	cup chopped kalamata olives
2	tablespoons balsamic vinegar	4	green onions, chopped
1	tablespoon Dijon mustard	4	boneless chicken breast halves, poached and chopped
¼	cup lemon juice		
½	cup extra virgin olive oil		Salt and pepper to taste
½	pound fresh asparagus, blanched, drained and cut in 1-inch pieces		

- Cook pasta according to package directions and drain. Rinse with cold water and set aside.

- Drain artichoke hearts and reserve marinade. Set aside artichokes.

- Whisk together marinade, garlic and next 4 ingredients in small bowl. Set aside.

- Toss artichokes, asparagus and next 5 ingredients with pasta. Drizzle with marinade mixture and mix well.

- Season with salt and pepper. Chill until ready to serve.

Yield: 8 servings

Mediterranean Pasta Salad

1 pound rigatoni pasta
¼ cup crumbled feta or goat cheese
¼ cup olive oil
2 tablespoons chopped fresh basil leaves
2 tablespoons chopped fresh parsley
2 tablespoons chopped kalamata olives
2 tablespoons chopped oil-packed sun-dried tomatoes
1 tablespoon capers, drained
4 teaspoons red wine vinegar
¼ teaspoon salt
⅛ teaspoon crushed red pepper flakes
1 medium tomato, seeded and coarsely chopped

- Cook pasta al dente and drain. Rinse with cold water and set aside.
- Combine feta cheese and remaining ingredients. Toss with pasta.
- Cover and chill about 2 hours. Toss before serving.

Yield: 6 servings

Chopped fresh basil leaves may be substituted with 2 teaspoons chopped dried basil leaves.

Just what are those delicious little capers? Native to the Mediterranean area, they are the unopened flower buds that bloom in spring. Pickled to perfection, they're the perfect addition to many salads and sauces.

~

Basil Tomato Couscous Salad

1¼ cups boiling water
1¼ cups couscous
2 cups chopped tomatoes
1 cup fresh basil, finely chopped
¼ cup finely chopped purple onion
¼ cup apple cider vinegar
2 tablespoons olive oil
¼ teaspoon salt
¼ teaspoon black pepper
3 slices cooked bacon, crumbled

- Combine boiling water and couscous in saucepan. Cover and allow to stand 5 minutes. Fluff with fork and cool.
- Combine couscous, tomatoes, basil and onions. Set aside.
- Combine vinegar, oil, salt and pepper. Drizzle over couscous mixture and toss gently.
- Chill and toss with bacon before serving.

Yield: 6 to 8 servings

In some cultures, couscous is believed to be a symbol of happiness and abundance. It's fast and very easy to prepare.

The shape of the pasta should dictate the type of sauce to be used. The longer the pasta, the thinner the sauce; the shorter the pasta, the thicker the sauce. Orzo is an exception because it is a small pasta usually served with a light sauce.

Orzo with Everything

1½	cups orzo
⅓	cup chopped, drained oil-packed sun-dried tomatoes
5	tablespoons extra virgin olive oil
¼	cup balsamic vinegar
¼	cup chopped kalamata olives

1	cup finely chopped radicchio
½	cup pine nuts, toasted
½	cup fresh basil, chopped
½	cup fresh Parmesan cheese
2	garlic cloves, minced
	Salt and pepper to taste

- Cook orzo in pot of boiling, salted water until just tender, but still firm to bite. Drain well and transfer to large bowl.

- Add tomatoes, oil, vinegar and olives, tossing well. Allow to stand until cool.

- Add radicchio and remaining ingredients to orzo mixture. Season with salt and pepper.

Yield: 6 to 8 servings

Shrimp Salad

1	pound fresh shrimp, peeled, deveined, cooked and chopped
3	cups white rice, cooked
½	cup chopped bell pepper
½	cup chopped yellow bell pepper
1	tomato, seeded and chopped

¼	cup chopped celery
¼	cup sliced green onions
½	cup mayonnaise
2	tablespoons lime juice
¼	teaspoon Old Bay seasoning
	Salt and pepper to taste

- Combine shrimp and next 6 ingredients in large bowl and set aside.

- Combine mayonnaise, lime juice and seasoning, mixing well. Toss with shrimp mixture, coating well. Season with salt and pepper and chill at least 2 hours.

- Serve over bed of greens or in hollowed tomatoes.

Yield: 6 to 8 servings

Shrimp and Orzo Salad

2 pounds fresh asparagus, trimmed and cut into 1-inch pieces
1½ pounds shrimp, peeled and deveined
2 tablespoons olive oil
1 pound orzo, cooked
1 (14-ounce) can artichoke hearts, drained and halved
1 red bell pepper, diced
½ cup fresh basil, chopped
2 tablespoons fresh oregano, chopped
   Fresh Herb Vinaigrette
6 cups fresh gourmet salad greens
½ cup feta cheese

- Cook asparagus in boiling salt water 4 minutes or until crisp tender. Plunge in cold water. Drain and chill.
- Sauté shrimp in olive oil until just pink.
- Combine asparagus, shrimp, orzo and next 4 ingredients in large bowl. Serve with Fresh Herb Vinaigrette over greens.
- Garnish with feta cheese.

Yield: 8 servings

FRESH HERB VINAIGRETTE

½ cup extra virgin olive oil

½ cup white wine vinegar

½ cup fresh basil, chopped

3 tablespoons fresh oregano, chopped

⅓ cup sliced green onions

½ teaspoon seasoning salt

½ teaspoon sugar

½ teaspoon crushed red pepper flakes

- Combine ingredients, blending well.

Island Shrimp Salad

½ cup cooking oil
2 tablespoons white vinegar
1 teaspoon freshly grated ginger
1 teaspoon honey
1 teaspoon coarsely ground mustard
1 tablespoon lemon juice
1 tablespoon chopped fresh dill
1 tablespoon chopped green onions
2 large avocados, chopped
3 medium mangoes, peeled and chopped
1½ pounds fresh shrimp, cooked, peeled and deveined
   Lettuce or baby greens
   Salt and pepper to taste

- Combine oil and next 7 ingredients in blender or food processor. Blend well and set aside.
- Place avocados, shrimp, and mango in large bowl. Toss lightly with oil mixture to coat.
- Serve on bed of lettuce or baby greens. Season with salt and pepper.

Yield: 6 servings

Wild-Rice Shrimp Salad

Oh, de swimp,
he taste so good.

I eat 'um all day
if I could.

Catch 'um fresh
right out de crick,

Pinch off dey head
an' cook 'um quick!

printed with the
kind permission of
Vida Miller

1½	pounds medium shrimp, peeled and deveined	¼	cup chopped yellow bell pepper
	Olive oil for sautéing	¼	cup chopped red bell pepper
	Butter for sautéing		
1	(6-ounce) package long grain and wild rice mix	12	black olives, sliced
1	(7-ounce) jar marinated artichoke quarters	1	celery rib, sliced
		⅓	cup mayonnaise
4	green onions, sliced	¼	teaspoon curry powder

- Sauté shrimp in oil and butter until pink.
- Cook rice according to package directions and cool.
- Drain artichokes, reserving 3 tablespoons liquid.
- Combine shrimp, rice, artichokes, onions and next 4 ingredients in large bowl and set aside.
- Combine reserved artichoke liquid, mayonnaise and curry powder. Toss with shrimp mixture.
- Cover and chill 5 hours. Serve on bed of baby greens.

Yield: 8 servings

Chicken may be substituted for shrimp.

Sea Island Shrimp Salad

8	ounces peeled and deveined shrimp	1	small cucumber, seeded and chopped
8	ounces scallops	2	tablespoons cilantro, chopped
2	tablespoons butter	1	green onion, diced
	Juice of 1 lemon		Dijon Dressing
1	(5-ounce) package saffron rice, cooked		Salt and pepper to taste
1	pint grape tomatoes, halved		

- Sauté shrimp and scallops in butter. Remove from heat and sprinkle with lemon juice. Transfer to small bowl and chill 2 to 3 hours.

- Combine rice and next 4 ingredients with shrimp mixture.

- Toss with enough Dijon Dressing to coat well. Salt and pepper to taste. Cover and chill overnight.

Dijon Dressing

⅓	cup red wine vinegar	1	teaspoon Worcestershire sauce
⅓	cup olive oil	1	teaspoon sugar
2	teaspoons Dijon mustard		
	Hot pepper sauce to taste		

- Combine ingredients in small bowl, mixing well.

Yield: 6 to 8 servings

Up and down the coast of South Carolina, cast-netting for shrimp is a favorite summer pastime. When the shrimp are "running" (scurrying under the surface of the water), it is a thrill to throw out your net, hear its soft "whoosh" and splash as it lands perfectly on top of the shrimp. The pleasure continues as the net is shaken over a large bucket to yield the catch for the day's meal!

Battery Creek Shrimp Salad

3	pounds medium shrimp (heads off)	1	small onion, finely chopped
1	onion, quartered	3	tablespoons fresh lemon juice
1	tablespoon Old Bay seasoning	½-¾	cup mayonnaise
4	hard-boiled eggs, finely chopped		Salt and pepper to taste
¾	cup finely chopped celery		Lettuce or parsley for garnish

- Boil shrimp with quartered onion and crab boil seasoning. Shrimp may be peeled and deveined before or after boiling.

- Add eggs, celery, chopped onion and lemon juice to shrimp. Add mayonnaise a spoonful at a time, lifting ingredients to mix. Use just enough mayonnaise to moisten; full amount may not be needed.

- Salt and pepper to taste. Garnish with lettuce or parsley.

Yield: 8 servings

Chopped tomatoes or pimiento may be added to salad for color.

Creole Shrimp Salad

½	cup olive oil	3	garlic cloves, minced
½	cup cooking oil	2	bay leaves
1	cup cider vinegar	2	pounds fresh shrimp, boiled, peeled and deveined
4	tablespoons Creole mustard		Mixed greens
2	tablespoons capers		Feta cheese
1	tablespoon caper juice		Grape tomatoes
1	small onion, grated		Cucumbers
3	tablespoons lemon juice		Black olives
¼	teaspoon crushed red pepper		Pepperoncini

- Blend oils and next 8 ingredients in food processor or blender until well blended. Add bay leaves.

- Place shrimp in container and cover with oil mixture. Marinate overnight.

- Combine mixed greens and remaining ingredients in large salad bowl. Top with shrimp and toss with marinade.

Yield: 8 servings

Shrimp may also be drained and served as an appetizer.

Crab Salad

4	tablespoons mayonnaise	1	cup seedless cucumber, cut into ¼-inch slices
4	tablespoons crème fraîche		
2	tablespoons lemon juice	4	cups lump crabmeat
2	tablespoons chopped fresh chives		Salt and pepper to taste
1	cup chopped, seeded tomato	4	medium tomatoes
			Leaf lettuce

- Combine mayonnaise, crème fraîche, lemon juice and chives. Mix well and set aside.

- Combine chopped tomatoes, cucumber and crabmeat with half of mayonnaise mixture. Season with salt and pepper.

- Core tomatoes and cut into sixths, forming tulip shape, being careful not to cut through all the way.

- Center tomato on leaf lettuce and mound the crab salad on top. Serve with remaining mayonnaise mixture on the side.

Crème fraîche

½	**cup heavy cream**	½	**cup sour cream**

- Whisk ingredients together in small bowl.

- Pour into jar, cover and allow to stand at room temperature 12 hours.

- Stir and chill 24 hours.

Yield: 4 servings

Crème fraîche may be stored in refrigerator for several weeks.

Once the crabs have been cooked, the tedious job of "picking" them comes. If you plan to eat them as you go, simply spread out newspaper on your picnic table. The back of the shell will easily lift off and reveal the treasure of the sea inside. Do away with the soft spongy parts and the hairy, finger-like filters. With hammer or nutcracker, lightly crush the large claws and legs. Remove the meat from shells and claws. The shell can be cleaned and used as a serving or baking dish for a stunning presentation.

The strong piney scent and flavor of the needle-like rosemary leaves are best released by mincing or crushing it in your hands, then adding a little at a time to the dish.

Rosemary Chicken Salad

4	chicken breast halves	1	teaspoon rosemary, finely minced
1	tablespoon extra virgin olive oil		Dash of Tabasco Sauce
	Salt and pepper to taste	3	thinly sliced green onions
¼	cup dry white wine	½	cup thinly sliced celery
½	cup mayonnaise	½	cup thinly sliced red bell pepper
2	tablespoons lemon juice		
1	garlic clove, minced		

- Sauté chicken in oil over medium high heat in large skillet 2 minutes on each side or until brown.

- Sprinkle with salt and pepper. Add wine and cover, simmering 4 minutes or until chicken is no longer pink. Cool, chop and set aside.

- Combine mayonnaise and next 4 ingredients in small bowl, mixing well, and set aside.

- Combine chicken, green onions, celery and red bell pepper in large bowl. Add mayonnaise mixture, coating well, and chill.

Yield: 4 servings

Szechuan Noodle Salad with Grilled Chicken

2	boneless, skinless chicken breasts	1	yellow bell pepper, cut in julienned strips
2	tablespoons sesame oil	4	green onions, chopped
1	tablespoon Chinese 5 spice powder	4	ounces snow peas
1	pound vermicelli, cooked al dente	1	cup cilantro, chopped
		2	tablespoons sesame seeds
1	red bell pepper, cut in julienned strips	¾	cups Szechuan sauce
		¼	cup sesame oil
			Hot chili oil to taste

- Slice chicken on the diagonal. Toss with sesame oil and Chinese 5 spice powder. Grill or stir-fry and set aside.

- Combine vermicelli and next 6 ingredients in large bowl, mixing thoroughly.

- Combine Szechuan sauce, sesame oil and hot chili oil, mixing well. Pour over salad, tossing to coat. Arrange chicken over salad in individual salad bowls. Serve at room temperature.

Yield: 4 servings

Mango Curried Chicken Salad

Mango Curry Mayonnaise

1   (8½-ounce) jar mango
     chutney
1½ cups mayonnaise

1½ rounded tablespoons curry
     powder

- Place chutney in food processor and pulse 15 to 20 seconds.
- Combine mayonnaise and curry powder in small bowl. Add chutney, blending well.

Chicken Salad

5-6 cups fresh broccoli florets
     (about 1 large bunch)
6   chicken breasts, poached,
     chilled, and cut into
     1-inch cubes

1   large red bell pepper,
     seeded and finely
     chopped

- Bring large pot of salted water to a rapid boil over high heat. Add broccoli and cook until crisp-tender (about 60 seconds). Drain, then plunge into cold water until thoroughly cooled. Drain and pat dry.
- Combine broccoli, chicken and red bell pepper in large salad bowl. Add 1½ cups Mango Curry Mayonnaise and mix well, adding more mayonnaise if desired. Chill until ready to serve.

Yield: 8 to 10 servings

Located on Craven Street, Beaufort's "Secession House" has an inscription on the basement wall that reads, "In this house the first meeting of Secession was held in South Carolina." After meeting in this historic house, the Beaufort delegates left for Charleston by boat to cast their ballots for secession.

Prince William's Parish (Old Sheldon) was built between 1745 and 1755. The name Sheldon was used in honor of the Bull family whose nearby plantation and ancestral home in England were both called Sheldon Hall. During the American Revolution, arms were hidden in the family vault, and Continental troops drilled on the churchyard grounds. Sheldon Church was burned by British troops in 1779 and was rebuilt in 1826, but it was burned again by Sherman's troops in 1865.

Cranberry and Wild Rice Salad

4	cups white rice, cooked	1	cup green onions, minced
4	cups wild rice, cooked	½	cup finely chopped celery
1	cup pecans, chopped and roasted	1	red bell pepper, chopped
1	cup dried cranberries, soaked in water 10 minutes and drained	⅓	cup parsley, minced
		¼	cup fresh chives, dill or tarragon

- Combine ingredients in large bowl. Cover and chill until ready to serve.
- Toss with Vinaigrette before serving.

Vinaigrette

4	tablespoons rice vinegar	⅓	cup cooking oil
4	tablespoons lemon juice	2	tablespoons sesame oil
1	garlic clove, minced		

- Combine ingredients in food processor, blending until smooth.

Yield: 8 to 10 servings

Picnic Potato Salad

1½	pounds small red new potatoes	1	tablespoon fresh oregano, chopped
⅔	cup extra virgin olive oil	1	tablespoon fresh chives
2	tablespoons Dijon mustard	2	tablespoons fresh dill, chopped
2	tablespoons lemon juice	2	tablespoons chopped shallots
4	tablespoons white wine vinegar		Salt and pepper to taste
2	garlic cloves, minced		Fresh dill or parsley for garnish
1	tablespoon fresh basil, chopped		

- Boil potatoes with skin on. Allow to cool. Cut into quarters and set aside.
- Combine olive oil and next 9 ingredients in food processor. Pulse until well blended.
- Combine potatoes and dressing. Season with salt and pepper. Chill at least 1 hour before serving. Garnish with dill or parsley.

Yield: 4 to 6 servings

Old Sheldon Potato Salad

3	pounds new potatoes	1½	tablespoons fresh dill, chopped
4	hard-boiled eggs, chopped	¾	cup mayonnaise
2	(16-ounce) jars marinated artichokes, drained and chopped	2	tablespoons Dijon mustard
½	cup chopped onion	1	tablespoon lemon pepper seasoning

- Boil potatoes in salted water 30 minutes or until tender. Cool and cut into quarters.

- Combine potatoes and next 4 ingredients in large bowl.

- Combine mayonnaise, mustard and lemon pepper, mixing well. Toss with vegetables to thoroughly coat. Chill overnight or at least 4 hours.

Yield: 10 servings

Fresh dill may be substituted with 2½ teaspoons dry dill.

On the second Sunday after Easter, a special service is held at the Old Sheldon Church. Among the majestic oaks and ancient tabby ruins, the annual worship service and picnic are enjoyed by young and old.

Cornbread Salad

1	(9-ounce) package cornbread mix	1	large Vidalia onion, chopped
1	(16-ounce) container sour cream	1	(16-ounce) can light red kidney beans, rinsed and drained
1	cup mayonnaise	1	(16-ounce) can corn, drained
1	(1-ounce) package ranch dressing mix	1	(3-ounce) jar real bacon bits
1	large tomato, chopped	2	cups shredded Mexican blend cheese
1	large bell pepper, chopped		

- Bake cornbread mix according to package directions. Cool, crumble and set aside.

- Combine sour cream, mayonnaise and dressing, mixing well, and set aside.

- Combine tomato and next 4 ingredients and set aside.

- Layer in large salad bowl half of vegetable mixture, cornbread, dressing, cheese and bacon bits. Repeat layers and chill.

Yield: 8 to 10 servings

Arugula grows wild in Asia and throughout southern Europe. The dark green plant is a staple in the Italian kitchen, adding a peppery, spicy tang to salads and pastas. The older the leaves, the stronger the flavor.

Spinach and Arugula Salad with Champagne Vinaigrette

1½	pounds spinach, trimmed	4	ounces enoki mushrooms
4	ounces Arugula, trimmed	8	ounces bacon, cooked and crumbled
2	small red onions, sliced	2	hard-boiled eggs, sliced
8	ounces white mushrooms, sliced	½	cup toasted sesame seeds.

- Combine ingredients in large bowl. Add warm Champagne Vinaigrette, tossing to coat well.

Champagne Vinaigrette

1	cup champagne vinegar	1	teaspoon Dijon mustard
2	tablespoons sugar	1	egg, beaten
1½	tablespoons all-purpose flour	3	tablespoons heavy cream
2	teaspoons dry vermouth	2	cups olive oil
			Salt and pepper to taste

- Heat vinegar and next 4 ingredients in saucepan over medium heat until simmering.
- Whisk in egg and heavy cream over low heat.
- Remove from heat and whisk in olive oil, salt and pepper.

Yield: 6 servings

Pear Stilton Salad with Candied Walnuts

3	heads Boston or Bibb lettuce	6	ounces Stilton cheese, crumbled
3	pears, peeled and sliced	1	cup Candied Walnuts

- Combine lettuce and pears in large salad bowl. Toss with Dijon Herb Vinaigrette. Sprinkle with cheese and Candied Walnuts.

Dijon Herb Vinaigrette

¼	cup red wine vinegar	1	teaspoon fresh basil, chopped
½	cup extra virgin olive oil		
1	shallot, finely chopped	½	teaspoon oregano
1	teaspoon Dijon mustard	½	teaspoon garlic powder
2	tablespoons water		Salt and pepper to taste
1	tablespoon fresh parsley, chopped		

- Combine ingredients in jar and shake well. Chill until ready to serve.

Yield: 10 servings

CANDIED WALNUTS

1 cup walnuts

2 tablespoons light corn syrup

1 tablespoon sugar

½ teaspoon salt

¼ teaspoon black pepper

⅛ teaspoon cayenne pepper

- Combine ingredients in small bowl, tossing well to coat.

- Spread mixture on prepared baking sheet and bake at 325° for 15 minutes or until nuts are deep golden brown and sugar mixture bubbles.

Stir to break clumps. Nuts may be stored in an air tight container.

Festive Apple and Blue Cheese Salad

6	cups mixed salad greens	2	large Granny Smith apples, cored and sliced
1	small red onion, thinly sliced and rings separated	4	ounces blue cheese, crumbled

- Combine ingredients in large salad bowl and toss with Mustard Dressing to coat.

Mustard Dressing

1	cup cooking oil	½	cup cider vinegar
½	cup sugar	½	teaspoon salt
½	teaspoon dry mustard	1	teaspoon paprika

- Combine ingredients in small bowl and whisk until thoroughly blended.

Yield: 8 servings

St. Helena's Salad

1	pound mixed salad greens	2	oranges, peeled and thinly sliced
4	ounces blue cheese, crumbled		**Balsamic Vinaigrette**
1	pint strawberries, hulled and quartered		**Seasoned Pecans**

- Toss greens with cheese and Balsamic Vinaigrette. Transfer to individual salad plates. Arrange strawberries and orange slices over greens. Top with Seasoned Pecans.

Balsamic Vinaigrette

⅓	cup balsamic vinegar	1	medium shallot, minced
3	tablespoons Dijon mustard	¼	teaspoon salt
3	tablespoons honey	¼	teaspoon black pepper
2	garlic cloves, minced	1	cup olive oil

- Combine vinegar and next 6 ingredients in food processor. Pulse until well blended. Add olive oil in a steady stream.

Seasoned Pecans

¼	cup sugar	2	tablespoons sugar
1	cup warm water	1	tablespoon chili powder
1	cup pecan halves	⅛	teaspoon cayenne pepper

- Preheat oven to 350°.

- Stir together ¼ cup sugar and water until sugar dissolves.

- Add pecans and soak for 10 minutes.

- Drain pecans and set aside, discarding sugar water.

- Combine 2 tablespoons sugar, chili powder and cayenne pepper. Add pecans, tossing to coat.

- Place pecans on baking sheet sprayed with nonstick cooking spray.

- Bake at 350° for 10 minutes or until pecans are golden brown, stirring once.

Yield: 6 servings

Supper Club Salad

1 bag romaine lettuce
1 bag mixed greens or
   spinach
1 cup toasted almonds
   Feta cheese, crumbled

2 (11-ounce) cans Mandarin
   oranges, drained
4 green onions, sliced
1 (8-ounce) can sliced water
   chestnuts, drained

- Combine ingredients in large bowl. Pour Red Wine Dressing over salad and toss well.

Red Wine Dressing
½ cup cooking oil
4 tablespoons sugar
4 tablespoons red wine
   vinegar

1 teaspoon salt
   Black pepper to taste

- Combine ingredients in jar and shake well.

Yield: 12 servings

For variation substitute almonds with pine nuts, feta with blue cheese, oranges with red grapes, green onions with red onions. Add a splash of raspberry vinegar to the Red Wine Dressing.

Summer Salad with Lemon Dressing

1 pound fresh pea pods
1 bag fresh baby spinach,
   washed and patted dry

2 ounces goat cheese,
   crumbled

- Shell pea pods and place peas into boiling water 2 minutes to blanch. Strain under running cold water and drain.
- Transfer peas and spinach to large bowl. Toss with Lemon Dressing, coating well, before serving. Sprinkle with goat cheese and serve.

Lemon Dressing
4 tablespoons fresh lemon
   juice
10 tablespoons extra virgin
   olive oil

1 teaspoon salt
1 teaspoon black pepper

- Combine ingredients, mixing well.

Yield: 8 servings

Fresh pea pods may be substituted with 1 (10-ounce) package frozen petits pois, thawed.

Good quality olive oil should be used for best results.

Tomatoes with
Mustard and Brown Sugar Dressing

3   tomatoes, peeled and   Salt and pepper to taste
     sliced   4   green onions, chopped

• Arrange tomato slices on serving platter. Drizzle with Mustard
  and Brown Sugar Dressing. Season with salt and pepper. Top
  with green onions.

Mustard and Brown Sugar Dressing
¼   cup cooking oil   2   teaspoons dark brown
1   tablespoon cider vinegar   sugar
                            1½ teaspoons Dijon mustard

• Combine ingredients in small bowl and whisk until thoroughly
  blended.

Yield: 4 servings

Tomato and Arugula Salad

*To peel tomatoes easily,
blanch in boiling water
for approximately 10
seconds. Remove with a
slotted spoon. Cool
slightly and peel.
Tomatoes may be
blanched in advance,
but to retain freshness
do not peel until they
are needed.*

4-5 large tomatoes   2   ounces fresh Parmesan
½   teaspoon salt   cheese
1   small bunch arugula,
     washed and torn into
     bite size pieces

• Peel, seed and dice tomatoes. Sprinkle with salt.

• Pour Garlic and Pepper Dressing over tomatoes and toss to
  coat. Allow to stand 5 minutes.

• Combine arugula and Parmesan cheese in large salad bowl.
  Add tomatoes and toss gently. Serve immediately.

Garlic and Pepper Dressing
2   tablespoons extra virgin 1   small garlic clove, minced
     olive oil   ⅛   teaspoon freshly ground
1   tablespoon balsamic   black pepper
     vinegar

• Combine ingredients in small bowl and whisk until thoroughly
  blended.

Yield: 6 servings

Taste of Summer Tomatoes

3-4 large tomatoes, peeled and sliced
1 Vidalia onion, sliced thinly and separated into rings
1 tablespoon fresh basil, chopped
1 tablespoon fresh parsley, chopped
1 tablespoon fresh oregano, chopped
4 ounces feta cheese, crumbled
2 tablespoons extra virgin olive oil
2 tablespoons red wine vinegar

- Layer half of tomatoes and onions in round pie plate. Sprinkle with half of basil, parsley, oregano and cheese. Repeat process.
- Drizzle with oil and vinegar and serve.

Yield: 6 servings

Fresh cucumbers may be added.

Southerners are famous for their vegetable gardens. Beans, cucumbers, squash, okra, peas and corn are bountiful in the summer. If you don't grow your own, there are numerous roadside vegetable stands to purchase fresh produce. Menus are planned around the fresh produce in season.

Asparagus Salad with Balsamic Vinaigrette

2 pounds asparagus
1 small red bell pepper, diced
Mixed baby greens
⅓ cup chopped pecans, toasted

- Cook asparagus in salted water until tender.
- Drain and rinse in cold water until asparagus is cold. Pat dry and cut into 2-inch pieces.
- Toss asparagus with red bell pepper and Balsamic Vinaigrette, coating well.
- Serve over baby greens and sprinkle with pecans.

Balsamic Vinaigrette
⅓ cup balsamic vinegar
3 tablespoons extra virgin olive oil
1 tablespoon Dijon mustard
1 tablespoon chopped fresh marjoram
1 tablespoon minced fresh garlic
Salt and pepper

- Boil vinegar in small saucepan over medium heat until reduced by half (about 3 minutes).
- Pour into large bowl. Whisk in oil, Dijon, marjoram and garlic. Season with salt and pepper.

Yield: 4 servings

Roasted Onion Salad

"No-See-Ums" (sand gnats) are insect pests found in the Lowcountry. They are so tiny, that they are able to squeeze through even the smallest of mesh screens. Anyone spending the "pleasant weather" months in Beaufort will "meet" our famed insect!

5	medium onions, unpeeled and sliced ½-inch	½	cup toasted walnuts
¼	cup extra virgin olive oil	1	(4-ounce) package crumbled blue cheese
8	cups mixed baby greens		

- Arrange onions slices on lightly greased roasting pan. Drizzle evenly with olive oil.

- Bake at 500° for 10 minutes or until onions are slightly charred. Allow to cool.

- Remove and discard outer skin of onions. Set onions aside.

- Combine greens, nuts and cheese. Add onions, tossing gently. Drizzle with Garlic and Pepper Vinaigrette.

Garlic and Pepper Vinaigrette

3	garlic cloves	½	teaspoon crushed red pepper flakes
2	shallots		
¼	cup chopped fresh parsley	2	tablespoons white wine vinegar
½	teaspoon salt		
½	teaspoon pepper	½	cup extra virgin olive oil

- Pulse garlic and shallots in food processor. Add parsley and next 4 ingredients and pulse. Add oil in a slow steady stream with food processor running until well blended.

Yield: 8 servings

Black-Eyed Pea Salad
with Sun-Dried Tomato Vinaigrette

1	(10-ounce) package frozen black-eyed peas	1	yellow bell pepper, chopped
1	cucumber, peeled, seeded and chopped	½	cup finely chopped green onions
1	large tomato, seeded and chopped	1	cup crumbled feta cheese

- Cook black-eyed peas according to package directions and drain.

- Combine peas and next 4 ingredients. Toss with enough Sun-Dried Tomato Vinaigrette to coat. Top with feta cheese.

Sun-Dried Tomato Vinaigrette

1	cup oil-packed sun-dried tomatoes, drained and chopped	6	tablespoons balsamic vinegar
4	teaspoons Dijon mustard	½	cup olive oil
4	teaspoons honey		Salt and pepper to taste

- Combine sun-dried tomatoes, Dijon and honey in small bowl. Whisk in vinegar and oil. Season with salt and pepper. Keep at room temperature.

Yield: 4 servings

In the past it was well accepted that the combination of peas and rice provided complete protein. This same fact holds true today, as we continue to enjoy variations of the West African dish, Hoppin' John.

Hoppin' John Vinaigrette

Hoppin' John

2	cups dried black-eyed peas	1	bay leaf
2	quarts water	1	teaspoon fresh oregano
½	pound ham (or 1 meaty ham bone)	1	teaspoon fresh rosemary
1	cup rice, uncooked	1	teaspoon sugar
1	cup chopped onion	2	teaspoons salt
1	cup chopped celery	½	teaspoon freshly ground black pepper

- Sort and wash peas. Transfer to heavy saucepan and add water to cover peas. Cover and bring to a boil. Remove from heat immediately.

- Soak peas covered 1 hour. Drain, rinse and set aside.

- Combine ham and water in large Dutch oven. Bring to a boil. Reduce heat, cover and simmer 45 minutes.

- Add peas and remaining ingredients to Dutch oven and bring to a boil. Reduce heat, cover and simmer 30 minutes or until black-eyed peas are done.

- Remove ham and cut into small pieces. Stir ham into pea mixture.

Vinaigrette

⅓	cup red wine vinegar	2	tablespoons chopped fresh basil
1	tablespoon Dijon mustard		
1	cup peanut oil	3-4	heads seasonal greens
	Salt to taste	4	slices cooked, crumbled bacon for garnish
	Freshly ground black pepper to taste		

- Mix vinegar and mustard in small bowl then slowly whisk in oil. Season to taste with salt and pepper.

- Combine Hoppin' John, basil and Vinaigrette and toss well.

- Arrange greens on serving plates. Spoon Hoppin' John Vinaigrette on center of leaves and garnish with bacon.

Yield: 10 to 12 servings

Hoppin' John may be served hot or chilled.

Summer White Corn and Pea Salad

2 cups fresh silver queen corn
2 cups fresh peas or frozen petits pois
⅔ cup chopped celery
½ cup finely chopped sweet onion
½ cup chopped red bell pepper

- Heat corn and peas in saucepan over medium high heat until tender. Drain and cool.
- Transfer corn and peas to large salad bowl. Add celery, onion and red bell pepper.
- Toss with Parsley Dressing, coating well. Cover and chill.

Parsley Dressing

½ cup seasoned rice vinegar
2 tablespoons fresh parsley, minced
1 tablespoon brown sugar
½ teaspoon salt
¼ teaspoon black pepper
1 tablespoon fresh mint, minced

- Combine ingredients in small bowl, mixing well.

Yield: 8 to 10 servings

The sugar in corn starts to break down as soon as it is picked. So, the quicker from field to table, the better!

~

Corn Salad

2 (10-ounce) cans yellow corn, drained
2 (10-ounce) cans shoepeg corn, drained
1-2 tomatoes, seeded and chopped
1 cucumber, seeded and sliced
¼ cup chopped bell pepper
¼ cup chopped green onions

- Combine vegetables in large bowl. Toss with Sour Cream Sauce and marinate overnight. Serve chilled.

Sour Cream Sauce

¼ cup sour cream
4 tablespoons mayonnaise
2 tablespoons vinegar
¼ teaspoon celery seed
2 teaspoons salt
¼ teaspoon black pepper
½ teaspoon dry mustard

- Combine ingredients in small bowl, blending thoroughly.

Yield: 8 to 10 servings

Canned corn may be substituted with 5 cups fresh, cooked and drained corn.

"If there were no other reason to live in the South, Southern cooking would be enough."

Michael
Andrew Grissom
Southern by the
Grace of God

Cabbage may be substituted with 1 large head of Bok Choy stalks and leaves. For a main course, add cooked chicken breasts.

~

Sweet and Sour Crunch

2	(3-ounce) packages Ramen noodles	4	green onions, chopped
½	cup sesame seeds	¾	cup cooking oil
1	(3-ounce) package sliced almonds	¼	cup red wine vinegar
1	head Napa cabbage, finely chopped	½	cup sugar
		2	tablespoons soy sauce

- Discard Ramen noodle seasoning packet and break noodles.

- Arrange noodles, sesame seeds and almonds on baking sheet. Heat at 325° until lightly golden. Allow to cool and transfer to serving bowl.

- Add cabbage and onions to noodles. Toss well and set aside.

- Combine oil, vinegar, sugar and soy sauce in small bowl, thoroughly blending. Pour over cabbage mixture before serving.

Yield: 10 to 12 servings

Japanese Cucumber Salad

"COOL AS A CUCUMBER..."

Do you know why we use that term? Cucumbers can be as much as 20 degrees cooler on the inside than its outer skin.

1	tablespoon dark soy sauce	4	cucumbers
¼	cup sherry vinegar or rice vinegar	1	tablespoon salt
		1¼	tablespoons sugar

- Whisk together soy sauce and vinegar and set aside.

- Peel and seed cucumbers. Slice to one-fourth inch thickness. Drain and toss with salt. Set aside in strainer 30 minutes.

- Rinse cucumber slices and pat dry.

- Toss with sugar and soy mixture.

Yield: 4 to 5 servings

English cucumbers may be substituted. If so, only 2 will be needed.

SEAFOOD

SEAFOOD

The waters surrounding Beaufort are brimming with an abundance of seafood. Lowcountry cooks enjoy the incredible bounty of the sea with gatherings that may feature Crab Pickings, Frogmore Stew, Fish Fries or Oyster Roasts. These and other seafood recipes found in this section are sure to delight your guests. The versatility and availability of seafood make it a Lowcountry favorite.

Grilled Island Dolphin

⅓ cup grated fresh ginger
⅓ cup horseradish
¼ cup soy sauce
2 teaspoons minced garlic
1 cup mayonnaise

6 tablespoons honey or
   brown sugar
4 (8-ounce) fresh dolphin
   fillets
   Salt and pepper
¼ cup unsalted butter, melted

- Process ginger and next 5 ingredients in food processor until well blended. Set aside.

- Season dolphin with salt and pepper. Brush with melted butter and grill until slightly opaque.

- Preheat broiler.

- Remove dolphin from grill and place on ovenproof platter.

- Spread ginger sauce on dolphin and broil until hot and bubbly.

Yield: 4 servings

This recipe calls for the dolphin fish. Highly sought after as a prize gamefish, its meat is white, flaky and tender.

Tomato Basil Grilled Fish

¾ cup olive oil
3 tomatoes, seeded and
   chopped
¼ cup balsamic vinegar
4 garlic cloves, minced
¼ cup minced fresh basil

1 teaspoon salt
1 teaspoon cayenne pepper
5 pounds fish fillets
   (grouper, tuna or
   dolphin)

- Combine oil and next 6 ingredients in bowl, blending well. Reserve ½ cup marinade and set aside.

- Place fillets in large zip-top plastic bag and pour remaining marinade over fillets. Chill at least 1 hour.

- Preheat grill.

- Bring fillets to room temperature and discard marinade. Grill fish until center is opaque.

- Spoon reserved marinade over fish and serve immediately.

Yield: 12 servings

Substitute fresh tomatoes with one (15-ounce) can diced tomatoes, drained.

Great summer supper when everything is in season!

Grilled Fish with
Corn, Tomato and Basil Salad

2	tablespoons chopped fresh basil	4	(6-ounce) firm white fish fillets
½	teaspoon minced garlic		Salt and pepper to taste
2	tablespoon minced chives		Olive oil
2	tablespoons olive oil		

- Combine basil, garlic, chives and oil in bowl and coat fillets. Place in large zip-top plastic bag and chill 2 to 3 hours.

- Season fillets with salt and pepper and brush with olive oil.

- Grill 3 minutes on flesh side, turn and grill 4 to 5 minutes on skin side.

- Mound Corn, Tomato and Basil Salad on each plate and top with fillet.

Salad

2	cups fresh corn, sautéed	½	cup chopped fresh basil
2	medium tomatoes, seeded and chopped	1	tablespoon fresh lime juice
1	green onion, thinly sliced	¼	cup extra virgin olive oil
½	cup chopped red bell pepper	¼	teaspoon crushed red pepper flakes
3	cups baby spinach leaves, washed and dried	1½	teaspoons salt

- Toss together sautéed corn and next 5 ingredients in large bowl and set aside.

- Whisk together lime juice, olive oil, pepper flakes and salt in small bowl. Pour over salad and toss thoroughly.

Yield: 4 servings

Fish in Caper's Island Sauce

4	medium tomatoes, seeded and chopped	3	teaspoons minced fresh basil
1	medium Vidalia or sweet onion, chopped	½	teaspoon garlic powder
2	teaspoons minced fresh oregano	1½	pounds fresh fish fillets
		2	tablespoons capers, drained
		1½	teaspoons dry sherry

- Combine tomatoes and next 4 ingredients in large skillet and sauté over medium heat 5 minutes or until onion is tender. Remove from skillet and set aside.
- Add fish and capers to same skillet and drizzle with sherry. Add tomato mixture, cover and simmer 10 to 12 minutes or until fish flakes easily with fork.

Yield: 4 to 6 servings

Grilled Tuna with Herb Vinaigrette

4	(6-ounce) tuna steaks		Salt and pepper to taste
¼	cup olive oil	1	(10-ounce) bag spinach or romaine lettuce
	Juice of ½ lime		Herb Vinaigrette
	Juice of ½ lemon		

- Preheat grill.
- Brush tuna with oil and juices. Season with salt and pepper.
- Grill tuna 4 to 5 minutes per side until medium rare and keep warm.
- Steam spinach until just wilted. Mound steamed spinach or torn romaine on plate. Top with tuna and Herb Vinaigrette.

Herb Vinaigrette

2	tablespoons Dijon mustard	2	tablespoons chopped basil
2	tablespoons white wine vinegar	2	tablespoons chopped chives
¼	cup fresh lemon juice	1	teaspoon minced garlic
¾	cup olive oil	¼	teaspoon freshly ground black pepper
2	tablespoons chopped parsley		

- Combine ingredients in small bowl, mixing well.

Yield: 4 servings

THE BALLAD OF THE HUMMOCK STEW

"Two fish that ain't quite swimmin',

A pound of bacon

Two potatoes,

Diced tomatoes."

Using only these ingredients, Ricky Akers, a Beaufort native and Beaufort Academy alumnae, makes THE most fabulous meal which over the years has fed many friends and family. To fully appreciate the dish, however, it must be eaten on a "hummock", a small island (of which there are many) tucked in among the waterways and marshes of coastal South Carolina.

Peppered Tuna Steak

¼	cup breadcrumbs	4	tablespoons finely minced shallots
4	tablespoons coarsely ground black pepper	2	garlic cloves, minced
4	(6-ounce) tuna fillets (1-inch thick)	¼	cup dry white wine
		½	cup chicken broth
	Salt to taste	2	pounds fresh spinach, washed and dried
5	tablespoons olive oil, divided	24	grape tomatoes, halved

- Combine breadcrumbs and pepper in small bowl and set aside.

- Season tuna with salt. Rub breadcrumb mixture over tuna, patting evenly to coat.

- Heat 3 tablespoons oil in heavy skillet over high heat. Sear tuna until crusty on both sides (about 3 minutes per side for rare). Remove from skillet and keep warm.

- Sauté shallots and garlic in same skillet over medium high heat about 2 minutes. Add white wine and cook until reduced. Add broth and cook until reduced by half. Remove sauce from skillet and set aside.

- Add remaining 2 tablespoons oil to same skillet and sauté spinach. Add tomatoes and cook until spinach begins to wilt. Season with salt and pepper to taste.

- Spoon spinach mixture onto plate. Top with tuna and drizzle with sauce.

Yield: 4 servings

Wasabi Tuna and Sesame Green Beans

¼ cup soy sauce
1 teaspoon wasabi powder
1 teaspoon minced garlic
   Salt and pepper to taste
4 (6-ounce) tuna steaks
   (¾-inch thick)

1 pound fresh green beans,
   trimmed and cooked
   until crisp tender
1 tablespoon sesame oil
¼ cup brown sugar

- Combine soy sauce, wasabi powder and garlic in large plastic zip-top plastic bag.

- Salt and pepper tuna and place in bag. Marinate 2 to 3 hours.

- Bring tuna to room temperature and reserve marinade.

- Heat oil in large skillet over medium high heat. Add tuna and cook 3 minutes per side for rare. Transfer to serving platter and keep warm.

- Add green beans, brown sugar and reserved marinade to same skillet and cook until sauce is reduced (about 4 minutes).

- Serve tuna with green beans topped with sauce.

Yield: 4 servings

Wasabi is a condiment originally used in Japanese cooking that has now become popular in Western cuisine. It is made from the above ground root of the wasabi vegetable. Because wasabi is one of the rarest and most difficult vegetables to grow, the majority of commercially prepared wasabi is artificial, made from horseradish, mustard and food coloring. If you can find it, use the real thing!

The South's rich legacy of fish gathering and eating began with Native American tribes. They used spears, bows and arrows or underwater traps. The Native Americans not only bestowed fish on the new white settlers as gifts of friendship, they gave the settlers a richer gift by teaching them how to fish. The fishermen today use a hook and line with a rod and reel. The joy of fishing in the waters of the Lowcountry is always worth a few memories and maybe a fish tale or two—even if there are no fish to show for it!

Glazed Fish with Ginger Butter Sauce

1	cup dry white wine	3	tablespoons honey
⅓	cup chopped shallots	3	teaspoons rice wine vinegar
⅓	cup peeled and thinly sliced fresh ginger	4	(6-ounce) firm white fish fillets
½	cup heavy cream	¼	cup chilled unsalted butter, cut into small pieces
1½	tablespoons cold water		
1½	teaspoons cornstarch		Salt and pepper to taste
6	tablespoons soy sauce		

- Combine wine, shallots and ginger in small heavy saucepan over high heat. Boil until liquid is reduced to one-fourth cup (about 5 minutes). Add cream and boil until liquid is reduced by half (about 3 minutes). Remove from heat and set aside.

- Combine water and cornstarch in small bowl until smooth and set aside.

- Combine soy sauce, honey and vinegar in heavy medium saucepan. Stir in cornstarch mixture over medium heat until glaze boils and thickens slightly (about 2 minutes). Remove from heat. Cool to room temperature.

- Preheat oven to 350°. Arrange fish on small baking sheet lined with parchment paper. Brush with half of glaze. Bake about 15 minutes or until opaque in center. Remove from oven.

- Bring remaining glaze to a boil. Spoon glaze over fish.

- Bring wine sauce to a simmer. Remove from heat. Add butter gradually to sauce, whisking until just melted. Strain sauce and season with salt and pepper.

- Spoon sauce onto plate. Top with fish and serve.

Yield: 4 servings

Baked Flounder Fillets

¼ cup unsalted butter, melted
2 medium onions, sliced
1½ pounds fresh flounder fillets or any firm white fish
¾ cup mayonnaise
1 teaspoon dried parsley flakes
Juice of 1 lemon
½ cup fresh Parmesan cheese, divided
Toasted almonds (optional)

- Preheat oven to 350°.

- Pour melted butter in glass baking dish. Arrange onions on bottom of baking dish. Top with flounder and set aside.

- Combine mayonnaise, parsley, juice and half of cheese in small bowl. Spread over fish and sprinkle with remaining cheese.

- Bake for 25 minutes. Toasted almonds may be added last 5 minutes of cooking.

Yield: 4 servings

"What I would miss most about Beaufort if I were to move away would be the cooking and eating of fish just 30 minutes after it was caught from the dock right behind my house."

Clay Danielson,
Grade 10
Beaufort Academy
student

~

Whale Branch Flounder

⅔ cups butter, divided
2 tablespoons all-purpose flour
1 teaspoon salt
Dash of cayenne pepper
¾ cup half-and-half
½ cup dry white wine
4 (6-ounce) flounder fillets
Salt and pepper to taste
½ cup toasted, slivered almonds for garnish
Chopped fresh parsley for garnish

- Melt ⅓ cup butter in heavy saucepan over medium heat. Stir in flour, salt and cayenne. Add half-and-half, stirring until thickened. Add wine, blending until smooth. Set aside and keep warm.

- Place flounder skin side down in greased shallow baking dish. Brush with remaining ⅓ cup butter. Season with salt and pepper and broil 5 to 6 minutes.

- Pour wine sauce over flounder and garnish with almonds and parsley.

Yield: 4 servings

A popular method of catching flounder is called "gigging". Using a lantern or flashlight, good ol' boys gather together to search in shallow water for the unsuspecting flounder. The flounder that have been speared or "gigged" delight the palate with a mild sweet taste.

Grouper Gourmet

*Oh, de fish,
he hard to hook,*

*But he taste so good
eenyway 'e cook,*

*Fried, baked,
broiled or stew.*

*Wid coleslaw an'
hushpuppy, too!*

Printed with the
kind permission of
Vida Miller

1	cup all-purpose flour	12	button mushrooms, sliced
	Salt and pepper	2	large tomatoes, seeded and chopped
2	eggs, beaten		
½	cup milk	1	bunch green onions, chopped
6	(6-ounce) grouper fillets		
3	tablespoons butter, divided	2	ounces dry sherry
2	tablespoons oil	1	ounce fresh lemon juice
12	shrimp, peeled and deveined		

- Preheat oven to 400°.

- Combine flour, salt and pepper and set aside.

- Combine eggs and milk. Dip fillets in milk mixture and dredge in flour mixture.

- Heat 2 tablespoons butter and oil in large heavy skillet over medium heat and brown fillets on both sides. Transfer to baking dish and bake 7 to 10 minutes, depending on thickness.

- Reheat same skillet. Add shrimp and mushrooms. Sauté about 1 minute or until shrimp are pink. Add tomatoes and onions, mixing well.

- Remove from skillet and deglaze pan with sherry. Add lemon juice and remaining butter and reduce.

- Serve fillets topped with shrimp mixture and lemon butter.

Yield: 6 servings

Serve with rice pilaf.

Lowcountry Salmon over Collard Greens

3	(15-ounce) cans collard greens	4	tablespoons soy sauce
1	(2½-pound) salmon fillet	4	tablespoons minced fresh thyme
4	teaspoons minced garlic	2	teaspoons lemon zest
1	teaspoon kosher salt	½	cup fresh lemon juice
2	tablespoons cracked black pepper	1	cup cooking oil
½	cup coarse-grain mustard		Tomato Salsa

- Preheat oven to 400°.

- Drain greens and place in greased 9x13-inch glass baking dish. Place salmon over greens and set aside.

- Combine garlic and next 8 ingredients in bowl, mixing well. Pour over salmon, coating both sides.

- Bake for 30 minutes or until golden brown. Serve salmon and greens topped with Tomato Salsa.

Tomato Salsa

¾	cup minced green onions	2	tablespoons fresh sage or thyme, minced
¾	cup chopped fresh tomatoes	1	tablespoon raspberry vinegar
2	tablespoons olive oil	½	teaspoon hot sauce

- Combine ingredients, tossing well.

Yield: 6 to 8 servings

In other parts of the world, "greens" may refer to the makings of a salad. In the Lowcountry, however, greens refer to the leaves of certain vegetables that are simmered for a long time with some type of pork as seasoning. Collards, mustard greens and turnip greens are traditional southern soul foods. Spinach, kale, beet tops and cabbage can also be found simmering in the Lowcountry kitchen.

This vinaigrette is also great on a salad!

Sesame-Crusted Salmon with Ginger Vinaigrette

6	small cucumbers, divided and peeled	1	tablespoon honey
½	cup plus 2 tablespoons rice wine vinegar	1	teaspoon dark sesame oil
		4	salmon fillets (1-inch thick)
⅛	teaspoon salt		
2	tablespoons sugar	2	tablespoons toasted sesame seeds
¼	cup water		Fresh mint sprigs
¼	cup low-sodium soy sauce		

- Slice 2 cucumbers and set aside.

- Chop remaining 4 cucumbers and process in food processor until smooth, scraping down sides. Pour through a wire mesh strainer into small bowl and discard pulp. Stir in ½ cup vinegar and salt and set aside.

- Combine sugar and water in small saucepan. Bring to a boil, stirring often (about 1 minute). Remove from heat. Stir in cucumber mixture and set aside.

- Combine soy sauce, 2 tablespoons vinegar, honey and sesame oil in small bowl. Brush over salmon.

- Place salmon in lightly greased 9x13-inch baking dish. Sprinkle with sesame seeds.

- Bake at 450° for 10 to 12 minutes or until just opaque.

- Divide cucumber slices among 4 shallow bowls. Spoon cucumber sauce onto cucumber slices and top with salmon. Garnish with fresh mint sprig. Serve with Ginger Vinaigrette.

Yield: 4 servings

Ginger Vinaigrette

1	(1½-inch) piece fresh ginger, peeled and coarsely chopped	1	tablespoon low-sodium soy sauce
		1	tablespoon honey
1	garlic clove, peeled	⅛	teaspoon crushed red pepper flakes
2	tablespoons rice wine vinegar		
		¼	cup peanut oil
		½	teaspoon dark sesame oil

- Process ginger and garlic in food processor until finely chopped, scraping down sides. Add vinegar, soy sauce, honey and red pepper flakes. Process 30 seconds. Pour oils slowly through feed tube while processor is running. Process until thoroughly blended.

Yield: ½ cup

Crisp Crusted Broiled Salmon

3	slices bread, crusts removed	1	teaspoon olive oil
1	cup coarsely crushed potato chip pieces	¾	teaspoon salt Freshly ground black pepper
6	tablespoons chopped fresh dill	3	tablespoons Dijon mustard
1	whole (3½-pound) salmon fillet, skinned and boned		

- Preheat oven to 400°. Place one oven rack in broiler position and one in center position.

- Pulse bread in food processor into ¼-inch pieces (about 10 one-second pulses). Spread crumbs evenly on baking sheet and toast on lower oven rack. Shake pan once or twice and bake 5 minutes or until golden brown and crisp. Toss breadcrumbs with potato chip crumbs and dill in small bowl. Set aside.

- Increase oven temperature to broil setting. Cut piece of foil 6 inches longer than fillet. Fold lengthwise into thirds and place on baking sheet.

- Position salmon lengthwise on foil, allowing excess foil to overhang.

- Rub fillet evenly with oil. Sprinkle with salt and pepper.

- Broil on upper rack until surface is spotty brown and thick portion is opaque (about 9 to 11 minutes).

- Remove fillet from oven and spread evenly with Dijon. Press crumb mixture onto fillet. Return to lower rack and continue cooking about 1 minute or until crust is deep golden brown.

- Transfer fillet and foil to cutting board. Remove foil and serve from board.

Yield: 8 servings

SALMON MARINADE

½ cup white wine

¼ cup honey

3-4 finely minced shallots

3 tablespoons teriyaki sauce

- Combine ingredients in small bowl. Pour over salmon and marinate 8 to 10 hours in refrigerator. Allow salmon to stand in marinade at room temperature 15 minutes before grilling or broiling.

Yield: ¾ cup

Marinade may also be used for beef.

Sea Island Fish Burgers

¼	cup fresh lemon juice	¼	cup olive oil
2	tablespoons soy sauce	4	(6-ounce) fish fillets
¼	teaspoon minced garlic	¼	cup Tartar Sauce
¼	teaspoon freshly ground black pepper		Hamburger buns
			Tomato slices for garnish
¼	teaspoon hot pepper sauce		Lettuce leaves for garnish

- Combine lemon juice and next 5 ingredients in large zip-top plastic bag. Add fillets and marinate 1 hour.
- Preheat grill or grill pan.
- Remove fillets from marinade. Grill until fillets are opaque.
- Spread tartar sauce on buns and top with fillets. Garnish with tomato slices and lettuce.

Yield: 4 servings

TARTAR SAUCE

1 cup Hellmann's Real Mayonnaise

1 tablespoon lemon juice

1 tablespoon chopped onion or green onion

1 tablespoon sweet pickle cubes, drained

1 tablespoon capers, rinsed and drained

1 tablespoon chopped parsley

Dash of hot pepper sauce

Salt and pepper to taste

- Combine ingredients in bowl, mixing well.

Yield: 1¼ cups

Tartar Sauce will keep in refrigerator about one week.

Joyce's Crab Burgers

1	pound jumbo lump crabmeat	⅛	teaspoon lemon pepper seasoning
½	cup finely chopped celery	4	English muffins, split
3	tablespoons chopped onion	1	tablespoon chopped fresh parsley for garnish
¾-1	cup shredded sharp Cheddar cheese	¼	teaspoon minced fresh dill for garnish
½-¾	cup mayonnaise	2	tablespoons unsalted butter for garnish

- Combine crabmeat and next 5 ingredients in large bowl, mixing well. Shape into 4 patties and broil until golden brown, turning once.
- Place crab burgers on buttered and toasted English muffins and garnish with parsley and dill.

Yield: 4 servings

Lowcountry Deviled Crab

¼ cup butter
½ small onion, chopped
½ green or red bell pepper, chopped
1 celery stalk, chopped
1 egg, beaten
1 heaping tablespoon mayonnaise
1 teaspoon mustard
1 tablespoon Worcestershire sauce

Dash of hot pepper sauce
¼ cup whole milk
½ teaspoon salt
Freshly ground black pepper to taste
1 pound white crabmeat
12 round buttery crackers, coarsely crumbled
Additional crumbs for garnish
Paprika

- Preheat oven to 325°.

- Melt butter in large skillet over medium high heat. Sauté onion, bell pepper and celery until tender, but not brown.

- Remove from heat and add next 10 ingredients, blending well. Spoon into 1-quart casserole or individual baking shells. Sprinkle with additional crumbs and paprika.

- Bake for 25 to 30 minutes or until firm. Decrease baking time if using individual shells.

Yield: 6 servings

"In Beaufort during the Depression, we didn't have an abundance of material things. What we did have were lots of good, simple pleasures with family and friends. We really didn't think about being poor because almost everyone was in the same boat. For entertainment we enjoyed band concerts by the Parris Island Military Band at the bandstand on the riverbank across from the courthouse. Unfortunately, the bandstand was lost during the hurricane in 1940."

Betty Logan Waskiewicz
Beaufort Academy
parent

One dozen large meaty crabs will yield about one pound of white lump crabmeat.

Crab Imperial

3	tablespoons butter	½	teaspoon Old Bay Seasoning
2	tablespoons chopped onions	¼	teaspoon freshly ground black pepper
2	tablespoons chopped bell pepper	¼	cup mayonnaise
2	tablespoons all-purpose flour	1	tablespoon dry sherry
½	cup whole milk	¼	teaspoon Worcestershire sauce
1	pound fresh lump crabmeat, drained		Paprika

- Preheat oven to 350°.

- Melt butter in large heavy skillet over medium high heat. Sauté onion and bell pepper, stirring constantly, until tender.

- Combine flour and milk, stirring well. Add to onion mixture, stirring often. Cook about 2 minutes or until thickened. Add crabmeat and next 5 ingredients, blending well.

- Remove from heat and spoon into 2-quart casserole or individual baking shells. Sprinkle with paprika.

- Bake in casserole for 20 to 25 minutes or until bubbly. Decrease time if baking in shells.

Yield: 6 servings

Baked Seafood Salad

¾	cup mayonnaise		Freshly ground black pepper to taste
1	teaspoon Worcestershire sauce	2	pounds cooked shrimp, peeled and deveined
1	teaspoon lemon juice	1	pound crabmeat
¼	cup chopped red bell pepper	½	cup shredded Swiss cheese
¼	cup chopped shallots		Round buttery cracker crumbs
½	teaspoon salt		

- Preheat oven to 350°.

- Combine mayonnaise and next 7 ingredients in food processor until thoroughly blended.

- Transfer to large bowl and stir in crab. Spoon into 2-quart casserole. Top with cheese and cracker crumbs.

- Bake for 30 minutes.

Yield: 8 servings

Lucy Creek Crab Cakes

1 pound lump crabmeat
1 cup round buttery cracker crumbs, divided
1 egg, beaten
½ cup butter, melted
¼ cup mayonnaise
1 tablespoon Worcestershire sauce
1 tablespoon fresh lemon juice
Dash of lemon pepper seasoning
Dash of Old Bay Seasoning
½ cup butter
1 tablespoon olive oil
Lemon wedges

- Combine crab, ½ cup cracker crumbs and next 7 ingredients, mixing well.

- Shape into 4-inch patties. Roll in remaining crumbs. Place on wax paper and chill until cooking time.

- Melt butter and oil in large skillet over medium high heat. Sauté crab cakes until golden brown on each side. Drain on paper towels and garnish with lemon wedges.

Yield: 4 servings

Crab cakes may be frozen.

"One time when we were cooking crabs that we had caught in the river, my dad forgot to close the lid and the crabs started climbing out of the pot! We spent ten minutes chasing crabs around the kitchen!"

Jenny Baldwin,
Grade 12
Beaufort Academy
student

~

Southern Crab Cakes with Lime Sauce

⅔ cup mayonnaise
1 cup dry breadcrumbs, divided
1 tablespoon fresh lime juice
¼-½ teaspoon cayenne pepper
12-16 ounces lump crabmeat
2 ounces chopped pimiento, drained
2 tablespoons minced green onion
2 tablespoons butter

- Combine mayonnaise, ½ cup breadcrumbs and next 5 ingredients in large bowl, mixing well.

- Shape into 8 (½-inch thick) patties and coat with remaining breadcrumbs.

- Melt butter in large heavy skillet over medium heat and sauté crab cakes about 3 minutes per side.

- Drain on paper towels and serve with Lime Sauce.

LIME SAUCE

½ cup mayonnaise

¼ cup sour cream

1 tablespoon fresh lime juice

2 teaspoons lime zest

• Combine ingredients in small bowl and blend thoroughly.

Yield: 8 servings

This Lime Sauce also makes a good crab salad. Toss with fresh crabmeat and stuff in an avocado half.

The Atlantic Blue crab's taxonomic name, Callinectes Sapidus, translates "savory beautiful swimmer". The name alone hints at its seductiveness.

Blend of Beaufort Seafood Casserole

½	cup butter	½	teaspoon salt
1	teaspoon minced garlic	¼	teaspoon freshly ground
1	cup sliced fresh mushrooms		black pepper
½	cup chopped onion	1	cup half-and-half
½	cup chopped bell pepper	1	tablespoon Worcestershire
1	cup chopped celery		sauce
1	pound crabmeat	1	tablespoon fresh lemon
1	pound cooked shrimp,		juice
	peeled and deveined	2	cups cooked rice
1	(2-ounce) jar pimientos		Round buttery cracker
1	cup mayonnaise		crumbs or breadcrumbs

- Preheat oven to 350°.
- Melt butter in large skillet over medium high heat. Sauté garlic and next 4 ingredients until tender, but not brown. Remove from heat.
- Add crab, shrimp and pimientos to garlic mixture and set aside.
- Combine mayonnaise and next 5 ingredients in small bowl, blending well. Stir into seafood mixture and add rice.
- Spoon into 3-quart casserole and top with crumbs.
- Bake for 30 minutes.

Yield: 8 servings

Casserole may be prepared ahead and refrigerated until ready to bake.

Fried Soft Shell Crab

	Peanut oil for frying		Salt and pepper
4	soft shell crabs, cleaned	½	cup all-purpose flour

- Heat enough oil to measure 2 inches deep in a Dutch oven or heavy stockpot.
- Rinse and pat crabs dry. Season with salt and pepper. Dredge in flour, shaking off excess.
- Deep fry crabs in 375° oil 2 at a time about 3 to 5 minutes or until golden brown, turning over once. Drain crabs.

Yield: 2 servings

Sautéed Soft Shell Crabs

4	soft shell crabs, cleaned	2	tablespoons cooking oil
	Salt and pepper	⅓	cup slivered almonds,
½	cup all-purpose flour		toasted
¼	cup unsalted butter		Lemon wedges for garnish

- Rinse and pat crabs dry. Season with salt and pepper. Dredge in flour, shaking off excess, and set aside.
- Melt butter in large skillet with oil. Sauté crabs over medium heat 3 to 4 minutes per side until golden brown.
- Drain crabs and sprinkle with toasted almonds. Serve with lemon wedge.

Yield: 2 servings

Soft shell crabs make delicious sandwiches. Serve on a sourdough roll with your favorite tartar sauce or homemade mayonnaise.

~

Grilled Soft Shell Crabs

	Juice of 4 limes	¼	cup chopped fresh cilantro
2	tablespoons tequila	½	cup olive oil
1	garlic clove, minced		Salt and pepper to taste
1	jalapeño pepper, seeded	8	soft-shell crabs, dressed
	and minced		Lime wedges

- Whisk together lime juice and next 4 ingredients. Whisk in olive oil gradually. Season with salt and pepper and set aside.
- Place crabs in single layer in shallow bowl. Pour lime juice mixture over crabs, cover and chill 3 hours.
- Preheat grill.
- Remove crabs from marinade and place 4 to 5 inches from heat. Grill 2 to 3 minutes per side or just until thoroughly cooked.
- Transfer to platter and serve immediately with lime wedges.

Yield: 4 servings

Soft shell crabs are a seasonal delicacy. They are available for only a few weeks each spring during the period when the blue crabs shed their old shells and before growing their new ones. Immediately after molting, they are most tender and are truly soft for only one hour!

Frogmore Spaghetti

¼	cup butter	1	(26-ounce) jar spaghetti
1	large Vidalia onion, chopped		sauce
			Salt and pepper to taste
1	large bell pepper, chopped		Garlic powder to taste or
2	cups sliced fresh mushrooms		1 teaspoon minced fresh garlic
2-3	pounds smoked sausage, sliced	2	pounds medium shrimp, peeled and deveined
1	(28-ounce) can crushed Italian plum tomatoes		Fresh Parmesan cheese
			Shredded Cheddar cheese
		2	pounds spaghetti, cooked al dente

- Melt butter in large skillet over medium high heat. Sauté onion, bell pepper and mushrooms until tender. Add sausage and sauté.
- Pour in tomatoes, spaghetti sauce, salt, pepper and garlic to taste. Reduce heat to medium and cook about 30 minutes or until sauce has thickened, stirring frequently.
- Add shrimp and cook until pink.
- Place spaghetti in serving bowl and top with shrimp sauce and cheeses.

Yield: 6 to 8 servings

There is an old settlement on St. Helena Island called Frogmore. Originally, it was a strategic crossroads connecting many of the Sea Island Plantations to Beaufort. It was named after an ancestral English country estate. In the early 1900s, Frogmore was noted for its diamondback terrapin and caviar business. Today Frogmore is a quaint place to stop and enjoy the food, crafts and history of Gullah culture. The official name has been changed to St. Helena, but to the locals, it will always be Frogmore.

~

This is a true Lowcountry specialty and great for a casual feast with friends. Simply put down newspaper, throw out stew and enjoy! Serve with crusty sourdough bread, your favorite cole slaw and beer.

Frogmore Stew

	Old Bay Seasoning to taste	1	ear of corn per person, shucked and halved
1	small onion per person, peeled	½	pound shrimp per person (31-35 count per pound)
¼	pound sliced kielbasa per person, sliced 1-inch thick		

- Fill large pot with enough water to cover ingredients. Add Old Bay Seasoning and onions.
- Bring water to a rapid boil and add sausage. Boil 5 minutes and add corn. Boil 5 minutes and add shrimp.
- Cook until shrimp begin to float and shells start to separate slightly from back of shrimp.
- Drain and serve.

Some cooks are known to add a can of beer to Frogmore Stew.

Szechuan Shrimp and Chicken Kabobs

2	tablespoons rice wine vinegar	½	pound shrimp, peeled and deveined
2	tablespoons olive oil	½	pound boneless chicken breasts, cubed
2	tablespoons soy sauce		
1	tablespoon chili paste with garlic	1	green or red bell pepper, cut into 1-inch squares
1	teaspoon sesame oil	2	green onions, cut into 2-inch length
1	teaspoon peeled and minced fresh ginger		

- Combine vinegar and next 5 ingredients in large zip-top plastic bag. Add shrimp and chicken and chill 1 to 2 hours.

- Remove shrimp and chicken from bag and set aside, reserving marinade. Boil marinade in small saucepan and set aside.

- Thread shrimp and chicken on skewers alternately with pepper and onion.

- Brush with marinade and grill 10 minutes, turning occasionally and basting.

Yield: 2 servings

The rise and fall of the tide played a significant role in early years. Large freight vessels could maneuver the waterways to plantation docks at high tide. The cotton could be loaded at low tide, and the vessel could head for the open sea at the next high tide.

Spicy Shrimp and Sesame Noodles

½	pound linguine	3	garlic cloves, minced
1	pound medium shrimp, peeled and deveined	2	tablespoons soy sauce
2	tablespoons sesame oil	2	green onions, chopped
1	teaspoon chili paste with garlic		Sesame seeds for garnish

- Cook linguine al dente in large pot of boiling, salted water. Rinse under cold water, drain and set aside.

- Sauté shrimp in large skillet over medium high heat in sesame oil. Add chili paste and garlic and sauté until shrimp are pink. Add soy sauce and pasta, tossing to coat, and heat. Sprinkle with onions and sesame seeds.

Yield: 4 servings

Asian Shrimp and Noodles

8	ounces spaghetti, broken	2	tablespoons sesame oil
1½	pounds fresh broccoli florets (5 cups)	1	tablespoon chili oil
1	pound shrimp, peeled and deveined	1	tablespoon peeled and grated fresh ginger
⅓	cup creamy peanut butter	3	garlic cloves, minced
⅓	cup soy sauce	4	green onions, chopped
3	tablespoons rice wine vinegar	⅓	cup chopped cashews or almonds

- Bring large amount of water to a boil in 4-quart Dutch oven. Add pasta and cook 4 minutes. Add broccoli and cook 2 minutes. Add shrimp and cook 2 to 3 minutes or until shrimp are pink.
- Drain spaghetti mixture and return to Dutch oven.
- Combine peanut butter and soy sauce in bowl. Stir in vinegar and next 4 ingredients, blending well.
- Add peanut butter mixture, green onions and nuts to spaghetti, tossing gently to coat.

Yield: 6 servings

Mango Grilled Shrimp

⅓	cup mango chutney	1	teaspoon olive oil
⅓	cup fresh lime juice	1	pound large shrimp, peeled and deveined
1	tablespoon peeled and minced fresh ginger		Mint sprigs
1	tablespoon minced garlic		Lime slices

- Combine chutney and next 4 ingredients in large zip-top plastic bag. Add shrimp and marinate 1 hour.
- Remove shrimp from bag and reserve marinade.
- Thread shrimp onto skewers and grill 3 to 5 minutes on preheated grill.
- Remove from grill and transfer to serving platter. Garnish with mint and lime slices.
- Boil reserved marinade in small saucepan and serve with shrimp.

Yield: 4 servings

Ginger Shrimp with Green Beans

2 pounds large shrimp, peeled and deveined (tails on)

4 tablespoons cooking oil, divided

2½ tablespoons grated ginger, divided

3 garlic cloves, minced and divided

2 pounds fresh green beans, trimmed

2 small white onions, chopped

¼ teaspoon crushed red pepper flakes

4 tablespoons soy sauce

2 tablespoons rice wine vinegar

4 tablespoons hoisin sauce

½ tablespoon sesame oil

4 cups cooked rice

For this spectacular dish, use only fresh ginger. Do not substitute with ginger powder or crystallized powder.

- Combine shrimp, 2 tablespoons cooking oil, 2 teaspoons ginger, and half of garlic in glass bowl. Toss and chill at least 1 hour.

- Cook beans until crisp tender (about 3 to 5 minutes). Drain and rinse with cold water. Set aside.

- Heat 2 tablespoons cooking oil in skillet over medium high heat. Add onions and sauté 4 to 5 minutes or until tender. Add remaining ginger and garlic. Add red pepper flakes and stir 2 minutes. Add soy sauce, vinegar, hoisin sauce and sesame oil and continue cooking 2 to 3 minutes or until thickened.

- Add beans, stirring until heated. Remove from heat and keep warm.

- Remove shrimp from marinade and thread onto skewers. Grill 2 to 3 minutes per side or until shrimp are pink.

- Remove shrimp from skewers.

- Toss shrimp with bean mixture and serve over rice.

Yield: 8 servings

*An easy way
to please a crowd!*

Broad River Shrimp Bake

7	tablespoons butter, divided	2	pounds cooked shrimp, peeled and deveined
4½	tablespoons plus ¼ teaspoon all-purpose flour	½-1	pound sliced portobello mushrooms
1	cup heavy cream	¼	cup dry sherry
½	cup half-and-half Salt and pepper to taste	1	tablespoon Worcestershire sauce
1	(14-ounce) can artichoke hearts, drained and halved	½	cup fresh Parmesan cheese Paprika

- Preheat oven to 375°.

- Melt 4½ tablespoons butter in skillet over medium heat. Stir in 4½ tablespoons flour. Add cream and half-and-half, stirring constantly until thickened. Season with salt and pepper and set aside.

- Place artichoke hearts in bottom of large casserole and top with cooked shrimp.

- Melt remaining butter in second skillet and sauté mushrooms over medium high heat until tender. Sprinkle ¼ teaspoon flour over mushrooms and stir. Remove from heat and spoon over shrimp.

- Add sherry and Worcestershire sauce to cream sauce and pour over shrimp and artichokes. Top with cheese and sprinkle with paprika.

- Bake for 20 minutes.

Yield: 6 servings

Shrimp Scampi

2½	pounds large shrimp, peeled and deveined (tails on)	1	teaspoon salt	
½	cup butter, melted	1	garlic clove, minced	
⅛	cup olive oil	1	teaspoon dried basil	
3	tablespoons fresh lemon juice	1	teaspoon dried oregano	
¼	cup chopped fresh parsley		Lemon pepper seasoning to taste	
			Hot cooked rice	

- Preheat oven to 450°.
- Place shrimp in single layer on jelly-roll pan.
- Combine butter and next 8 ingredients in small bowl, mixing well. Pour over shrimp.
- Bake for 5 minutes then broil 4 inches from heat for 5 minutes.
- Serve over cooked rice.

Yield: 6 servings

Dried basil and oregano may be substituted with 1 tablespoon fresh basil and oregano.

Company Shrimp

¼	cup butter, melted	½	cup sour cream	
¾	cup chopped onion	¼	cup dry white wine or sherry	
¾	cup sliced fresh mushrooms	1	pound shrimp, peeled and deveined	
3	tablespoons all-purpose flour		Hot cooked rice	
1	cup chicken broth			

- Melt butter in large skillet over medium high heat. Sauté onion and mushrooms until tender.
- Blend in flour. Add broth gradually, whisking constantly until mixture is thickened.
- Add sour cream, wine and shrimp. Continue cooking about 5 minutes or until shrimp are pink.
- Serve over cooked rice.

Yield: 4 servings

"When I was a young child, Beaufort still had street vendors who would make regular rounds to houses to sell fresh vegetables and seafood. The 'Shrimp Man' rode a bike with a wide basket in front that was lined with newspaper. When the cook heard 'swimps e raw', she would get one of grandmother's pots and meet him on the back porch. The shrimp had just been caught with a cast net and still had their heads and long whiskers on. Some were still jumping. It doesn't get any fresher than that!"

Charles Webb, III
Beaufort alumnae
and parent

~

An old time favorite on Pawley's Island!

In the South, many stew dishes contain tomatoes and sweet peppers—these are Creole dishes. When okra is added, it becomes gumbo.

The Best Shrimp Creole

4	tablespoons olive oil	1	(14-ounce) can whole
1	medium onion, chopped		tomatoes
1	yellow or red bell pepper,	1	(6-ounce) can tomato paste
	chopped	1	tablespoon sugar
¾	cup chopped celery	¾	cup water
2	garlic cloves, minced		Salt and pepper to taste
1	(28-ounce) can whole		Hot sauce to taste
	tomatoes	2	pounds cooked shrimp,
			peeled and deveined

- Heat oil in large skillet over medium high heat. Sauté onion, bell pepper, celery and garlic until tender, but not brown.

- Add tomatoes, tomato paste, sugar, water, salt, pepper and hot sauce. Bring to a boil, reduce heat and simmer 1 to 2 hours. Add shrimp and simmer until thoroughly heated.

Yield: 6 servings

Serve over rice.

Creamy Shrimp Risotto

2	tablespoons olive oil	1	cup frozen petits pois
2	tablespoons chopped red	1	teaspoon lemon zest
	onion	1	tablespoon fresh lemon
1¼	cup Arborio rice		juice
⅓	cup dry white wine		Salt to taste
4-5	cups unsalted chicken		Freshly ground black
	broth, divided		pepper to taste
1	pound medium shrimp,		Fresh basil or parsley,
	peeled and deveined		finely chopped

- Heat oil in skillet over medium high heat and sauté onion until tender. Stir in rice, coating with oil.

- Increase heat to high. Add wine and bring to a boil, stirring constantly, until liquid is reduced.

- Stir in 1 cup broth and bring to a boil. Cover and cook over low heat 5 minutes. Stir in 1 cup broth and bring to a boil. Cover and cook 10 minutes. Stir in 1 cup broth, shrimp, peas and zest. Cook uncovered, stirring constantly, until rice is tender and creamy. Shrimp should be cooked thoroughly.

- Add broth as needed to keep rice creamy. Stir in lemon juice, salt and pepper. Garnish with basil or parsley before serving.

Yield: 4 servings

Nana's Shrimp Delight

1½ cups long grain white rice
3 tablespoons butter
1 cup chopped onions
½ cup chopped yellow bell pepper
3 tablespoons all-purpose flour
1 (14.5-ounce) can diced tomatoes with garlic, drained
1 (14-ounce) can vegetable-tomato juice or tomato juice
1 tablespoon fresh lemon juice
2 tablespoons white wine
Pinch of sugar
1 teaspoon salt
1 teaspoon Worcestershire sauce
Dash of hot pepper sauce
¼ cup shredded Cheddar cheese
1 pound shrimp, peeled and deveined
Minced fresh basil or oregano

- Preheat oven to 350°.

- Cook rice according to package directions and set aside.

- Melt butter in heavy large skillet over medium high heat. Sauté onion and bell pepper until tender.

- Blend in flour. Stir in tomatoes and next 4 ingredients, stirring until thickened. Add salt, Worcestershire sauce, hot pepper sauce and cheese.

- Remove from heat and add shrimp. Transfer to casserole dish and sprinkle with basil or oregano.

- Bake for 30 minutes.

Yield: 6 servings

"If you are familiar with just some of 'Bubba Gump's' recitation of the variety of ways to prepare shrimp, you have a great starting point! From shrimp burgers to shrimp salad, shrimp and red rice to plain old fried shrimp, shrimp can please the palate of just about anyone!"

Claudia Gay
Beaufort Academy
parent

Shrimp with Orzo

1	tablespoon olive oil	1	cup dry white wine
2	garlic cloves, minced		Juice of 1 lemon
1	pound medium-large shrimp, peeled and deveined	5	tablespoons unsalted butter Zest of 1 lemon
¼	cup finely chopped parsley, divided	1	tablespoon capers, rinsed and drained
	Salt and pepper to taste	1	cup uncooked orzo, cooked al dente

- Heat oil in large skillet over medium high heat. Sauté garlic and shrimp until done. Sprinkle 2 tablespoons parsley over shrimp and season with salt and pepper. Remove from pan and keep warm.

- Add wine and lemon juice to same skillet and bring to a boil. Lower heat and reduce by half.

- Remove from heat and add remaining parsley. Stir in butter, lemon zest and capers, blending well. Pour over shrimp and serve on bed of orzo.

Yield: 4 servings

Shrimp Feta

2	eggs, beaten	1	(8-ounce) package angel hair pasta, cooked and divided
1½	cups half-and-half		
1	cup sour cream		
½	cup shredded Swiss cheese	1	(16-ounce) jar mild salsa
1	cup crumbled feta cheese	2	pounds shrimp, peeled and deveined
½	cup fresh parsley, chopped		
1	teaspoon dried basil	1	cup shredded Monterey Jack cheese
1	teaspoon dried oregano		

- Combine eggs and next 7 ingredients in medium bowl and set aside.

- Place half of pasta in greased 9x13-inch casserole. Spread salsa evenly over pasta. Top with shrimp and sprinkle with Monterey Jack cheese. Layer with remaining pasta.

- Pour egg mixture evenly over pasta. Shake gently until mixture soaks bottom pasta layer.

- Bake at 350° for 35 to 40 minutes or until heated thoroughly.

Yield: 8 to 10 servings

Judy's Jambalaya

¼ cup all-purpose flour
¼ cup bacon drippings or
olive oil
1½ cups chopped onions
1 cup chopped green onions
1 cup chopped celery with
leaves
1 cup chopped green or red
bell pepper
2 garlic cloves, minced
1 (6-ounce) can tomato paste
1 (16-ounce) can chopped
tomatoes
1 (8-ounce) can tomato sauce
1 cup water
1 teaspoon salt

1 teaspoon freshly ground
black pepper
½ teaspoon cayenne pepper
Hot pepper sauce to taste
2-3 bay leaves
1 teaspoon sugar
1 teaspoon Worcestershire
sauce
1 tablespoon fresh lemon
juice
2 cups uncooked rice
1 pound cooked, drained
and sliced kielbasa
2 pounds cooked shrimp,
peeled and deveined
½ cup chopped parsley

- Cook flour and bacon drippings in Dutch oven over medium heat until flour begins to brown. Add onions and next 4 ingredients and sauté until tender.

- Add tomato paste and next 12 ingredients. Cook until thoroughly heated. Remove bay leaves.

- Remove from heat and add remaining ingredients. Transfer to 3-quart casserole.

- Bake at 350° for 30 to 45 minutes or until liquid is absorbed and rice is cooked.

Yield: 6 to 8 servings

Jambalaya is a Creole dish of seasoned rice mixed with meat, seafood or both. Rice is the main ingredient, making it a Lowcountry crowd pleaser.

Southern Shrimp & Grits

No dish is more typical of the Lowcountry than shrimp and grits. The different versions for the gravy may range from simple sautéing of shrimp in bacon grease to complicated sauces made with fresh local ingredients. The dish may be found served as breakfast for the crew on shrimp boats as they head to sea or as a dinner entrée in Beaufort's finest restaurants.

3	tablespoons butter, divided		Pinch of Cajun seasoning
4	ounces country ham, thinly sliced	2	green onions, chopped
8	ounces smoked pork sausage	1	tomato, seeded and chopped
2	cloves garlic, minced	1	pound shrimp, peeled and deveined
		1	tablespoon water

- Melt 1 tablespoon butter in large skillet over medium high heat. Slice sausage into patties. Sauté ham and sausage until sausage is brown.

- Add garlic and Cajun seasoning and sauté 30 seconds. Add green onions, tomato and shrimp. Cook 2 minutes. Stir in water and remaining butter. Heat thoroughly and serve over grits.

Grits

4	cups water	1½	cups stone-ground grits
½	teaspoon salt	¼	cup heavy cream
1	tablespoon butter		

- Bring water, salt, butter and grits to a boil. Reduce heat to low and cook about 30 to 40 minutes, stirring occasionally, until grits are thick and creamy. Stir in cream, mixing well.

Yield: 4 servings

Shrimp Gravy

½ pound bacon, cut into 2-
   inch squares
1 large yellow onion,
   chopped
1 bell pepper, chopped

2-3 tablespoons all-purpose
     flour
2   pounds shrimp, peeled
     and deveined
     Salt and pepper

- Cook bacon until crisp in large heavy skillet over medium heat. Remove and set aside.

- Add onion and bell pepper to bacon drippings in skillet and sauté until tender. Remove and set aside.

- Brown flour in bacon drippings, adding just enough water to make a thick gravy.

- Reduce heat and add bacon, onion, bell pepper and shrimp. Season with salt and pepper. Serve over grits.

Grits

2 cups water
2 cups milk
3 beef bouillon cubes
1 cup quick grits
   Dash of garlic powder

Salt to taste
Butter (optional)
Fresh Parmesan or
   shredded Cheddar
   cheese (optional)

- Bring water, milk and bouillon to a near boil in heavy saucepan. Add grits, salt and garlic powder.

- Bring to a boil, reduce heat and simmer 10 to 15 minutes. Add butter or cheese if desired.

Yield: 6 servings

The annual Shrimp Festival sponsored by the Greater Beaufort Chamber of Commerce at the Waterfront Park salutes rich Lowcountry traditions and celebrates the bounty of shrimp. You may buy shrimp directly from local shrimp boats, try your luck with raffles for 100 pounds of shrimp or savor the shrimp treats from area restaurants. The blessing of the fleet, a 5K run-walk, music, arts and crafts are also part of the festivities.

Shrimp and Scallops
with Angel Hair Pasta

¼	cup plus 1 tablespoon olive oil	2	tablespoons butter
1	garlic clove, minced	1	pound scallops, washed and patted dry
1½	pounds shrimp, peeled and deveined	¼	cup dry white wine
6-8	plum tomatoes, seeded and chopped	1	pound angel hair pasta, cooked al dente
4	green onions, chopped		Fresh Asiago or Parmesan cheese
	Salt and pepper to taste		Fresh basil, minced
¼	cup fresh lemon juice		Fresh dill, minced

- Heat 1 tablespoon oil over medium high heat. Sauté garlic and shrimp until pink. Season with salt and pepper and remove from heat.

- Combine shrimp, tomatoes, onions, ¼ cup olive oil and lemon juice in large bowl, mixing well. Cover and chill at least 1 hour.

- Poach scallops in butter and wine in large skillet until opaque. Add shrimp mixture and slowly reheat.

- Stir in hot pasta, cheese, basil and dill and toss well.

Yield: 6 servings

Shrimp and Scallops Au Gratin

1	package frozen puff pastry shells	2	garlic cloves, minced
½	cup butter, divided	2	tablespoons all-purpose flour
½	pound medium shrimp, peeled and deveined	1½	cups whole milk
½	pound scallops	1	cup shredded Swiss cheese
	Salt and pepper to taste	2	tablespoons chopped fresh parsley
2	cups sliced fresh mushrooms		

- Bake pastry shells according to package directions and set aside.

- Melt ¼ cup butter in large skillet over medium high heat. Sauté shrimp until pink and scallops until opaque. (This may need to be done in separate processes.) Season with salt and pepper. Remove from skillet and set aside.

- Add mushrooms and garlic to same skillet and sauté until tender. Remove and set aside.

- Add remaining butter to same skillet and stir in flour until smooth. Add milk and bring to a boil, stirring constantly, until thickened (about 2 minutes).

- Reduce heat and add cheese and parsley, stirring until cheese melts. Return shrimp, scallops and mushrooms to skillet and heat thoroughly. Spoon into baked shells and serve.

Yield: 6 servings

A little bit labor intensive, but well worth the effort!

Sea Island Seafood Strudel

½	cup breadcrumbs	1	cup sour cream
¼	cup plus 2 tablespoons fresh Parmesan cheese	¼	cup plus 4 tablespoons chopped fresh parsley
¼	teaspoon dry mustard	¼	cup chopped shallots
½	pound shrimp, peeled, deveined and cooked	2	teaspoons chopped fresh chives
½	pound crabmeat, cooked	1	pound frozen phyllo dough sheets, thawed
½	pound small scallops, cooked	1	cup butter, melted
¾	cup shredded Swiss cheese		White Sauce
2	hard-boiled eggs, chopped		

- Preheat oven to 375°. Line baking sheet with parchment paper or grease baking sheet lightly.

- Combine breadcrumbs, ¼ cup Parmesan cheese and dry mustard in small bowl and set aside.

- Combine shrimp and next 5 ingredients in bowl and set aside.

- Combine ¼ cup parsley, shallots and chives in small bowl and set aside.

- Thaw phyllo according to package directions. Carefully remove 1 sheet. Brush with melted butter before layering next sheet and repeat 4 to 5 times. (Keep remaining phyllo sheets covered with a damp cloth until ready to use.)

- Place 1 cup seafood mixture in center of phyllo, spreading to a 4x4-inch square. Top with 2 to 3 tablespoons breadcrumb mixture, 1 teaspoon parsley mixture and a heaping tablespoon White Sauce.

- Fold long ends of pastry toward center, making a 5x15-inch rectangle. Fold short ends toward center, making a 5x5-inch square. Place seam side down on prepared baking sheet.

- Brush with butter. Repeat process, making 3 more strudels.

- Bake 30 to 35 minutes, basting often with melted butter until pastry is light golden brown.

- Allow to stand 5 to 10 minutes before slicing diagonally to form 2 triangular servings. Garnish with Parmesan cheese and chopped parsley.

White Sauce

3	tablespoons unsalted butter	¾	cup milk
3	tablespoons all-purpose flour	1	teaspoon Dijon mustard
		¼	teaspoon cayenne pepper
		2	tablespoons heavy cream

- Melt butter in small saucepan and stir in flour until roux forms.

- Whisk milk into butter mixture, stirring constantly, until thickened. Stir in Dijon and cayenne. Add cream, stirring just to incorporate.

- Cover and set aside until ready for use.

Yield: 8 servings

Scallops with Tomato–Mango Salsa

Tomato-Mango Salsa

1	medium tomato, seeded and chopped	2	tablespoons finely chopped fresh basil
¾	cup finely chopped mango	2	tablespoons red wine vinegar
3	tablespoons finely chopped red onion	1	tablespoon capers, rinsed and drained

- Combine ingredients in medium bowl, cover and chill at least 30 minutes.

Scallops

1	tablespoon olive oil	Fresh basil sprigs for garnish
12	sea scallops	Avocado slices for garnish
	Salt and pepper to taste	
	Fresh mint sprigs for garnish	

- Heat oil in heavy skillet over medium high heat until hot. Add scallops and cook 3 minutes or until opaque, turning once. Remove scallops from skillet and season with salt and pepper.

- Spoon ½ cup Tomato-Mango Salsa on plate and arrange scallops on top. Garnish with mint, basil and avocado slices.

Yield: 2 servings

In the winter it is a common sight to see pick-up trucks piled high with collard greens for sale along Highway 21. Always buy more than you think you'll need because once cleaned and stemmed, 5 pounds of greens will yield only about 3 pounds.

Southern Scallops

2	pounds collard greens, washed	1	pound fresh sea scallops
4	slices bacon or seasoned pork	1	cup balsamic vinegar
5	tablespoons butter, divided	2	tablespoons honey
		2	tablespoons chopped fresh basil
		½	teaspoon salt

- Cook collard greens with bacon or seasoned pork until tender and set aside.

- Melt 3 tablespoons butter in heavy skillet over medium high heat. Add scallops and sear 2 to 3 minutes per side, depending on thickness. Remove from skillet and keep warm.

- Pour vinegar into heavy small saucepan and bring to a boil. Continue cooking until vinegar is reduced to ¼ cup.

- Pour vinegar into small bowl. Add 2 tablespoons butter, honey, basil and salt and blend well. Return to saucepan and heat thoroughly.

- Mound ½ cup cooked collard greens on each plate and top with 4 to 5 scallops. Drizzle with balsamic reduction and serve.

Yield: 4 servings

Scallop Scampi

2	tablespoons olive oil, divided	2	tablespoons fresh lemon juice
2	tablespoons unsalted butter, divided	2	tablespoons heavy cream or half-and-half
1	pound large sea scallops, rinsed and dried	½	cup chopped and seeded plum tomatoes
¼	cup chopped shallots	2	tablespoons chopped fresh basil
1	garlic clove, minced		

- Melt 1 tablespoon oil and 1 tablespoon butter in heavy large skillet over medium high heat. Add scallops and sauté about 2 to 3 minutes per side or until golden. Remove from skillet and set aside.

- Reduce heat and add remaining oil and butter, shallots and garlic to same skillet. Cook until shallots and garlic are tender.

- Stir in lemon juice and cream. Return scallops to skillet and add tomatoes. Heat thoroughly and garnish with basil.

Yield: 4 servings

Serve over pasta or rice.

Oyster and Rice Casserole

¼ cup butter
2 cups sliced fresh
 mushrooms
½ cup chopped red bell
 pepper
½ cup chopped onion
 Salt and pepper
1 cup dry white wine
2 cups fresh oysters
1 cup cooked wild rice

- Preheat oven to 350°.

- Melt butter in large skillet over medium high heat. Add mushrooms, red bell pepper and onion. Sauté until slightly brown. Season with salt and pepper.

- Reduce heat and add wine. Simmer 15 minutes and add oysters.

- Spoon cooked rice into shallow 2-quart casserole. Spoon oyster mixture over rice and bake for 30 minutes.

Yield: 4 servings

Local oysters are harvested in months containing the letter "R". The tidal saltwater is cooler at this time, and the meat is firmer and saltier.

~

Lowcountry Oyster Pie

½ cup butter, melted
2 cups crushed crackers,
 divided
1 quart oysters, undrained
 Juice of 1 lemon
1 teaspoon mace
1 teaspoon black pepper
 Salt and pepper to taste
2 tablespoons
 Worcestershire sauce
1 cup heavy cream

- Preheat oven to 350°.

- Combine butter and cracker crumbs in small bowl. Layer bottom of prepared casserole with ⅓ crumb mixture and set aside.

- Drain oysters, reserving juice. Arrange half of oysters on top of crumbs and set aside.

- Combine lemon juice and next 4 ingredients in small bowl. Season oysters with half of lemon juice mixture and set aside.

- Repeat layers and top with remaining crumbs.

- Combine cream and 1 cup oyster juice in small bowl and pour over casserole.

- Bake 30 minutes until bubbly.

Yield: 6 servings

In the Lowcountry, no Thanksgiving dinner is complete without an oyster pie. To maximize the flavor of the oysters, wait until the last moment to prepare and serve immediately!

Oyster Roast

Fresh single or select oysters in the shell
Gloves
Oyster knives

Melted butter
Crackers
Cocktail sauce

This recipe can be used for gatherings of 2 to 2,000. Purchase fresh oysters from your local seafood market. Shells should be tightly closed and kept cool until cooking time. Clean mud and sand from shells with a garden hose!

- Fill steamer half full of water and bring to a boil. Place oysters in steamer basket and steam for about 10 minutes or until oysters begin to open.

- Hold oyster in gloved hand. Insert oyster knife into opened edge and separate to expose meat. Use knife to cut meat away from shell.

- Serve oysters plain, dipped in melted butter or placed on cracker and dipped in cocktail sauce.

Yield: 1 bushel serves 8

Round blunt knives or flat screwdrivers may be used if oyster knives are unavailable.

The traditional roasting method calls for steaming oysters open by placing them on metal sheets that have been heated over oak fires and covering them with wet burlap bags until they are steamed open.

POULTRY

POULTRY

Beaufort is a city blessed with rich history and tradition. It attracts thousands of visitors each year to explore its charm and beauty. Beaufort residents warmly welcome these visitors by opening their homes and plantations throughout the year. The Historic Beaufort Foundation Kitchen and Garden Tour, St. Helena's Episcopal Church Candlelight and Plantation Tour, and the Beaufort Academy Designer Showhouse have allowed visitors a firsthand glimpse of the Lowcountry way of life.

Sunset–Sherried Tomato Cream
over Chicken Breasts

4	chicken breast halves	¼	cup chopped fresh parsley
½	teaspoon salt	2	teaspoons chopped fresh basil
½	teaspoon freshly ground black pepper	⅓	cup dry sherry
½	teaspoon nutmeg	1	teaspoon Dijon mustard
1	tablespoon olive oil	1	medium tomato, peeled, seeded and chopped
1	tablespoon unsalted butter		
¼	cup chopped shallots	½	cup heavy cream

- Season chicken breasts with salt, pepper and nutmeg.

- Heat olive oil and butter in large heavy skillet over medium high heat and sauté chicken until light golden brown.

- Add shallots, parsley, basil and sherry. Bring to a boil. Reduce heat, cover and simmer 15 minutes.

- Transfer chicken to serving platter, keep warm and set aside.

- Stir mustard, tomato and cream into skillet and bring to a boil. Cook and stir until liquid has thickened slightly.

- Spoon sauce over chicken and serve.

Yield: 4 servings

SUNSET ON THE WATER

You see the water flowing by.

You see the sun go down.

You see the sunset on the water

Reflecting beautiful colors like

Red, blue, orange, yellow and purple.

Then you see the sky go dim,

And then go dark

Then you can get into bed,

And you long for the sunset over the water.

Nicole Aitken, Grade 5
Beaufort Academy
student

Lemon Chicken
with Artichoke Hearts and Mushrooms

4	chicken breast halves, skinned and boned	3-4	tablespoons fresh lemon juice
½	teaspoon crushed black peppercorns	1	tablespoon chopped fresh parsley
	Salt to taste	4	tablespoons dry white wine
½	cup butter, divided	2	tablespoons chicken broth
1	(14-ounce) can artichoke hearts, rinsed, drained and halved	½	pound fresh mushrooms, sliced

- Preheat oven to 300°.

- Pound chicken breasts between sheets of wax paper to ¼-inch thickness.

- Rub both sides of chicken with crushed peppercorns and sprinkle with salt.

- Heat 2 tablespoons butter in large heavy skillet over medium heat. Add chicken and sauté 3 to 5 minutes on each side. Transfer chicken to baking pan and keep warm.

- Add 2 tablespoons butter to same skillet. Stir in artichokes and mushrooms and sauté 1 minute. Add lemon juice, wine, chicken broth and parsley. Sauté 2 to 3 minutes.

- Return chicken to skillet, heat thoroughly and serve.

Yield: 4 servings

Lady's Island Chicken Breasts

1	cup dry breadcrumbs	¼	cup minced shallots
½	teaspoon salt	½	cup chicken broth
½	teaspoon freshly ground black pepper	½	cup dry white wine
¼	teaspoon dried tarragon	½	pound fresh mushrooms, sliced
6	chicken breast halves	2	cups seedless grapes
7	tablespoons butter, divided		

- Preheat oven to 375°.

- Combine breadcrumbs, salt, pepper and tarragon, blending well. Dredge chicken lightly in mixture.

- Melt ¼ cup butter in large heavy skillet over medium high heat. Brown chicken on both sides.

- Place chicken in single layer in shallow baking pan and set aside.

- Add shallots to skillet and sauté 3 minutes or until tender. Stir in broth and wine and bring to a boil. Pour over chicken and bake for 30 minutes.

- Melt remaining 3 tablespoons butter in same skillet. Sauté mushrooms and grapes 3 to 4 minutes. Add to chicken in baking pan and bake additional 8 to 10 minutes.

Yield: 6 servings

When they built Beaufort Academy on Lady's Island in the 1960s, it was considered "out in the boonies", but today Lady's Island is fast growing with neighborhoods and businesses popping up everywhere.

Cheesy Chicken Strudel

2　tablespoons olive oil
1　onion, chopped
2　cups fresh spinach
2　cups shredded Monterey
　　　Jack cheese
2　tablespoons white wine
½　teaspoon salt
¼　teaspoon black pepper

6　chicken breast halves,
　　　cooked and cubed
10　sheets frozen phyllo
　　　dough, thawed
¼　cup butter, melted
½　cup dry breadcrumbs
　　Paprika

- Preheat oven to 375°.

- Heat olive oil in heavy skillet over medium high heat. Sauté onion until transparent. Add spinach and cook about 3 minutes or until wilted.

- Remove from heat; add cheese and next 4 ingredients and set aside.

- Prepare 5 phyllo sheets by brushing each with melted butter. Sprinkle each layer with breadcrumbs and stack.

- Spoon half of chicken mixture along long edge of phyllo sheet. Roll up tightly in jelly roll fashion.

- Place seam side down on baking sheet and brush with melted butter. Repeat process with remaining ingredients. Sprinkle with paprika.

- Bake for 15 to 20 minutes or until light golden brown.

Yield: 6 servings

Herb Cheese Stuffed Chicken

8	chicken breast halves, skinned and boned	½	cup peeled and shredded carrots
½	cup chopped fresh basil	½	cup chopped walnuts
½	cup chopped fresh parsley	⅓	cup plain breadcrumbs
2	(5-ounce) packages cheese with herbs and garlic	4	tablespoons fresh Parmesan cheese
2	tablespoons all-purpose flour	¼	cup butter, melted

- Preheat oven to 350°.

- Pound each chicken half into a square by placing in a zip-top plastic bag and pounding with a mallet.

- Combine basil and parsley in small bowl and set aside.

- Mix herb cheese and flour until smooth. Add carrots, walnuts and 4 tablespoons parsley-basil mixture.

- Place 1 to 2 heaping tablespoons of cheese mixture in center of each chicken breast. Fold chicken around cheese mixture, pressing edges together. Secure with a toothpick.

- Combine breadcrumbs, Parmesan cheese and remaining parsley-basil mixture in small bowl. Dredge chicken in melted butter, then breadcrumb mixture.

- Place on baking sheet and bake for 30 minutes.

Yield: 8 servings

HERBED CHEESE SPREAD

1 (8-ounce) container whipped butter

2 (8-ounce) packages cream cheese, softened

½ teaspoon marjoram

½ teaspoon oregano

2 garlic cloves, minced

½ teaspoon dried basil

½ teaspoon dill

½ teaspoon black pepper

½ teaspoon thyme

¼ teaspoon salt

- Combine ingredients thoroughly and serve with crackers or on endive leaves.

Company Chicken Stuffed with Crabmeat

The Lewis Reeve Sams House was the home of the Beaufort Academy Designer Showhouse in March 2000. This magnificent house is a classic example of the summer homes built by sea island plantation owners on the banks of the Beaufort River. The marble steps warmly welcomed the many visitors from near and far, and the double porches with their cool and prevailing breezes took them back in time as they gazed at the river.

8	chicken breasts, skinned and boned	8	ounces fresh mushrooms, sliced
2	tablespoons unsalted butter, softened	¼	teaspoon dried thyme
2	teaspoons salt, divided	¼	teaspoon cayenne pepper
¼	teaspoon black pepper	1	teaspoon prepared mustard
	Dash of paprika	¼	teaspoon dried sage
½	cup unsalted butter	2	tablespoons unsalted butter, melted
½	cup sherry	2	cups fresh breadcrumbs
1	teaspoon garlic salt	⅓	cup half-and-half
½	cup ketchup	1	pound crabmeat

- Preheat oven to 350°.

- Rinse chicken and pat dry. Rub with 2 tablespoons butter, 1 teaspoon salt, pepper and paprika. Place in a 9x13-inch baking pan and bake for 35 minutes.

- Combine ½ cup butter and next 4 ingredients in small heavy saucepan, heating thoroughly. Pour over chicken.

- Baste chicken breasts every 2 minutes with sauce and continue baking 10 minutes. Remove and set aside.

- Combine remaining 1 teaspoon salt, thyme, cayenne, mustard, sage and 2 tablespoons melted butter, mixing well. Stir in breadcrumbs and half-and-half. Add crabmeat and mix well.

- Stuff each chicken breast with crab mixture. Bake for 30 minutes, basting frequently with mushroom mixture.

Yield: 8 servings

Chicken-Crab Divan

2 (10-ounce) packages frozen artichoke hearts, thawed and drained
7 tablespoons unsalted butter, divided
6-8 chicken breast halves, skinned and boned
1 (6.5-ounce) can crabmeat
¼ cup sherry
Salt
Freshly ground black pepper

½ cup small button mushrooms
¼ cup minced onions
3 tablespoons all-purpose flour
1⅓ cups heavy cream
1 cup milk
½ cup chopped fresh parsley
Dash of cayenne
¼ cup fresh Parmesan cheese
Paprika
Slivered almonds, toasted

- Preheat oven to 375°.

- Place artichokes on bottom of greased 12x8-inch baking dish and set aside.

- Heat ¼ cup butter in large skillet over medium heat. Cook chicken in butter 15 minutes.

- Add crabmeat and cook 5 minutes. Pour in sherry and cook until reduced. Season with salt and pepper. Remove from skillet and keep warm.

- Add remaining 3 tablespoons butter to same skillet and drippings. Sauté mushrooms and onions until tender. Sprinkle with flour and stir until smooth. Slowly add cream and milk, stirring constantly. Stir in parsley and cayenne. Remove from heat and add Parmesan cheese.

- Cover artichokes with half of sauce. Arrange chicken and crab mixture over sauce. Top with remaining sauce. Sprinkle with paprika and almonds.

- Bake for 20 to 30 minutes.

Yield: 6 to 8 servings

Fresh, blanched asparagus may be substituted for artichoke hearts.

Supper clubs are very popular in the South, and Beaufort is no different. The evenings may vary, ranging from casual cookouts to elegant gourmet meals, but the opportunity to relax and dine with friends is the main attraction.

Sheldonia's Chicken Curry

½	pound bacon, cut into pieces	2	chicken fryers or 1 hen, cut up
3	cups chopped bell pepper	1	tablespoon Worcestershire sauce
3	cups chopped celery		Salt and pepper to taste
3	cups chopped onion	½	cup all-purpose flour
2-3	cups cubed ham	3	tablespoons curry powder
2	cups water		Cooked rice

- Fry bacon in skillet over medium high heat until crisp. Remove with slotted spoon and set aside.

- Sauté bell pepper, celery and onions until translucent. Remove from heat and set aside.

- Boil ham in 2 cups water until ham broth is reduced by half and set aside.

- Cover chicken with water in large saucepan and bring to a boil. Continue cooking until tender. Remove chicken and cool. Drain chicken stock, reserving 2½ cups. Cube chicken and set aside.

- Combine 1 cup ham stock, 2½ cups chicken stock, bell pepper mixture, bacon, Worcestershire sauce, salt and pepper. Stir in flour with 1 cup stock to thicken. Add curry powder, chicken and ham.

- Transfer to serving bowl. Serve over rice.

Yield: 8 to 10 servings

Offer pear chutney, chopped bell pepper, chopped peanuts, chopped celery and crumbled bacon as toppings for curry.

Easy Chicken Kiev

6	chicken breasts, skinned and boned	½	cup unsalted butter, melted
	Salt and pepper to taste	¼	cup dry white wine or chicken broth
1	cup Italian breadcrumbs		
½	cup fresh Parmesan cheese	2	tablespoons chopped fresh parsley, for garnish

- Preheat oven to 350°.
- Rinse chicken and pat dry. Sprinkle with salt and pepper and set aside.
- Combine breadcrumbs and Parmesan cheese in bowl and set aside.
- Dip chicken in butter and dredge in breadcrumbs, coating evenly.
- Place in shallow prepared baking dish. Bake for 25 minutes.
- Pour wine around chicken and bake additional 15 minutes. Garnish with fresh parsley and serve immediately.

Yield: 6 servings

Herbed Chicken Sauté

2	tablespoons olive oil	2	tablespoons whole grain mustard
2	tablespoons red wine vinegar	2	teaspoons Worcestershire sauce
1	tablespoon dried tarragon	6	chicken breast cutlets
2	tablespoons dried thyme		Salt and pepper to taste

- Combine oil and next 5 ingredients in small bowl, mixing well. Pour into large heavy skillet and heat over medium heat.
- Season chicken with salt and pepper. Place in skillet and sauté 2 to 3 minutes on each side or until done.

Yield: 6 servings

Beaufort Marine Corps Air Station, nicknamed "Fightertown", sits on 6900 acres that at one time were parts of the prominent Clarendon and Edgerly plantations. This area has played a significant role in South Carolina Lowcountry history. With the reactivation of the airfield in 1956 and designation of the Marine Corps Air Station in 1960, it will continue to play a vital role in our future.

Fightertown Florentine

1	(10-ounce) bag fresh spinach, stems removed	3	tablespoons unsalted butter
½	cup sour cream	1	teaspoon paprika
¼	mayonnaise	½	teaspoon dried sage
1	tablespoon finely chopped onion	½	teaspoon dried thyme
4	chicken breast halves, skinned and boned	1	garlic clove, minced
		2	tablespoons chicken broth
½	teaspoon salt	2	tablespoons fresh lemon juice, divided
¼	teaspoon freshly ground black pepper		

- Preheat oven to 325°.

- Steam spinach until wilted and set aside.

- Mix together sour cream, mayonnaise and onion in medium bowl. Add spinach, blending gently.

- Spread spinach mixture evenly on bottom of prepared baking pan.

- Season chicken breasts with salt and pepper and set aside.

- Melt butter in large heavy skillet over medium heat. Add paprika, sage, thyme and garlic, stirring about 2 to 3 minutes or until hot.

- Add chicken and cook about 7 minutes or until brown on both sides. Remove chicken and arrange on top of spinach mixture.

- Add chicken broth and 1 tablespoon lemon juice to drippings in skillet, stirring well. Pour over chicken in baking dish.

- Cover and bake for 30 minutes. Pour remaining lemon juice over chicken before serving.

Yield: 4 servings

Chicken with Caramelized Onions

1	teaspoon olive oil	1½	teaspoons fresh lemon juice
2	large white onions, thinly sliced	½	teaspoon freshly ground black pepper
3	tablespoons brown sugar	1	teaspoon Worcestershire sauce
¾	cup dry red wine		
3	tablespoons balsamic vinegar	1	teaspoon minced fresh garlic
4	(4-ounce) chicken breasts, skinned and boned	4	ounces Brie, rind removed and quartered
3	tablespoons Dijon mustard		

- Preheat oven to 350°.

- Heat olive oil in large skillet over medium heat. Add onions and brown sugar, stirring frequently, and sauté about 15 minutes or until onions begin to caramelize.

- Stir in wine and vinegar. Increase heat to medium high and bring to a boil.

- Reduce heat and cook 30 minutes or until most of liquid has been absorbed and set aside.

- Arrange chicken in baking dish coated with cooking spray and set aside.

- Combine mustard and next 4 ingredients in small bowl. Pour over chicken.

- Bake uncovered for 30 minutes or until chicken is no longer pink in center. Top chicken with Brie during last 10 minutes of baking.

- Transfer chicken to serving platter and top with caramelized onions.

Yield: 4 servings

The purpose of the Open Land Trust of Beaufort County is to protect and preserve scenic, open vistas in Beaufort County. These vistas provide the opportunity for visitors and locals alike to see and enjoy what lies beyond on any fine sea island day.

A quick pulse of herbs with a little garlic and some olive oil in the food processor and "presto"—pesto! You have a flavorful sauce that can transform plain pasta, chicken or bread into company fare.

Pesto Baked Chicken

1	(7-ounce) container pesto sauce or 1 cup pecan pesto	3	tablespoons white wine
6	boneless, skinless chicken breasts	¾	cup chicken broth, divided
	Salt and pepper to taste	2	tablespoons all-purpose flour
		3	tablespoons heavy cream

- Spread pesto over each chicken breast, reserving 1 tablespoon for sauce.

- Season chicken with salt and pepper. Place in casserole and bake at 375° for 45 minutes or until juices run clear when pierced with fork.

- Transfer chicken to serving platter and set aside.

- Bring wine, scrapings and juices from baking pan to a boil in skillet. Add ½ cup chicken broth and set aside.

- Whisk together flour and 2 tablespoons chicken broth. Add to skillet and boil about 5 minutes or until thickened, stirring constantly. Add remaining broth, pesto and cream. Serve over chicken.

Yield: 6 servings

Pecan Pesto

½	cup pecans, lightly toasted and chopped	1	large garlic clove, minced
½	cup fresh parsley	½	cup olive oil
½	cup fresh cilantro		Salt and pepper

- Combine ingredients in food processor until smooth.

- Cover and refrigerate up to 10 days.

Yield: 2 cups

Marshlands Chicken Marinara

4	chicken breast halves, skinned and boned	1	cup sliced fresh mushrooms (optional)
¼	teaspoon salt	1	cup marinara sauce
¼	teaspoon freshly ground black pepper	1	tablespoon chopped fresh parsley
¼	cup all-purpose flour	1	medium zucchini, cut lengthwise into eighths
1	egg, lightly beaten		Shredded Mozzarella cheese
½	cup dry breadcrumbs		
2	tablespoons olive oil		

- Preheat oven to 375°.

- Pound chicken breasts between sheets of wax paper to ½-inch thickness. Season with salt and pepper and set aside.

- Place flour, egg and breadcrumbs in 3 separate shallow dishes. Dredge chicken in flour, shaking off excess, then in egg and breadcrumbs, pressing firmly to coat.

- Heat olive oil in large skillet over medium high heat. Add chicken and cook 3 to 4 minutes on each side or until golden. Remove from skillet. Transfer to large baking pan and set aside.

- Add mushrooms to skillet and sauté 30 seconds. Stir in marinara sauce and parsley. Cook 3 minutes, stirring frequently.

- Place zucchini slices in shallow microwave dish. Sprinkle with 1 tablespoon water. Cover and microwave on high 2 minutes. Remove and drain.

- Arrange 2 zucchini slices on each chicken breast to form an "X". Pour marinara sauce evenly over each chicken breast. Sprinkle with Mozzarella cheese.

- Bake for 10 to 15 minutes or until cheese melts.

Yield: 4 servings

Marshlands was built by Dr. James Robert Verdier around 1814. Dr. Verdier was noted for his successful treatment of yellow fever. During the Civil War, this national historic landmark served as the headquarters of the United States Sanitary Commission.

Dancing Chicken

1	cup kosher salt	3	tablespoons Spice Rub
2	quarts cold water	1	(12-ounce) can beer
1	(3½-pound) whole fryer		

Allspice is not a blend at all. It is a single spice. Although it can be bought whole, it is best to purchase the ground variety, as it is difficult to grind.

Tired of grilling the same thing all of the time? Grill a Dancing Chicken for a new mouth-watering experience!

- Dissolve salt in water in container large enough to hold chicken. Immerse chicken in salt water and chill 1 hour. Remove chicken and rinse with cold water. Pat dry and set aside.

- Preheat gas grill; light all burners. Cover with lid and heat 15 minutes. Turn off all burners except one.

- Rub Spice Rub on inside and outside of chicken, including under breast skin.

- Open beer can and discard ¼ cup beer. Punch 2 large holes in top of can with bottle opener. Slide chicken over can so drumsticks reach down to bottom of can and chicken stands upright.

- Place chicken on cool part of grill, using drumstick ends to steady it. Cover and roast, rotating chicken 180° after 35 to 45 minutes.

- Continue roasting another 35 to 45 minutes or until meat thermometer registers 170° to 175°.

- Transfer chicken to cutting board, keeping can upright. Allow to rest 15 minutes. Carefully lift chicken off of can and onto cutting board.

Yield: 4 to 6 servings

Spice Rub

2	tablespoons cumin	1	tablespoon freshly ground black pepper
2	tablespoons curry powder		
2	tablespoons chili powder	1	teaspoon cinnamon
1	tablespoon allspice		

- Combine all ingredients in small bowl, blending well. Spice Rub may be stored or frozen in an air-tight container for several weeks.

Federal Chicken

1	cup lowfat plain yogurt	1	garlic clove, minced
1	tablespoon fresh lemon juice	6	chicken breast halves, skinned and boned
½	teaspoon dried oregano	4	ounces feta cheese, crumbled
½	teaspoon dried rosemary		
¼	teaspoon freshly ground black pepper	2	teaspoons chopped fresh parsley

- Preheat broiler.

- Combine yogurt and next 5 ingredients in medium bowl, mixing well. Place chicken in bowl, tossing to coat. Cover and chill 30 minutes.

- Cover broiler pan with foil and spray with nonstick cooking spray.

- Place chicken breasts on broiler pan and broil about 7 minutes. Turn chicken and sprinkle with cheese. Broil additional 7 minutes or until chicken is done.

- Transfer to serving platter and garnish with parsley. Serve warm.

Yield: 6 servings

Beaufort was occupied by Federal troops during the Civil War. This is the major reason Beaufort is so well preserved today. It did not receive the destruction that many other Southern towns experienced.

Grilled Chicken with Soy-Lime Sauce

¼	cup soy sauce	4	chicken breast halves, skinned and boned
¼	cup fresh lime juice		
1	tablespoon minced garlic	1	cup low-sodium chicken broth
1	tablespoon minced fresh ginger	1	small onion, sliced
1½	teaspoons curry powder		

- Place chicken breasts in large zip-top plastic bag and set aside.

- Combine soy sauce and next 4 ingredients in small bowl, mixing well. Pour over chicken and chill 3 hours.

- Preheat gas grill.

- Remove chicken from marinade and set aside.

- Pour marinade into medium saucepan. Add broth and onion. Bring to a boil and cook about 15 minutes or until sauce coats a spoon.

- Grill chicken until done. Spoon sauce over chicken and serve.

Yield: 4 servings

A seaport was erected at Port Royal in 1710. The town of Beaufort was named one year later. It is pronounced "bew" as in "beautiful" rather than the French "beau" that Beaufort, North Carolinians use.

Beaufort Bruschetta

1	teaspoon garlic powder	1	small zucchini, quartered lengthwise and sliced
½	teaspoon salt, divided		
¼	teaspoon freshly ground black pepper, divided	4	garlic cloves, minced
		1	cup chopped plum tomato
4	(4-ounce) chicken breast halves, skinned and boned	½	cup chopped red onion
		½	cup chopped fresh basil
		4	teaspoons balsamic vinegar
1	tablespoon olive oil		
8	ounces mushrooms, sliced	¼	cup fresh Parmesan cheese

- Preheat broiler.

- Combine garlic powder, ¼ teaspoon salt and ⅛ teaspoon pepper and sprinkle over chicken.

- Spray broiler pan with nonstick cooking spray and place chicken on broiler pan. Broil 6 minutes on each side or until done. Remove chicken from pan and keep warm.

- Heat olive oil in large skillet over medium high heat. Add ¼ teaspoon salt, mushrooms, zucchini and garlic; sauté 2 minutes. Add ⅛ teaspoon pepper, tomato, red onion, basil and vinegar; sauté 3 minutes.

- Serve vegetable mixture over chicken and sprinkle with cheese.

Yield: 4 servings

Chicken Satay

8	boneless, skinless chicken breasts, cut into ¼-inch strips		**Spicy Peanut Sauce**

- Soak 12 wooden grilling skewers in water for 1 hour.
- Thread chicken strips onto skewers and arrange in one layer on foil-lined baking sheet.
- Pour Spicy Peanut Sauce over chicken. Cover tightly with plastic wrap and chill several hours.
- Remove satays from marinade. Bring half of marinade to a simmer in small saucepan.
- Baste chicken constantly with remaining half while grilling.
- Pour heated marinade over chicken before serving.

Yield: 8 servings

Spicy Peanut Sauce

2	tablespoons minced garlic	¼	cup hoisin sauce
2	tablespoons grated fresh ginger	¼	cup soy sauce
		2	tablespoons sesame oil
2	tablespoons unseasoned rice vinegar	2	tablespoons creamy peanut butter
2	green onions, minced	2	tablespoons honey
¼	cup minced fresh cilantro	1	teaspoon crushed red pepper flakes
½	cup dry sherry		

- Combine all ingredients, mixing thoroughly.

Thai Chicken Curry

4	medium onions, chopped	2	tablespoons apricot jam
½	cup unsalted butter, divided	8	chicken breasts, skinned and boned
2	teaspoons fresh ginger, minced	2	(14-ounce) cans diced tomatoes, drained
2	garlic cloves, finely sliced Curry Mix	1	(16-ounce) can coconut milk
1	(6-ounce) can tomato paste		Salt and pepper to taste

- Preheat oven to 350°.

- Sauté onions in ¼ cup butter until tender. Add ginger and garlic, cooking 10 minutes. Add Curry Mix and gently stir in tomato paste and apricot jam.

- Melt remaining butter in Dutch oven over medium high heat. Sauté chicken until golden brown on each side. Add tomatoes, coconut milk and onion-curry mixture, stirring 5 minutes.

- Season with salt and pepper. Cover and bake for 2 hours.

Yield: 8 servings

Offer chopped tomato, chutney, raisins and diced pineapple as toppings for curry. Also, substitute equal amount prepared minced ginger for fresh ginger.

Curry Mix

1	teaspoon ground coriander	1	teaspoon cumin
1	teaspoon garam masala	½	teaspoon cinnamon
1	teaspoon turmeric		

- Combine all ingredients, blending well. Curry Mix may be substituted with 1 teaspoon mild curry paste.

Millennium Chicken Pot Pie

2½ cups chicken broth, divided
2 sprigs fresh rosemary,
    divided
2 cups ½-inch sliced carrots
½ pound sugar snap peas
1 (15-ounce) jar pearl onions,
    drained
2 tablespoons unsalted butter

2 tablespoons all-purpose
    flour
2 cups cooked chicken, cut
    into bite-size pieces
2 sheets frozen puff pastry,
    thawed
¼ cup unsalted butter, melted

Quaker missionaries founded Penn School on St. Helena's Island during the occupation of Beaufort by Union troops. This school gave freed black men the opportunity for an education.

- Preheat oven to 450°.

- Bring 1 cup chicken broth to a boil in small saucepan. Add 1 sprig rosemary and carrots; boil 4 minutes. Drain and reserve liquid. Set carrots aside and discard rosemary.

- Bring ½ cup water to a boil in small saucepan. Add sugar snap peas and cook 1 minute. Drain and rinse under ice cold water to stop the cooking process.

- Combine carrots, peas and onions in medium bowl and set aside.

- Melt 2 tablespoons butter in small saucepan. Whisk in flour and cook over medium low heat about 3 minutes. Add reserved carrot liquid and remaining chicken broth, stirring until thickened. Add rosemary sprig and set aside to cool.

- Spray eight (4-inch) ramekins with nonstick cooking spray. Place ¼ cup of chicken in each ramekin followed by a layer of vegetables. Pour sauce over vegetables.

- Roll out puff pastry sheet to 16-inch square. Cut into eight (4-inch) squares. Place one square on each ramekin and trim edges. Brush with melted butter.

- Bake for 18 to 20 minutes or until pastry is light golden brown.

Yield: 8 servings

Pot pies may be prepared ahead and then baked.

Influences of Africa have touched Beaufort since the earliest days of exploration. The Africans brought their skills, music, food and language. The words "Gullah" and "Geechee" have come to describe that legacy. The Gullah language is a Creole blend of European and African tongues born on Africa's slave coast and matured on isolated plantations in South Carolina.

Chicken Enchiladas

1 small onion, chopped
2 tablespoons cooking oil
2 garlic cloves, minced
½ teaspoon cumin
2 (8-ounce) cans tomato
     sauce
½ cup chicken broth
2 tablespoons chili powder
¼ teaspoon dried oregano
     Dash of salt
12 white corn tortillas
     Oil, for frying

3 cups cooked, chopped
     chicken breast
6 ounces shredded Monterey
     Jack cheese
6 ounces shredded Cheddar
     cheese
1 (2.25-ounce) can sliced
     black olives, drained
1 bunch chopped green
     onions for garnish
1 cup sour cream for garnish
     Shredded lettuce for
     garnish

- Preheat oven to 350°.

- Sauté onion in oil in Dutch oven over medium heat until tender. Add garlic and cumin, cooking 1 minute. Add tomato sauce and chicken broth. Gradually stir in chili powder. Add oregano and salt. Cover and simmer 30 minutes, stirring frequently to prevent burning.

- Heat 1-inch of oil in small skillet. Lightly fry tortillas to soften. Drain on paper towels.

- Place chicken in center of tortilla and layer with cheeses. Roll tightly. Spoon sauce into bottom of baking dish and arrange enchiladas side by side.

- Pour remaining sauce over enchiladas. Top with remaining cheeses and olives.

- Cover with foil and bake for 30 minutes or until hot throughout. Garnish with green onions, sour cream and lettuce.

Yield: 4 servings

Crunchy Baked Chicken

½ cup sour cream
2 tablespoons fresh lemon juice
1½ tablespoons Worcestershire sauce
1 teaspoon celery salt
1 teaspoon minced garlic
½ teaspoon onion salt
½ teaspoon freshly ground black pepper
6 chicken breast halves, skinned and boned
½ cup butter, melted
40 round buttery crackers, crushed

- Combine sour cream and next 6 ingredients in medium bowl, mixing well. Dredge chicken in sour cream mixture, coating well. Cover and chill overnight.

- Preheat oven to 350°.

- Dip chicken in butter and roll in cracker crumbs. Arrange in greased baking dish. Drizzle remaining butter over chicken.

- Bake for 45 minutes to 1 hour.

Yield: 6 servings

"The best thing about my kitchen is I can watch dolphins swim and play while I sit at the kitchen table."

Sarah Simmons, Grade 5
Beaufort Academy
student

~

Castle Cacciatore

1 cup all-purpose flour
1 teaspoon salt
1 teaspoon freshly ground black pepper
1 teaspoon garlic powder
¼ cup fresh parsley, chopped
4 boneless, skinless chicken breasts, cut into bite-size pieces
2 tablespoons olive oil
2 (14-ounce) cans Italian plum tomatoes, undrained
6 fresh basil leaves
2 garlic cloves, minced
1 cup sliced fresh mushrooms

- Combine flour and next 4 ingredients in large zip-top plastic bag. Add chicken, shaking until lightly coated.

- Heat olive oil over moderately high heat in large sauté pan. Brown chicken on each side until medium brown. Add tomatoes, basil leaves, garlic and mushrooms. Season with salt and pepper.

- Cover and simmer 45 minutes or until chicken is tender. Serve over pasta.

Yield: 4 servings

The Johnson-Danner house, often called "the Castle", was built by Dr. Joseph Johnson in the mid-1800s. The home and gardens were not destroyed during the Civil War probably because the house served as a hospital during this time. It was the site for some scenes in the filming of the movie Forces of Nature.

"The kitchen is my very favorite place in the house. It's a place where the family stops whatever they are doing to come together to enjoy a meal."

Danielle deVillier,
Grade 10
Beaufort Academy
student

Parmesan-Crusted Chicken

4	chicken breasts, skinned	¼-½ teaspoon cayenne pepper
1	egg	¼-½ teaspoon garlic powder
1	tablespoon milk	¼ cup unsalted butter,
1½	cups seasoned breadcrumbs	melted
1	cup fresh Parmesan cheese	

- Wash and pat chicken dry. Set aside.

- Whisk together egg and milk in small bowl and set aside.

- Combine breadcrumbs, cheese, cayenne and garlic powder in flat dish. Dip chicken in egg mixture, then dredge in breadcrumbs.

- Arrange chicken in square glass baking dish with thickest parts toward the outside of the dish and thinner parts toward the center.

- Pour butter over chicken and sprinkle with remaining breadcrumbs.

- Cover with wax paper and microwave on high 10 to 15 minutes, turning several times. Check for doneness after 10 minutes and microwave again if necessary.

Yield: 4 servings

Craven Street Chicken

6 tablespoons butter, divided
3 tablespoons olive oil, divided
1 pound chicken breasts, skinned, boned and cut into bite-size pieces
1 (14.5-ounce) can diced tomatoes, undrained
¾ cup half-and-half
1 tablespoon fresh lemon juice
¼ teaspoon crushed red pepper flakes
6 ounces button mushrooms, sliced
¾ cup oil-packed julienne sun-dried tomatoes, drained
1 (14-ounce) can artichoke hearts, drained and quartered
1 tablespoon chopped shallots
½ cup chopped fresh basil
Salt and pepper to taste
1 pound penne pasta, cooked al dente
Fresh Parmesan cheese

- Heat 2 tablespoons butter and 1 tablespoon oil in Dutch oven over medium heat. Add chicken and cook, stirring occasionally about 5 minutes or until done. Remove and keep warm.

- Melt remaining ¼ cup butter in same pan over medium heat. Add tomatoes, half-and-half, lemon juice and red pepper flakes. Reduce heat and simmer about 7 to 10 minutes or until mixture begins to thicken slightly. Set aside.

- Heat remaining 2 tablespoons oil over medium heat. Add mushrooms, sun-dried tomatoes, artichokes and shallots. Cook, stirring constantly, about 5 minutes or until shallots are tender.

- Add tomato mixture and chicken. Cook about 5 minutes or until heated throughout. Season with salt and pepper. Stir in fresh basil.

- Toss with pasta and sprinkle with Parmesan cheese.

Yield: 6 to 8 servings

At the end of the Civil War, 500 black members of the Baptist Church of Beaufort bought "the Tabernacle" on Craven Street. They created Tabernacle Baptist Church, which is still active today. In the churchyard lies the grave of Robert Smalls and a bust of his likeness. Smalls was born a slave. Later he was the captain of the "Planter", which carried Confederate troops up and down the Atlantic coast. Robert Smalls became the first black congressman in South Carolina.

Goat Cheese Chicken over Angel Hair Pasta

4	chicken breast halves, skinned and boned	3	ounces goat cheese, softened
½	teaspoon salt	½	cup chopped fresh basil
½	teaspoon freshly ground black pepper	8	ounces angel hair pasta, cooked al dente
8	large fresh basil leaves		Tomato-Basil Sauce

- Preheat oven to 350°.

- Place chicken breasts between sheets of heavy duty plastic wrap. Flatten to ¼-inch thickness. Season with salt and pepper. Place 2 basil leaves and 2 tablespoons cheese in center of each chicken breast.

- Roll up jelly roll fashion starting with short end and secure with toothpick. Place rolls seam side down in lightly greased 8-inch square baking dish.

- Bake for 30 to 35 minutes. Let stand 10 minutes. Cut into ½-inch slices.

- Toss pasta with half of Tomato-Basil Sauce. Serve chicken over pasta and top with remaining sauce.

Yield: 4 servings

Tomato–Basil Sauce

1	small onion, chopped	¼	teaspoon freshly ground black pepper
4	garlic cloves, minced		
2	tablespoons olive oil	2	(28-ounce) can diced tomatoes, drained
1	cup dry red wine		
½	teaspoon salt	½	cup fresh shredded basil leaves

- Sauté onion and garlic in hot oil in large saucepan until tender. Add wine, salt and pepper. Cook, stirring occasionally, about 5 minutes.

- Add tomatoes; reduce heat and simmer, stirring often, about 30 minutes. Cool slightly.

- Process half of tomato mixture in food processor or blender until smooth, stopping once to scrape down sides. Return to saucepan. Repeat process with remaining tomato mixture. Cook over medium heat until sauce is thoroughly heated. Stir in shredded basil.

Yield: 5 cups

Sauce may be prepared a day ahead of serving.

Prime Time Pasta

½ cup all-purpose flour
4 tablespoons fresh Parmesan cheese
½ teaspoon garlic powder
Salt and pepper to taste
1½ pounds chicken breasts, skinned, boned and cut into 1-inch pieces
¼ cup unsalted butter
1 (6-ounce) jar marinated artichoke hearts
½ cup white wine
1 cup chicken broth
¼ cup fresh lemon juice
2 tablespoons capers, drained
2 tablespoons chopped fresh parsley
2 tablespoons chopped fresh basil
Dash of crushed red pepper flakes
12 ounces angel hair pasta, cooked al dente and drained
Fresh Parmesan cheese, for garnish

"Al dente" means *"firm to the bite but cooked through".* Use the time given on the package as a guide, but ALWAYS taste the pasta to determine if it is done.

- Combine flour, 4 tablespoons Parmesan, garlic powder, salt and pepper in large zip-top plastic bag. Place chicken in bag, shaking until well coated.

- Melt butter in large skillet over medium high heat. Add chicken and sauté about 5 to 8 minutes or until browned. Remove and set aside.

- Drain artichoke hearts, reserving marinade, and chop.

- Add artichokes, wine, chicken broth and lemon juice to skillet. Stir in 1 to 2 tablespoons of reserved artichoke marinade, capers, parsley, basil and red pepper flakes. Simmer 5 to 10 minutes. Return chicken to sauce.

- Serve over hot pasta and garnish with Parmesan cheese.

Yield: 4 servings

Honey Hill Roasted Chicken

1	(4-pound) chicken	1	tablespoon olive oil
1	garlic clove, minced	¼	teaspoon kosher salt
1	tablespoon chopped fresh thyme		Feta Stuffing
1	teaspoon chopped fresh oregano or marjoram	1	bunch fresh rosemary, crushed

- Preheat oven to 375°.

- Wash and pat chicken dry.

- Mash garlic and next 4 ingredients together in small bowl. Rub chicken with garlic mixture, being careful to place some between breast meat and skin.

- Fill cavity with Feta Stuffing. Sprinkle top of chicken with rosemary.

- Roast chicken, breast side up, 25 minutes. Turn over and roast additional 25 minutes. Return chicken to breast side up and roast 30 minutes longer.

- Remove from oven and let rest, covered loosely with foil, 15 minutes. Carve and serve.

Yield: 4 servings

Feta Stuffing

3-4	cups day-old French bread, cubed	¼	cup chopped onion
¾	cup feta cheese, crumbled	1	teaspoon garlic salt
½	cup chopped celery		Dash of black pepper
½	cup chopped apple		Olive oil

- Combine bread and next 6 ingredients. Fill chicken cavity and drizzle olive oil over exposed stuffing.

Chicken Lasagna

A real crowd pleaser!

8-10 chicken breasts, skinned, boned and cubed
3 tablespoons olive oil
6 tablespoons butter
8 tablespoons all-purpose flour
1½ cups buttermilk
1 cup milk
Salt and pepper to taste
3 (10-ounce) packages frozen chopped spinach, thawed and drained

4 (5-ounce) containers ricotta cheese
2 (3-ounce) packages cream cheese, softened
8 ounces shredded Swiss cheese
2 cups dry white wine, divided
Nutmeg
1 (16-ounce) package uncooked lasagna noodles
½ cup fresh Parmesan cheese

- Preheat oven to 350°.

- Heat oil in large skillet on medium high. Sauté chicken in skillet until golden and set aside.

- Melt butter in heavy saucepan and whisk in flour. Add buttermilk, milk, salt and pepper. Whisk until sauce is thickened and set aside.

- Combine chicken, spinach, ricotta cheese, cream cheese and Swiss cheese. Moisten with 4 tablespoons white wine. Season with salt, pepper and nutmeg.

- Layer white sauce, uncooked noodles, ¼ cup wine and chicken mixture in a 9x13-inch baking dish. Continue layers, ending with white sauce and topping with Parmesan cheese.

- Bake uncovered for 1 hour.

Yield: 14 servings

Lasagna may be prepared ahead.

Fried Turkey

Specialty shops and hardware stores feature turkey frying pots. They have a spike and hanger that help lower the turkey into the hot oil. Some cooks use extra long forks and tongs to lower turkeys while others rely on a broomstick.

1 (12- to 14-pound) turkey
Large (10-gallon) cooking
  pot
Creole seasoning
Large trash bag

5 gallons peanut oil
Outdoor gas cooker
Long handle cooking
  thermometer

Do not attempt this recipe indoors!

- Place frozen, wrapped turkey in cooking pot two days before serving. Fill pot with enough water to cover turkey.

- Remove turkey from pot and mark water level on the side with an indelible pen. Discard water and return turkey to refrigerator to thaw.

- Remove turkey from plastic wrap when thawing is complete and discard neck and giblets.

- Coat cavity and outside of turkey with Creole seasoning.

- Place seasoned turkey in clean trash bag and refrigerate overnight.

- Fill the pot to previously marked line with peanut oil when ready to cook. Heat oil to 425°.

- Remove turkey carefully from trash bag. Use extreme caution and lower turkey slowly into hot oil. Do not cover the pot.

- Cook turkey about 4 minutes per pound or until meat thermometer registers 180° when inserted in thickest portion of turkey and not touching bone. (The oil temperature will cool to 300° to 375° when turkey is placed in pot and should remain there until the turkey is cooked. Do not allow the oil to go over 400°.)

- Remove turkey from grease carefully. Allow to rest before carving.

One (5-pound) turkey breast may be substituted for a whole turkey. Cook in a 5-gallon stockpot with about 2 gallons of oil.

MEAT & GAME

MEAT & GAME

On any given weekend, you can find a group of people gathered around a crackling fire at their small island "fish camp." To those fortunate enough to go "down the river," oysters, barbecue, fish tales and libations abound! Mustard Fried Venison, found in this section, is a favorite fish camp delicacy.

These wonderful weekend retreats are only accessible by boat. They usually feature a rustic cabin with luxuries of ocean breezes and rainwater showers. They serve as relaxing getaways and great fun for "down the river trips."

Beef Tenderloin with Bordelaise Sauce

3	tablespoons unsalted butter	1	shallot, chopped ¼-inch
2	(6-ounce) beef filets	1	thyme sprig
	Salt and pepper to taste	1	bay leaf
1	cup sliced carrots (¼-inch)	1	tablespoon fresh flat leaf parsley, chopped

- Melt butter in heavy skillet over medium high heat.
- Season beef with salt and pepper. Add filets to skillet and sear about 2 minutes or until golden. Turn filets and add carrots, shallot, thyme and bay leaf. Cover and cook 3 minutes for medium rare or until desired doneness.
- Transfer to serving plate and keep warm.
- Continue cooking vegetables uncovered 1 minute or until just tender. Add Bordelaise Sauce and bring to a boil.
- Stir in remaining 2 tablespoons butter. Cook 8 to 10 minutes or until Bordelaise Sauce thickens, stirring occasionally.
- Spoon Bordelaise Sauce and vegetables around filets and sprinkle with parsley. Serve immediately.

Yield: 2 servings

BORDELAISE SAUCE

1½ tablespoons unsalted butter

2 shallots, chopped

1 tablespoon cracked pepper

1 bay leaf

6-8 fresh sprigs thyme

1⅓ cups Cabernet Sauvignon

2 cups unsalted beef broth

- Melt butter in 3-quart saucepan over medium high heat. Add shallots and sauté 6 minutes or until tender and lightly golden.
- Add pepper, bay leaf and thyme, stirring until well blended. Add wine and bring to a boil. Cook 15 to 20 minutes, stirring occasionally, until liquid is reduced to ½ cup.
- Add broth and bring to a simmer. Cook 15 minutes and skim excess fat from top.
- Strain sauce through a fine mesh strainer into clean saucepan and keep warm over low heat.

"As an operator on the Woods Memorial Bridge in Beaufort, I enjoy the time of year when the magnificent osprey return to make their nests and raise their young on the fender system of the bridge. Year after year, these beautiful birds have been making the bridge their home, and whether you are passing over or under the bridge, they are a sight to behold. The one thing I like the most is watching young osprey grow and 'earn their wings' after learning to fly. After they have learned, they hang around through the summer, then fly off for yet another return to the Woods Bridge next year."

Malcolm C. MacGregor
Woods Memorial
Bridge Operator
Beaufort,
South Carolina

Peppered Beef Tenderloin

1	(8-ounce) container sour cream	2	teaspoons coarse salt
6	tablespoons Dijon mustard, divided	1	(3½-pound) beef tenderloin, trimmed
2	tablespoons horseradish	1	cup chopped fresh flat leaf parsley
2	tablespoons whole green peppercorns	¼	cup butter, softened
2	tablespoons whole red peppercorns		Baby artichokes
			Fresh rosemary

- Combine sour cream, 3 tablespoons Dijon and horseradish; cover and chill.

- Place peppercorns in blender or pepper mill; cover and pulse until chopped. Transfer to bowl and stir in salt.

- Place beef on lightly greased rack in shallow roasting pan.

- Combine parsley, butter and remaining Dijon; rub mixture evenly over tenderloin. Pat peppercorn mixture evenly over beef.

- Cover and chill up to 24 hours.

- Bake at 350° for 50 minutes or 425° for 30 minutes until meat thermometer inserted in thickest portion of beef registers 145° (medium-rare) to 160° (medium).

- Transfer beef to serving platter; cover loosely with foil. Allow to stand 10 minutes before slicing.

- Serve with sour cream mixture. Garnish with baby artichokes and rosemary.

Yield: 8 servings

Mushroom Stuffed Beef Tenderloin

1	(5- to 6-pound) beef tenderloin	3	tablespoons butter, melted
1	pound fresh mushrooms, chopped	½	cup Marsala cooking wine
⅓	cup sliced green onions	1½	cups soft, whole wheat bread crumbs
2	garlic cloves, crushed		Salt and pepper
		4	garlic cloves, crushed

- Slice tenderloin lengthwise, but not through center, leaving one long side connected. Set aside.

- Sauté mushrooms, onions and garlic cloves in butter over medium heat until tender. Add wine and simmer until liquid evaporates.

- Remove from heat. Add breadcrumbs and toss gently.

- Spoon mushroom mixture into opening of tenderloin. Fold top side over stuffing and tie securely with heavy cotton string at 1½-inch intervals. Coat with salt, pepper and crushed garlic.

- Place tenderloin seam side down on roasting rack. Insert meat thermometer into thickest portion of tenderloin.

- Bake uncovered at 425° for 30 minutes until thermometer registers 140° (rare), but no higher than 150°.

Yield: 10 to 12 servings

The three basic elements essential to sautéing are the correct pan, high heat and the right fat. Use a pan wide enough to accommodate all ingredients in a single layer. The pan sides must be low enough that the liquid evaporates quickly. Always use a heavy pan for even heat. High heat is essential for sautéing. Since butter burns at a high temperature, blend the butter with oil to get the flavor of butter. Once the pan and the fat are hot, add the ingredients. A crust will form on the food that prevents sticking and allows for caramelizing.

Herb and Spice Roasted Tenderloin with Red Wine Sauce

2	tablespoons minced fresh rosemary	1	teaspoon freshly ground black pepper
2	tablespoons minced fresh thyme	½	teaspoon ground nutmeg
4	large garlic cloves, peeled	¼	teaspoon ground cloves
2	bay leaves	2	tablespoons olive oil
1	large shallot, peeled and quartered	2	(2-pound) beef tenderloin pieces, trimmed
1	tablespoon orange zest	¼	cup unsalted butter, softened
1	tablespoon coarse salt		Salt and pepper to taste

- Process rosemary and next 9 ingredients in food processor. Add oil with processor running and blend well.

- Spread mixture evenly over tenderloins. Place in large glass baking dish. Cover and chill at least 6 hours.

- Preheat oven to 400°.

- Place beef on rack in large roasting pan. Roast about 35 minutes until meat thermometer inserted into thickest portion registers 140°.

- Remove from oven and cover with foil. Allow to stand 10 minutes. Transfer beef to cutting surface and set aside.

- Pour accumulated pan juices into Red Wine Sauce. Bring to a boil. Remove from heat and whisk in butter. Season with salt and pepper.

- Slice beef and serve with Red Wine Sauce.

Red Wine Sauce

2	tablespoons olive oil	2	teaspoons minced fresh rosemary
2½	cups sliced shallots	1	bay leaf
2	tablespoons minced garlic	1	teaspoon orange zest
1	teaspoon sugar	¼	teaspoon nutmeg
1	tablespoon all-purpose flour	¼	teaspoon ground cloves
1	tablespoon minced fresh thyme	3¼	cups beef broth
		1½	cups dry red wine
		¼	cup brandy

- Heat oil in large saucepan over medium low heat. Add shallots and garlic; sauté about 10 minutes or until tender.

- Stir in sugar and sauté about 15 minutes or until shallots are golden. Add flour and next 6 ingredients, stirring 1 minute.

- Pour in broth, wine and brandy. Boil about 20 minutes until sauce is reduced to 1¾ cups. Discard bay leaf.

Yield: 8 to 10 servings

Herb and Garlic Crusted Beef Tenderloin

2 (2¼- to 2½-pound) beef tenderloin pieces, trimmed

½ cup olive oil, divided
Salt and pepper to taste

6 tablespoons Dijon mustard

6 garlic cloves, minced

3 tablespoons fresh thyme, minced and divided

3 tablespoons minced fresh rosemary, divided

- Preheat oven to 375°

- Rub tenderloin with ¼ cup oil. Season with salt and pepper. Brown beef in large nonstick skillet over high heat about 5 minutes on each side.

- Transfer beef to large roasting pan. Brush tops and sides of beef with Dijon and set aside.

- Combine remaining ¼ cup oil, garlic, 2½ tablespoons thyme and 2½ tablespoons rosemary in small bowl. Coat beef with herb mixture.

- Roast about 40 to 45 minutes until meat thermometer inserted into thickest portion registers 140°.

- Transfer to serving platter and allow to stand 10 minutes before slicing. Top slices with remaining thyme and rosemary.

Yield: 8 servings

The beautiful beaches of Fripp Island were once rumored to have been a favorite hideaway of the notorious pirate Blackbeard. It is thought that somewhere beneath the sand dunes on Fripp are many buried treasure chests. Today Fripp Island is a modern development with condos, beach homes, restaurants and golf courses.

Reduce the recipe to two filets for a wonderfully romantic dinner!

Tournedos Sautés Aux Champignons
or Filets with Mushrooms

¼	cup butter, divided	½	cup dry white wine
3	tablespoons minced shallots	¼	cup brandy
8	ounces mushrooms, sliced		Freshly ground black pepper to taste
1	teaspoon marjoram	6	(1-inch thick) filet mignons
2	tablespoons chives, chopped		Chopped parsley
	Salt to taste		

- Melt 2 tablespoons butter in skillet over medium heat. Add shallots and cook slowly 1 minute. Add mushrooms and cook 1 minute. Stir in marjoram and next 4 ingredients. Cook over medium high heat about 3 minutes or until wine has reduced substantially.

- Pound steaks to ¼-inch thickness. Season with pepper on both sides.

- Melt remaining 2 tablespoons butter in second skillet over high heat until butter foam begins to subside. Sauté filets about 2 minutes. Turn the filet and pour small amount mushroom sauce over each filet.

- Garnish with parsley and serve immediately.

Yield: 6 servings

~

Peppered Flank Steak

OUTDOOR COOKING TIP

Bring meat to room temperature before cooking. It will cook somewhat faster.

1½	pounds flank steak	1	teaspoon crushed red pepper flakes
3	tablespoons fresh lime juice	½	cup dry red wine
2	garlic cloves, minced	1	tablespoon sugar
½	teaspoon hot chili oil	3	tablespoons soy sauce
¼	cup cooking oil		

- Place steak in large glass baking dish and set aside.

- Combine lime juice and remaining ingredients in small bowl, mixing well. Pour over steak and marinate 8 to 12 hours.

- Grill 10 to 12 minutes. Slice thinly on the diagonal.

Yield: 4 servings

Lemon juice may be substituted for lime juice.

Flank Steak with Corn-Tomato Relish

⅓	cup dry red wine	2	garlic cloves, minced
¼	cup chopped Vidalia onion	¼	teaspoon salt
2	teaspoons low-sodium soy sauce	¼	teaspoon pepper
		1	(16-ounce) flank steak

- Combine wine, onion, soy sauce and garlic in large zip-top plastic bag. Add beef to bag and marinate 4 to 6 hours.
- Remove steak from bag. Sprinkle with salt and pepper.
- Grill 5 minutes on each side. Serve with Corn-Tomato Relish.

Corn-Tomato Relish

1	teaspoon olive oil	1	tablespoon lime juice
1	cup chopped Vidalia onion	1	teaspoon sugar
1½	cups fresh corn kernels (about 3 ears)	¼	teaspoon salt
1½	cups seeded, chopped tomatoes	¼	teaspoon crushed red pepper flakes
⅓	cup basil, thinly sliced	⅛	teaspoon black pepper

- Heat olive oil in large nonstick skillet over medium heat. Add onion and sauté 5 minutes or until tender. Add corn and cook 8 minutes until tender, stirring frequently.
- Combine corn mixture with remaining ingredients, tossing well.

Yield: 4 servings

Grilled Flank Steak

3	cups dry red wine	1	tablespoon plus 1½ teaspoons dry mustard
3	cups chopped onion		
2¼	cups soy sauce	1	tablespoon plus 1½ teaspoons ginger
¾	cup olive oil		
8	large garlic cloves, chopped	4½	pounds flank steak

- Combine wine and next 6 ingredients in large bowl, mixing well. Pour over steak, turning to coat. Cover and chill 3 to 6 hours.
- Grill steaks 4 minutes on each side for rare or to desired doneness.
- Slice thinly on the diagonal before serving.

Yield: 12 servings

Beaufort has many generations of tomato farmers who toil during the hot and humid summer months to produce a delicious tomato. We are proud of the islands and their beauty... the rich soil, cooling breezes and the spirit of working people!

~

A simple guideline for determining the temperature of your charcoal fire is to hold your hand, palm side down, five inches above the cooking grate. If you can stand the heat for only two to three seconds, the fire is medium-hot. If you can keep your hand in place for four to five seconds, the fire is medium-low.

Monterey Flank Steak

Marinades and flavor mixes are composed of three key elements— acids, oils and flavorings. They perform three distinct functions—tenderize, moisten and flavor.

Red Wine Vinegar Marinade

6	tablespoons red wine vinegar	1	teaspoon black pepper
2	tablespoons olive oil	2	garlic cloves
2	teaspoons oregano	2	bay leaves
1½	teaspoons salt	¼	teaspoon cloves

• Combine ingredients, blending well.

Steak

2	(1½-pound) flank steaks	1	teaspoon chili powder
3	tablespoons butter	1	teaspoon cumin
¾	cup chopped onion	½	teaspoon salt
¾	cup shredded zucchini	½	teaspoon black pepper
2	garlic cloves, minced	1	cup breadcrumbs
3	tablespoons chopped cilantro	8	(¼-inch) slices Monterey Jack cheese

• Place each steak in separate zip-top plastic bag. Pour Red Wine Vinegar Marinade evenly into both bags. Marinate 8 to 12 hours.

• Melt butter in skillet over medium heat. Add onions, zucchini and garlic and sauté 4 minutes. Add cilantro and next 4 ingredients. Stir in breadcrumbs and sauté until golden. Allow to cool.

• Spread half of onion mixture on steak. Place 4 cheese slices on upper third of steak. Roll and tie with cotton string, securing at 1-inch intervals.

• Grill 10 to 15 minutes, turning frequently for even degree of doneness. Allow to stand 5 minutes.

Yield: 8 servings

Grilled London Broil

2	teaspoons seasoned salt flavor enhancer	4	tablespoons dry sherry
2	teaspoons salt	2	tablespoons sugar
2	tablespoons honey	4	tablespoons meat tenderizer
4	tablespoons soy sauce	1	(2½-pound) London broil

- Combine seasoned salt and next 6 ingredients in small bowl, mixing well.
- Place beef in large zip-top plastic bag. Pour marinade into bag and chill 8 to 12 hours.
- Grill beef to desired doneness. Slice thinly across the grain before serving.

Yield: 6 servings

Beaufort Beef

1	tablespoon olive oil	1	cup beer
1	(2-pound) chuck steak, cut into 2-inch strips	1	large garlic clove
¾	pound onions, peeled and sliced into rings	1	thyme sprig
1	tablespoon all-purpose flour	1	bay leaf
			Salt and pepper to taste

- Heat oil in flame-proof casserole over medium high heat. Sear beef a few pieces at a time until well browned.
- Remove and transfer to plate.
- Add onions to casserole and brown.
- Return beef and accumulated juices to casserole. Reduce heat, add flour and stir. Stir in beer and bring slowly to a simmer. Add garlic, thyme, bay leaf, salt and pepper. Cover tightly with lid.
- Cook in middle of oven at 275° for 2 hours, 30 minutes. Do not open oven door while cooking.

Yield: 4 servings

Crock Pot Beef

1½	pounds beef stew meat	1	teaspoon oregano
7	new red potatoes, cubed	1	teaspoon thyme
½	cup chopped celery		Chopped fresh parsley
½	cup chopped carrots		Salt and pepper
½	cup chopped green onions	2	bay leaves
1	(8-ounce) package baby	4	cups beef broth
	portobello mushrooms	1	(8-ounce) container sour
2	garlic cloves, minced		cream
1	tablespoon mixed	¼	cup all-purpose flour
	peppercorns		Egg noodles, cooked

- Place beef and next 13 ingredients in crock pot. Cook on low 7 to 8 hours or high 5 to 6 hours.
- Combine sour cream and flour in small bowl 1 hour before serving. Stir in ½ cup hot liquid from crock pot, whisking well.
- Add sour cream mixture to crock pot and cook 1 hour until thick and bubbling.
- Serve over egg noodles.

Yield: 6 servings

What a treat to come home from a busy day and be greeted by the wonderful aroma of dinner when you walk in the back door! Slow cookers, once popular in the 1970s, have made a comeback over the last few years with families who are always on the go.

~

Yankee Pot Roast

1	cup all-purpose flour	2	medium onions, peeled
	Salt and pepper to taste		and quartered
1	(3-pound) chuck roast	4	carrots, peeled and thickly
2	tablespoons cooking oil		sliced
1	(8-ounce) jar horseradish	4	large potatoes, peeled and
	sauce		cut into chunks
1	cup water		

- Preheat oven to 350°.
- Mix flour with salt and pepper. Lightly dust entire roast with flour mixture.
- Brown roast in heated cooking oil until crusty on all sides.
- Combine horseradish sauce with water.
- Place roast in cooking bag and cover with sauce mixture.
- Close bag; cut slits in top and place in baking dish and bake for 1 hour, 30 minutes to 2 hours.
- Open bag carefully and add vegetables. Close bag and continue cooking for 1 hour or until vegetables are tender.

Yield: 4 to 6 servings

The Yankee Restaurant, a colorful Beaufort landmark, once stood where the Boys and Girls Club is located today on Boundary Street. Though not famous for its ambiance, you couldn't find a better place to catch up on the happenings in Beaufort.

Mexican Lasagna

A big hit with the teenage crowd!

1   pound ground beef
1   cup salsa
1   (15-ounce) can tomato
    sauce
1   (1.25-ounce) package taco
    seasoning

1   (16-ounce) container
    cottage cheese
2   eggs
1   teaspoon oregano
8   flour tortillas
1½ cups shredded Mexican
    cheese blend

- Preheat oven to 375°.

- Brown beef in large skillet and drain. Return beef to skillet and stir in salsa, tomato sauce and taco seasoning. Simmer on low, stirring frequently.

- Combine cottage cheese, eggs and oregano in medium bowl and set aside.

- Lightly grease a 13x9-inch baking dish. Place 4 tortillas in pan, covering bottom.

- Spoon half of beef mixture over tortillas. Spoon cottage cheese mixture over beef. Top with 4 remaining tortillas. Spoon remaining beef mixture over tortillas. Top with cheeses.

- Bake 30 to 35 minutes.

Yield: 4 to 6 servings

Cottage cheese may be substituted with 1½ cups sour cream and 3 tablespoons mayonnaise or 3 ounces cream cheese.

Beaufort is home to the United States Marine Corps Recruit Depot. The Marine Base at Parris Island transforms 20,000 recruits each year into Marines. The Parris Island Museum offers a fascinating exhibit of local and military history.

~

Parris Island Pasta

2	tablespoons olive oil	1	(28-ounce) can Italian plum tomatoes, drained and chopped
1	pound sweet Italian sausage, casings removed	1½	cups heavy cream
⅛-¼	teaspoon crushed dried red pepper flakes	12	ounces bowtie or rotini pasta
½	cup chopped onion	1	cup frozen peas (optional)
3	garlic cloves, minced		Fresh chopped parsley

- Heat oil in large skillet. Add sausage and pepper flakes. Cook about 7 minutes or until sausage is no longer pink.

- Add onion and garlic and cook 7 minutes or until onion is tender and sausage has browned. Add tomatoes and cream and simmer 4 minutes.

- Cook pasta al dente, adding peas last 2 minutes of cooking, if desired. Drain and rinse under warm water.

- Combine pasta and peas with sausage mixture. Heat thoroughly, sprinkle with fresh parsley and serve.

Yield: 6 servings

"Did you know whole wheat spaghetti won't stick to the ceiling like the usual kind of spaghetti noodles?"

Lindsey Frazier,
Grade 10
Beaufort Academy
student

Million Dollar Spaghetti

1½	pounds ground beef	¼	cup sour cream
¼	teaspoon garlic salt	1	cup cottage cheese
1	teaspoon salt	⅓	cup chopped green onions
½	teaspoon black pepper	¼	cup minced bell pepper
2	(8-ounce) cans tomato sauce	1	(8-ounce) package spaghetti, cooked
1	(8-ounce) package cream cheese, softened	1	cup shredded Cheddar cheese

- Brown beef in large skillet. Drain well. Add salts, black pepper and tomato sauce. Remove from heat.

- Combine cream cheese with sour cream and cottage cheese. Add green onions and bell pepper.

- Place half of cooked spaghetti on bottom of 2-quart casserole. Spread half of beef mixture over spaghetti. Spread half of cheese mixture over beef. Repeat layers and top with shredded cheese.

- Bake at 325° for 25 to 30 minutes.

Yield: 6 to 8 servings

Grandma's Italian Favorite

2	pounds mixture ground beef, pork and veal	3	(6-ounce) cans tomato paste
1	large onion, finely chopped	2	tablespoons sugar
2	eggs, beaten	5	(28-ounce) cans whole plum tomatoes with basil
1	cup whole milk		
2	cups Italian seasoned breadcrumbs	1	tablespoon basil
	Olive oil for frying	1	tablespoon oregano
8-10	sweet Italian sausages	1	tablespoon garlic powder
		1	tablespoon salt or to taste

- Combine meat and next 4 ingredients, blending well. Shape into 1-inch balls.

- Heat oil in skillet over medium high heat. Add meatballs and cook until dark brown, turning constantly, being careful not to burn. Set meatballs aside. Do not drain skillet.

- Add sausages to skillet and cook until done. Set sausages aside. Do not drain skillet.

- Add tomato paste and sugar to skillet. Cook until oil is absorbed into paste, stirring constantly. Set aside.

- Combine plum tomatoes and remaining ingredients in large stockpot. Add meatballs, sausages and tomato paste mixture, stirring gently.

- Cover and simmer at least 3 hours.

Yield: 10 to 12 servings

GREEK POTATOES

¼ cup olive oil

½ cup lemon juice

1 teaspoon salt

1 teaspoon pepper

2 teaspoons
minced garlic

2 teaspoons oregano

4-6 russet potatoes,
quartered

1 onion, sliced

1 tomato, seeded and
chopped

• Combine olive oil
and next 5 ingredients in
small bowl, blending
thoroughly.

• Place potatoes, onion
and tomato in prepared
baking dish. Pour oil
mixture over vegetables
and cover.

• Bake at 350° for 45
minutes. Stir 2 times
while baking.

Yield: 6 servings

Rosemary Lamb Chops

3	large garlic cloves, minced	3	tablespoons olive oil
4	teaspoons chopped fresh rosemary	2	tablespoons Dijon mustard
½	teaspoon salt	2	tablespoons lemon juice
½	teaspoon freshly ground black pepper	6	lamb chops

- Combine garlic and next 6 ingredients in small bowl, blending well.

- Pour over lamb chops and marinate at least 2 hours.

- Grill lamb chops to desired doneness.

Yield: 6 servings

Butterflied Leg of Lamb with Parmesan Crust

¼	cup olive oil	3	tablespoons minced fresh parsley
2	teaspoons minced garlic		
1	teaspoon dried tarragon, crumbled	2	tablespoons dried breadcrumbs
1	(7-pound) leg of lamb, boned and butterflied	2	tablespoons unsalted butter, melted
¼	cup Dijon mustard, divided		Fresh mint or parsley sprigs
½	cup fresh Parmesan cheese		

- Combine oil, garlic and tarragon in small bowl, blending well. Brush over lamb. Allow to stand at room temperature 2 hours.

- Preheat broiler. Arrange lamb fat side down in shallow baking pan. Brush with 1 tablespoon Dijon.

- Broil 6 inches from heat 5 minutes. Turn meat, brush with remaining Dijon and broil 5 minutes.

- Heat oven to 450°.

- Combine cheese, minced parsley and breadcrumbs in small bowl. Sprinkle over lamb, patting gently so that crumbs adhere. Drizzle with melted butter.

- Roast until crumbs are crisp and brown and thermometer inserted in thickest portion of lamb registers 140° for rare.

- Let stand about 10 minutes before slicing. Garnish with fresh mint or parsley sprigs.

Yield: 8 to 10 servings

Rack of Lamb Persille

1   6-rib rack of lamb (about 1¼ pounds), trimmed of fat

Dijon Marinade

1   tablespoon minced shallot
1   garlic clove, minced
3   tablespoons unsalted butter
½   cup breadcrumbs
1   tablespoon minced fresh parsley
¼   teaspoon dried thyme
¼   teaspoon dried rosemary
   Salt to taste
   Freshly ground black pepper to taste
   Watercress sprigs for garnish

- Rub lamb with Dijon Marinade. Cover, chill and marinate 30 minutes or overnight.

- Sauté shallot and garlic in butter in small skillet over moderate heat, stirring occasionally, until tender.

- Add breadcrumbs and next 5 ingredients. Heat 2 minutes, stirring, and remove from heat.

- Sear lamb in large hot skillet, browning on all sides. Sprinkle breadcrumbs over lamb, patting gently so that crumbs adhere.

- Cook at 450° for 12 to 15 minutes for medium rare. Garnish with watercress and serve.

Dijon Marinade

2   teaspoons Dijon mustard
1   teaspoon olive oil
1   garlic clove, crushed to paste
   Pinch of dried thyme
   Pinch of dried rosemary, crumbled
   Salt and pepper

- Combine ingredients in small bowl, blending well.

Yield: 2 servings

Indigo is a plant that produces a brilliant blue dye. It became the most important cash crop for Port Royal Island plantations and brought immense wealth to the planters in the early years. The British markets for indigo disappeared when the United States gained their independence and cotton became the crop of choice.

Beaufort College was chartered in 1795 by influential citizens of Beaufort. Their goal was to educate the sons of Sea Island planters before sending them to Harvard, Yale or England in order to complete their education. The college is now part of the University of South Carolina system.

Veal Piccata

2	large lemons	1	small shallot or garlic clove, minced
1½	pounds veal cutlets, thinly pounded	1	(10½-ounce) can beef broth
	Salt and pepper	2	tablespoons small capers, drained
½	cup all-purpose flour		
4	tablespoons olive oil, divided	3	tablespoons unsalted butter
		2	tablespoons minced fresh parsley

- Slice 1 lemon thinly and set aside. Juice remaining lemon to extract ¼ cup juice and set aside.

- Sprinkle each side of cutlets with salt and pepper. Coat with flour, shaking off excess.

- Heat heavy 12-inch skillet over medium high heat about 2 minutes. Add 2 tablespoons oil and swirl to coat pan. Sauté cutlets about 1 to 2 minutes per side. Remove from pan and keep warm.

- Add remaining oil and repeat process with remaining cutlets. Set cutlets aside.

- Add shallot or garlic to same skillet. Sauté over medium low heat until fragrant (about 30 seconds for shallot and 15 seconds for garlic).

- Add broth and lemon slices. Increase heat to high and scrape skillet to loosen brown bits. Simmer 3 to 4 minutes or until liquid reduces to ⅓ cup.

- Add lemon juice and capers and simmer about 1 minute or until sauce reduces to ⅓ cup.

- Remove from heat and whisk in butter until it melts and thickens sauce. Stir in parsley. Spoon sauce over veal and serve immediately.

Yield: 4 servings

Grilled Veal Chops

½ cup olive oil
1 cup chopped fresh basil
Juice and zest of 1 lemon
2-3 garlic cloves, minced
1 tablespoon Dijon mustard
4 veal chops, 1-inch thick

- Process oil, basil, juice, zest, garlic and Dijon in blender or food processor until basil is minced.
- Transfer basil mixture to glass bowl. Add veal chops and marinate 30 minutes at room temperature or 2 hours chilled.
- Grill over medium-hot coals about 7 minutes per side, turning once and basting with marinade.

Yield: 4 servings

"Every time my dad cooks, you can't see because of the smoke!"

Abby Kraft, Grade 5
Beaufort Academy
student

Roasted Dijon Pork Tenderloin

4 large garlic cloves, minced
8 teaspoons chopped fresh rosemary
½ teaspoon salt
½ teaspoon black pepper
6 tablespoons olive oil
4 tablespoons Dijon mustard
4 tablespoons fresh lemon juice
3-4 pork tenderloins
2 pounds fresh asparagus

- Preheat oven to 400°.
- Combine garlic and next 6 ingredients in small bowl, blending well. Spread half of mixture over pork. Set aside remaining mixture.
- Place pork on wire rack in roasting pan. Transfer to oven and reduce heat to 325°. Cook uncovered 35 to 45 minutes or until meat thermometer inserted in thickest portion registers 155°.
- Steam asparagus until crisp tender and toss with remaining mustard mixture.

Yield: 8 to 10 servings

SWEET HOT
MUSTARD

1 cup dry mustard

1 cup sugar

1 cup vinegar

2 eggs, well beaten

• Combine mustard,
sugar and vinegar in
small bowl overnight.

• Add eggs, mixing well.

• Cook over hot water in
double boiler, stirring
until thickened.

**Sauce will keep several
weeks in refrigerator.**

Grilled Pork Tenderloin

1½	cups soy sauce	¼	cup bourbon
3	tablespoons dark molasses	1	(3-pound) pork tenderloin
½	cup dark brown sugar		

• Combine soy sauce, molasses, sugar and bourbon in small
bowl, blending well. Pour over pork and marinate overnight.

• Sear pork on all sides on grill. Lower heat, cover and grill until
done.

• Serve with Sweet Hot Mustard.

Yield: 6 to 8 servings

Pork Tenderloin in Red Wine Marinade

½	cup olive oil	½	teaspoon onion powder
½	cup dry red wine	2	dashes of Tabasco Sauce
½	cup soy sauce	2	(1-pound) pork tenderloins
1	teaspoon minced garlic	2	tablespoons all-purpose
¼	cup ketchup		flour
¼	teaspoon ginger		

• Combine oil and next 7 ingredients in large bowl and mix well.

• Place pork in large baking dish. Pour marinade over pork.
Cover and chill overnight, turning several times.

• Drain, reserving ½ cup for baking dish and pouring remaining
marinade in saucepan for gravy.

• Return pork to baking pan with ½ cup marinade. Cover with
foil and bake at 350° for 50 minutes.

• Pour any juices from cooked pork into reserved saucepan of
marinade. Sprinkle flour over surface. Bring to a boil, whisking
constantly. Reduce heat and simmer 1 minute until thickened.

• Transfer pork to warm serving platter. Cut into ½-inch slices
and serve with gravy.

Yield: 6 servings

Honey-Lime Marinated Pork Tenderloin

1	(2-pound) pork tenderloin	⅛	teaspoon cayenne pepper
⅓	cup lime juice	2	tablespoons Dijon mustard
¼	cup olive oil		
2	tablespoons honey	1	teaspoon finely chopped garlic
½	teaspoon salt		
1	teaspoon black pepper	½	teaspoon cumin

- Pierce pork several times with fork and set aside.
- Combine lime juice and remaining ingredients in small bowl and mix well.
- Place pork in large zip-top plastic bag. Pour marinade into bag. Marinate 1 hour or overnight.
- Grill pork, basting and turning until done.

Yield: 6 servings

Skewered Honey-Orange Pork

1	cinnamon stick	¼	cup honey
2	tablespoons fennel seeds	1	tablespoon balsamic vinegar
½	teaspoon black peppercorns		Zest of 2 oranges
1	cup orange juice	1	(2½- to 3-pound) pork tenderloin
½	cup Dijon mustard		

- Combine cinnamon stick, fennel seeds and peppercorns in blender or food processor and pulse. Transfer to bowl. Add orange juice and next 4 ingredients, mixing well. Pour into glass baking dish.
- Cut pork into 1-inch chunks and thread onto skewers. Place skewers in marinade, turning to coat well. Cover loosely with plastic wrap and chill 6 hours. Rotate skewers occasionally.
- Preheat grill to medium high.
- Remove skewers from marinade. Grill skewers 6 to 10 minutes, depending on size of chunks. Serve slightly pink.

Yield: 6 servings

The ACE Basin is where the Ashepoo, Combahee and Edisto Rivers converge to form the largest pristine estuarine preserve on the East coast. On either a private or guided boat ride, you will see dolphins, alligators, eagles, ospreys, raccoons, minks, otters, deer and many different birds that make the ACE Basin their home.

Pork Medallions in Mustard Sauce

4	tablespoons cooking oil	3½	pounds pork tenderloin
4	tablespoons coarse mustard	½	cup dry white wine or
1	teaspoon salt		chicken broth
1	teaspoon coarsely ground black pepper		Mustard Sauce

- Combine oil, mustard, salt and pepper in small bowl. Rub mixture over pork and place in large zip-top plastic bag. Chill 8 hours or overnight.

- Place pork in shallow roasting pan. Bake at 450° for 15 minutes. Baste with wine or broth every 10 minutes. Reduce temperature to 400° and bake 30 minutes or until meat thermometer inserted into thickest portion registers 160°.

- Cut into 16 slices and serve with Mustard Sauce.

Mustard Sauce

3	cups heavy cream	½	teaspoon salt
½	cup coarse-grained mustard	¼	teaspoon ground white pepper

- Cook cream in heavy saucepan over medium heat until reduced to 2½ cups (about 20 minutes). Do not boil. Stir in remaining ingredients and cook 1 minute.

Yield: 8 servings

Honey–Gingered Pork Tenderloins

2	(¾-pound) pork tenderloins	1	tablespoon minced garlic
¼	cup honey	1	tablespoon ketchup
¼	cup soy sauce	¼	teaspoon onion powder
¼	cup oyster sauce	¼	teaspoon cayenne pepper
2	tablespoons packed brown sugar	¼	teaspoon cinnamon
1	tablespoon plus 1 teaspoon minced fresh ginger		Fresh flat leaf parsley sprigs for garnish

- Pat pork dry and place in large zip-top plastic bag.

- Whisk together honey and next 9 ingredients, blending well. Pour into bag over pork. Chill 8 hours or overnight, turning occasionally.

- Preheat grill.

- Remove pork from marinade. Reserve marinade and set aside.

- Arrange pork on lightly greased rack set 5 to 6 inches over glowing coals. Grill 10 minutes, basting with reserved marinade. Turn pork every 3 minutes.

- Discard marinade. Continue cooking pork about 10 minutes or until meat thermometer inserted into center registers 155°.

- Allow pork to stand 5 minutes. Slice thinly, garnish with parsley and serve.

Yield: 4 servings

Pork may also be cooked in preheated 500° oven for 20 minutes, basting frequently.

Pork tenderloins are usually packaged in pairs. Place thick and thin sides opposite each other in the baking dish for more even cooking.

Pork Tenderloin
with Cranberry-Apple Chutney

2	**(1-pound) pork tenderloins**	1	**cup apple brandy**
	Salt and pepper to taste	1	**cup water**

- Preheat oven to 425°.

- Rub pork with salt and pepper. Place in prepared broiler pan.

- Pour brandy and water in pan. Bake for 30 minutes or until meat thermometer registers 160°.

- Remove from oven and cover with foil. Allow to stand 10 minutes. Serve 4 ounces pork with ¼ cup Cranberry-Apple Chutney.

Cranberry-Apple Chutney

2	**cups sweetened dried cranberries**	⅓	**cup white wine vinegar**
1½	**cups boiling water**	3	**tablespoons sugar**
⅓	**cup diced dried apple**	⅛	**teaspoon cayenne pepper**
¼	**cup golden raisins**		**Dash of allspice**
1	**tablespoon crystallized ginger**		**Dash of cinnamon**
			Dash of ginger
		¼	**cup red plum jam**

- Combine cranberries and next 4 ingredients. Cover and allow to stand 30 minutes.

- Combine vinegar and next 5 ingredients in saucepan. Bring to a boil, stirring frequently. Add cranberry mixture and bring to a boil. Reduce heat and simmer 5 minutes.

- Stir in jam and cool to room temperature.

Yield: 8 servings

Okatie Venison
with Mango and Mint Sauce

½	cup garlic infused olive oil	1	zucchini
½	cup soy sauce		Salt and pepper
½	teaspoon crushed celery seed, divided		Butter
1	pound venison tenderloins	1	bell pepper, finely chopped
14	ounces fresh mango	1	red bell pepper, finely chopped
½	cup cooking oil		
½	cup rice wine vinegar	1	yellow bell pepper, finely chopped
2	fresh mint leaves		Fresh mint sprigs

- Combine olive oil, soy sauce and ¼ teaspoon crushed celery seed in small bowl, mixing well. Pour over venison and marinate 2 hours.

- Grill venison over hot coals until charred but rare. Transfer to platter, slice and keep warm.

- Combine mango, cooking oil and vinegar in blender or food processor and process until mango is smooth. Add mint leaves, salt, pepper and remaining celery seed. Pulse until mint is finely chopped and set aside.

- Cut zucchini in half lengthwise. Cut the halved zucchini in diagonal slices ¼-inch thick. Season with salt and pepper and sauté in butter.

- Sauce the plate to the rim with mango sauce. Place 4 ounces sliced venison in plate center. Add zucchini crescents and rim plate with bell peppers. Garnish with mint sprigs.

Yield: 4 servings

Spring Island, a 3000 acre island that lies along the south shore of Port Royal Sound, is unexcelled in its natural beauty and commitment to environmental education and preservation. Only 400 homesites have been carefully woven into the natural tapestry of the island. This allows more than one-half of the island to remain in nature preserves, protecting the thousands of plant and animal species, which for centuries have made Spring Island their home.

Mustard Fried Venison

1½ pounds venison cubed steak, cut into bite size pieces	Mustard
	Cooking oil
	Self-rising flour
White wine	Salt and pepper to taste

- Place venison in container with tight lid. Fill container one-fourth full of white wine. Add mustard until venison is half covered, mixing well until thoroughly coated.
- Chill overnight, turning once.
- Heat oil in skillet to 350°.
- Combine flour, salt and pepper in zip-top plastic bag. Place venison in bag, coating well.
- Cook in hot oil 4 minutes until golden brown.

Yield: 4 servings

"Mustard Fried Venison is a standard favorite at the annual 'Jelly Q', a favorite local 'down the river' weekend held at Pritchards Island fish camp. It sets the mood (along with chosen libations) for a full weekend of story telling, oyster eating and friendship renewing. I'm glad the walls can't talk, or we would all have to leave town!"

Charles Webb, III
Beaufort Academy
alumnae and parent

Venison Kabobs

1½	cups cooking oil	½	cup bourbon (optional)
¾	cup cider vinegar	1-2	pounds venison loin (remove bone and membrane)
¾	cup soy sauce		
½	cup Worcestershire sauce		
⅓	cup lemon juice	2	bell peppers, seeded and sliced
2	teaspoons dry mustard		
1½	teaspoons parsley flakes	1-2	large portobello mushrooms, sliced
2	teaspoons white pepper		
2	teaspoons garlic powder	1	pound bacon slices, cut in half
2	garlic cloves, crushed		

- Combine cooking oil and next 10 ingredients in blender or food processor. Blend on high 1 minute.
- Cut venison into ½-inch strips. Marinate overnight.
- Wrap venison, bell pepper and mushroom with bacon strips. Secure with toothpicks.
- Place "kabobs" in marinade 30 minutes.
- Grill over hot coals, turning once.

Yield: 4 to 6 servings

Palmetto Bluff Game Birds

12	quail or doves, picked and dressed	8	ounces mushrooms
½	cup butter	2	cups chicken broth
1	pound bacon	½	cup dry sherry
2-3	tablespoons all-purpose flour		Salt and pepper to taste
½	medium onion, chopped		Vegetable-tomato juice or Bloody Mary mix
			Cooked white rice

- Melt butter in large skillet over medium high heat. Add birds and brown.

- Remove birds from skillet and wrap in bacon slice. Arrange in casserole and set aside.

- Add flour to butter in skillet and blend well. Add onions and mushrooms and sauté. Stir in chicken broth. Add sherry, salt and pepper.

- Pour onion mixture over birds in casserole, reserving small amount. Bake covered 1 hour, 30 minutes at 350°.

- Add vegetable-tomato juice to remaining onion mixture to thin as desired. Heat and pour over birds. Serve over rice.

Yield: 4 to 6 servings

Quail with Portobello Sauce

12	quail	3	tablespoons flour
6	tablespoons butter	2	cups chicken broth
4-6	large portobello mushrooms, sliced		Salt and pepper to taste
			Cooked wild rice

- Split quail and brown in melted butter in heavy skillet. Transfer quail to baking dish.

- Sauté mushrooms in same skillet and add to quail.

- Whisk in flour with remaining butter in skillet until firm. Add chicken broth, salt and pepper and blend well. Pour over quail. Cover and bake at 325° for 1 hour. Serve with wild rice.

Yield: 6 servings

Quail Breasts in Sour Cream and Wine

Many plantations in the Lowcountry have large tracts of land maintained as quail preserves. A habitat improvement program, as well as the latest in wildlife management techniques, are utilized to ensure a good quail population. Lowcountry hunts are traditionally on horseback or mule-drawn wagons, however, jeep hunts and walks are becoming more popular.

1	cup all-purpose flour	8	ounces fresh mushrooms, sliced
1	teaspoon salt	2	cups low-fat sour cream
¼	teaspoon black pepper	1	cup Sauterne or white wine
8	quail breasts	1	teaspoon crushed basil leaves
3	tablespoons cooking oil, divided		Salt to taste
1	medium onion, chopped		Cooked rice

- Combine flour, 1 teaspoon salt and pepper in zip-top plastic bag. Add quail to bag, coating well.

- Heat 2 tablespoons oil in large skillet on medium high heat. Sauté quail quickly, turning to lightly brown both sides.

- Transfer quail to 2-quart casserole and set aside.

- Add 1 tablespoon oil to same skillet and sauté onions and mushrooms about 2 to 3 minutes. Remove from heat and spoon over quail.

- Lower heat and add sour cream and wine to same skillet, stirring to blend well. Add basil and salt to taste. Pour over quail. Cover and bake at 350° for 45 minutes. Pour sauce over quail and rice before serving.

Yield: 4 servings

Hunting Island Game Hen with Wild Rice

¼   cup chopped onion
2   tablespoons chopped celery
6   tablespoons butter, melted
      and divided
1   cup sliced water chestnuts
¼   cup golden raisins
1   small apple, peeled and
      cubed

2   Cornish game hens
      Onion salt
      Freshly ground black
      pepper
¼   cup undiluted orange juice
¼   cup light corn syrup

Wild rice is actually not a rice, but the seed of a native grass. The long unpolished kernels provide an intense earthy, nutty flavor. It is usually seen in combination with other rices for salads, stuffings and side dishes.

- Sauté onion and celery in 2 tablespoons butter in skillet over medium high heat. Remove from heat and add water chestnuts, raisins and apples. Set aside.

- Cut hens in half. Season with onion salt and pepper. Brush hens with melted butter.

- Place each hen over mound of stuffing (breast side up) in prepared baking pan.

- Bake at 350° for 1 hour, 30 minutes. Baste with remaining melted butter.

- Combine orange juice and corn syrup in small bowl. Brush hens twice during last 30 minutes of cooking.

Yield: 4 servings

Wild Rice

1¼   cups wild rice, rinsed
      thoroughly
5½   cups chicken broth
1   cup chopped pecan halves
      Zest of 1 orange

4   green onions, including
      bulbs, thinly sliced
¼   cup olive oil
⅓   cup fresh orange juice

- Bring rice and chicken broth to a rapid boil in large saucepan over high heat. Reduce heat and simmer uncovered. Begin checking for doneness at 30 minutes.

- Drain and transfer to large bowl. Add pecans and remaining ingredients, tossing well. Allow to rest 2 hours.

Yield: 12 servings

Cranberry Roasted Duck

1	cup dried cranberries	½	cup all-purpose flour
1	cup white breadcrumbs		Salt and pepper to taste
1	cup scalded milk	4	small ducks (such as teal)
¼	cup butter, melted	4	bacon slices, cut in half

- Soak cranberries in water about 15 minutes. Drain and set aside.
- Soak breadcrumbs in milk until just moistened. Add butter and cranberries, blending gently.
- Stuff duck with cranberry mixture.
- Combine flour, salt and pepper. Coat duck with flour mixture. Top each duck with 2 bacon strips.
- Roast at 325° for 45 minutes.

Yield: 4 servings

To make scalded milk, heat until small bubbles appear on sides of saucepan. Stir about 2 minutes.

Orange Sauce for Cranberry Roasted Duck

1	cup sugar	1	(6-ounce) can frozen
1	cup plus 1 tablespoon		orange juice concentrate
	water	¼	teaspoon allspice
		1	tablespoon cornstarch

- Place sugar in skillet and cook until sugar caramelizes. Add 1 cup water and cook until caramelized sugar is dissolved. Add juice and allspice and bring to a slow boil.
- Combine cornstarch with 1 tablespoon water and add to sauce to thicken.

Yield: 1½ to 2 cups

VEGETABLES & SIDES

VEGETABLES & SIDES

Beaufort is a town with much to celebrate!
We celebrate the rich bounty of the sea with the
Shrimp Festival. We celebrate a wealth of cultural
traditions with the Gullah Festival. We celebrate
history with the Fall Festival of Homes. But probably
the most celebrated festival of all is the
Water Festival. Locals and tourists alike join in the
fun and fellowship of the many Beaufort
festivals year after year.

Asparagus and Tomatoes with Herb Vinaigrette

1	pound fresh asparagus	¼	teaspoon salt
⅓	cup olive oil	¼	teaspoon freshly ground black pepper
¼	cup red wine vinegar		
1	tablespoon chopped fresh chives	4-6	plum tomatoes, sliced Fresh chives, for garnish
2	teaspoons dried oregano, crushed		

- Snap off tough ends of asparagus.
- Blanch in boiling water about 4 minutes or until crisp tender.
- Plunge into ice water and drain.
- Cover and chill 3 hours.
- Whisk together olive oil and next 5 ingredients.
- Drizzle vinaigrette over blanched asparagus and sliced tomatoes. Garnish with additional chives.

Yield: 4 servings

This wonderful sauce will add flavor to steamed broccoli, asparagus or your favorite vegetable.

½ cup butter
½ cup fresh lemon juice
¼ cup chopped pecans
2 tablespoons chopped fresh chives
½ teaspoon salt
½ teaspoon black pepper
¼ teaspoon marjoram

- Combine ingredients in a saucepan and heat until bubbly. Drizzle over vegetables.

Asparagus with Shallots and Red Bell Pepper

2	pounds fresh asparagus, trimmed	1	teaspoon kosher salt
⅓	cup unsalted butter	½	teaspoon freshly ground black pepper
3	shallots, chopped	½	teaspoon garlic powder
1	red bell pepper, cut into thin strips		

- Blanch asparagus in boiling water about 3 to 4 minutes or until crisp tender. Drain and set aside.
- Sauté shallots and red bell pepper strips in butter about 3 to 4 minutes or until tender.
- Add asparagus and toss with salt, pepper and garlic powder.

Yield: 8 to 10 servings

Fresh green beans may be substituted for asparagus.

In 1863 President Lincoln authorized the purchase of land in both the North and the South for the establishment of twelve national cemeteries. The Beaufort National Cemetery was purchased for $75 at an 1863 tax sale.

Sesame Asparagus Stir-Fry

2	pounds asparagus	2	tablespoons sesame oil
2	tablespoons soy sauce	2	garlic cloves, minced
2	teaspoons sugar	4	teaspoons sesame seeds

- Trim and cut asparagus diagonally into 2-inch pieces and set aside.
- Whisk together soy sauce and sugar in small bowl until sugar is dissolved and set aside.
- Heat sesame oil in skillet over medium heat. Add garlic and sauté 15 seconds.
- Add asparagus and stir-fry for about 4 minutes or until crisp tender.
- Toss asparagus with soy mixture and continue stirring about 1 minute.
- Transfer to serving bowl and toss with sesame seeds.

Yield: 4 to 6 servings

Fresh green beans may be substituted for asparagus.

Roasted Asparagus and Potatoes

1	pound small red potatoes, cut into ½-inch cubes	1	tablespoon extra virgin olive oil, divided
2	pounds fresh asparagus, peeled and trimmed	1	tablespoon balsamic vinegar
			Salt and pepper to taste

- Preheat oven to 500°.
- Gently toss potatoes and asparagus with 1½ teaspoons olive oil. Season generously with salt and pepper.
- Spread potatoes and asparagus in 2 shallow baking pans. Place first pan in upper third of oven and second in lower third. Switch pans once during roasting. Roast 15 minutes or until crisp tender and golden.
- Transfer to serving platter and drizzle with balsamic vinegar and remaining olive oil.

Yield: 6 servings

Mushroom and Artichoke Sauté

1	garlic clove, minced	1	(14-ounce) can artichoke
½	cup unsalted butter		hearts, drained and
½	pound fresh mushrooms,		quartered
	thinly sliced		Salt and pepper to taste

- Sauté garlic in butter over medium heat 1 to 2 minutes, careful not to brown. Add mushrooms and sauté until golden brown.
- Reduce heat and add artichoke hearts. Season with salt and pepper.
- Simmer 20 minutes or until liquid from mushrooms has reduced.

Yield: 4 to 6 servings

Delicious side with trout, grouper or flounder.

NOONDAY STORM

Feel de rain a comin'
Creepin' in dem bones,
Don wanna work
Wanna go back home.
When de rains be bad,
Makes me wanna sleep.
Dat low down feelin'
Makes me sleep so deep.
De clouds comin' in
Fast as dey kin
Need to warn my family
And de boss man.

Erika Dorr Marshall
Beafort Academy
alumnae and parent

Broccoli with Dijon Vinaigrette

1½	pounds fresh broccoli,	2	tablespoons red wine
	trimmed		vinegar
3	teaspoons olive oil	1	tablespoon water
¼	cup finely chopped green	1	tablespoon Dijon mustard
	onions	¼	teaspoon freshly ground
½	teaspoon dried tarragon		black pepper
½	teaspoon dry mustard	¼	teaspoon salt
2	garlic cloves, minced		

- Steam broccoli spears covered 5 to 7 minutes or until crisp tender.
- Heat olive oil in small saucepan over medium heat and sauté green onions, tarragon, dry mustard and garlic about 2 to 3 minutes.
- Remove from heat; add vinegar and remaining ingredients, stirring until well blended.
- Toss broccoli with vinaigrette in large bowl and serve immediately.

Yield: 4 to 6 servings

Sesame seeds are known as benne seeds in the South. They are a symbol of good luck. These tiny unassuming seeds are far more dynamic than their size might suggest, giving a deep nutty flavor to a wide range of dishes.

Benne Broccoli

1½	teaspoons sesame oil	1	tablespoon water
1½	teaspoons cooking oil	½	teaspoon crushed red
2	garlic cloves, minced		pepper flakes
⅓	cup soy sauce	2	pounds fresh broccoli
1	tablespoon sugar		spears
1	tablespoon fresh lemon	1	tablespoon toasted benne
	juice		or sesame seeds

- Combine oils in small saucepan and heat until hot.
- Add garlic and next 5 ingredients, stirring until sugar dissolves. Keep warm.
- Steam broccoli spears about 5 minutes or until crisp tender.
- Toss broccoli with garlic sauce. Sprinkle with seeds and serve hot.

Yield: 6 servings

Broccoli with Balsamic Vinegar Sauce

1½	pounds fresh broccoli florets	1	teaspoon chopped fresh tarragon
2	tablespoons balsamic vinegar	6	tablespoons butter, cut into 1-inch cubes
2	tablespoons dry red wine		

- Steam broccoli about 5 minutes or until crisp tender and set aside.
- Combine vinegar and wine in small saucepan over medium high heat and cook until reduced by half. Add tarragon and reduce heat to low.
- Whisk in butter 1 tablespoon at a time until sauce is creamy.
- Drizzle over broccoli and serve warm.

Yield: 6 servings

Fresh tarragon may be substituted with ½ teaspoon dried tarragon.

Green Beans with Roasted Onions

6	medium onions	3	tablespoons sugar
6	tablespoons butter, divided	2	tablespoons red wine
	Salt and pepper to taste		vinegar
2	cups low-salt chicken	3	pounds slender green
	broth		beans, trimmed

- Preheat oven to 450°.

- Peel and cut onions vertically through root ends into 12 to 14 wedges and set aside.

- Spray 2 large baking sheets with nonstick cooking spray. Arrange onion in single layer and dot with ¼ cup butter, dividing equally. Season with salt and pepper.

- Bake for 35 minutes or until onions are dark brown on bottom.

- Bring chicken broth to a boil in large heavy skillet over high heat until reduced to ½ cup (about 6 minutes). Add sugar and vinegar, whisking until sugar dissolves and mixture comes to a boil.

- Reduce heat to medium low and add onions. Simmer about 5 minutes until liquid is slightly reduced. Season with salt and pepper.

- Cook green beans in large pot of salted boiling water until crisp tender (about 10 minutes). Drain well and return to pot. Add remaining 2 tablespoons butter, tossing to coat.

- Mound green beans in large shallow bowl. Top with roasted onion sauce and serve.

Yield: 8 to 10 servings

Onion sauce may be prepared ahead and refrigerated. Reheat over low heat before tossing with green beans.

The St. Helena's Episcopal Church Tour of homes and gardens is held in the spring of each year. Historic properties dating back to the late 1700s are open for the Friday night Candlelight Tour. The Lowcountry Tour, featuring nearby plantations and properties, is held on Saturday. This 45-year-old tradition is a favorite for tourists and locals alike.

Basil has "come along way, baby!" It now comes in many varieties: sweet basil, Genovese, lime basil, lemon basil, purple basil, hot and spicy basil and cinnamon basil.

Marinated Green Beans with Basil and Feta

3	pounds fresh green beans, trimmed	¾	teaspoon salt
1½	teaspoons Dijon mustard	½	teaspoon freshly ground black pepper
3	tablespoons red wine vinegar	1	(4-ounce) package feta cheese, crumbled
½	cup olive oil	½	cup chopped basil leaves

- Cook green beans in large pot of boiling water until crisp tender (about 10 minutes). Plunge immediately into ice water to stop the cooking process.

- Whisk together Dijon mustard and next 4 ingredients in large bowl. Add green beans and basil.

- Marinate at least 1 hour. Top with feta before serving.

Yield: 8 to 10 servings

Green Bean and Potato Puree

1	pound white potatoes, peeled and cubed	5	tablespoons butter
			Nutmeg to taste
1	teaspoon salt	2	tablespoons sour cream
1	pound fresh green beans, trimmed and broken	1	cup shredded Cheddar cheese

- Cover potatoes with water in large saucepan over medium high heat. Season with salt and bring to a boil.

- Add green beans and cook about 10 minutes or until crisp tender, then drain.

- Place into food processor fitted with a steel blade. Add butter, nutmeg and sour cream. Puree, scraping down the sides of bowl.

- Pour puree into deep baking dish and top with Cheddar. Bake for 20 minutes.

Yield: 8 to 10 servings

Green Beans Parmesan

2   pounds fresh green beans, trimmed
6   tablespoons unsalted butter, melted
1   teaspoon onion salt
2   teaspoons seasoning salt
½   teaspoon salt
¼   teaspoon freshly ground black pepper
¼   cup fresh Parmesan cheese
    Juice of ½ lemon

A great accompaniment for a special meal.

- Cook green beans in large pot of boiling water for about 20 minutes. Drain and set aside.

- Combine butter and remaining ingredients in small bowl, mixing well.

- Pour over green beans and serve.

Yield: 6 to 8 servings

Sugar Snap Peas and Snow Peas with Lemon Thyme

½   pound fresh snow peas, strings removed
1   pound fresh sugar snap peas, strings removed
2   tablespoons butter, melted
½   teaspoon fresh lemon juice
1   teaspoon chopped fresh parsley
2   teaspoons chopped fresh lemon thyme
½   teaspoon salt
¼   teaspoon freshly ground black pepper

- Cook snow peas in boiling water until crisp tender (about 1 minute). Rinse and set aside.

- Cook sugar snap peas in boiling water until crisp tender (about 3 minutes). Rinse and set aside.

- Combine butter and remaining ingredients in small bowl, mixing well.

- Toss together peas and butter mixture in large bowl, coating well. Serve warm.

Yield: 4 servings

I was born on a mountain in the Pacific

On a beach where the waves were terrific.

But this week, I moved

To a place that has proved

That chiggers and gnats are prolific.

James Mozley, Grade 2
Beaufort Academy
student

Sugar Snap Peas with Champagne Dressing

¼	cup egg substitute
¼	cup champagne vinegar
2	teaspoons Dijon mustard
½	teaspoon salt
¼	teaspoon freshly ground black pepper
⅔	cup cooking oil
3	pounds fresh sugar snap peas, strings removed

- Process egg substitute and next 4 ingredients in blender or food processor about 1 minute. Add oil in a steady stream until well blended.
- Cover and chill at least 1 hour.
- Bring water to a boil in large skillet over high heat. Add peas and cook 3 minutes then drain.
- Plunge into ice water to stop the cooking process and drain.
- Drizzle peas with champagne dressing and serve.

Yield: 12 servings

Sugar Snap Peas and Carrots

8	ounces baby carrots
8	ounces sugar snap peas, strings removed
2	teaspoons sugar
¼	cup butter, softened
2	teaspoons lime zest
1	teaspoon minced ginger
	Salt and pepper to taste

- Blanch carrots and peas in separate saucepans. Rinse under cold water and allow to cool.
- Combine sugar, butter, zest and ginger in medium skillet over low heat, cooking until blended.
- Add carrots and peas, cooking until thoroughly heated. Season with salt and pepper.

Yield: 4 servings

Balsamic Braised Red Cabbage

4	tablespoons cooking oil	¼	cup water
2½	pounds red cabbage, thinly sliced	½	cup balsamic vinegar
		5-6	tablespoons sugar
1½	medium red onions, thinly sliced		

- Heat cooking oil in large stockpot over medium high heat.
- Cook cabbage and onions about 15 minutes. Reduce heat and stir in water, vinegar and sugar.
- Simmer until liquid evaporates and cabbage is tender (about 30 minutes).

Yield: 10 servings

The cabbage palmetto is South Carolina's state tree. It is seen on the state flag and the state seal. Palmetto trees dot the landscape throughout the Lowcountry.

Moroccan Carrots

6	carrots, peeled and sliced	1	teaspoon brown sugar
1	garlic clove, minced	¼	cup water
1	teaspoon Hungarian paprika	1	tablespoon red wine vinegar

- Combine carrots and next 4 ingredients in small saucepan. Cover and cook over medium low heat until carrots are lightly caramelized (about 12 minutes). Add vinegar and cook 1 minute.

Yield: 4 servings

Roasted Carrots

12	carrots, peeled and sliced lengthwise	½	teaspoon freshly ground black pepper
3	tablespoons olive oil	½	teaspoon minced dill, for garnish
1½	teaspoons kosher salt		

- Preheat oven to 400°.
- Toss carrots with olive oil, salt and pepper in medium bowl.
- Place on baking sheet and bake for 20 minutes. Garnish with dill.

Yield: 4 servings

Minced dill may be substituted with parsley or tarragon.

Locally grown corn is available from June to September. Corn boil parties are popular during this time. Guests armed with grocery sacks head to the fields to pick corn. The corn is shucked and boiled for dinner. Although barbecue and slaw may round out the menu, the star of the meal is the fresh corn. Guests are rewarded for their labors with a bag of fresh picked corn to take home.

Corn Pie

¼	cup sugar	6	eggs
3	tablespoons all-purpose flour	1	pint heavy cream
		½	cup butter, melted
2	teaspoons salt	6	cups fresh or frozen corn kernels
2	teaspoons baking powder		

- Preheat oven to 350°.

- Combine sugar, flour, salt and baking powder in small bowl and set aside.

- Beat eggs with wire whisk in large bowl. Stir in cream and butter until smooth. Add sugar mixture and corn. Combine thoroughly and pour into lightly greased 13x9-inch baking dish.

- Bake for 45 minutes or until brown. Allow to rest 5 minutes before serving.

Yield: 8 servings

Balsamic Onions

4	pounds medium onions, peeled and cut through root ends into ¾-inch wedges	6	tablespoons butter
		3	tablespoons sugar
		6	tablespoons balsamic vinegar
¼	cup olive oil	1	tablespoon chopped fresh parsley
	Salt and pepper to taste		

- Preheat oven to 500°. Position rack in center and bottom third of oven.

- Toss onions with olive oil. Line 2 baking sheets with foil and arrange onion cut side down. Season with salt and pepper.

- Roast until brown and tender, rotating pans in oven and turning once (about 45 minutes).

- Melt butter in small heavy saucepan over medium high heat. Add sugar, stirring until dissolved.

- Remove from heat. Add vinegar and return to heat. Simmer until mixture thickens (about 2 minutes).

- Arrange onions on serving platter, drizzle with vinegar sauce and sprinkle with parsley.

Yield: 8 servings

Vidalia Onion Casserole

5	Vidalia onions, sliced into rings	¼	cup milk
½	cup butter	12	crushed buttery crackers
		¼	cup fresh Parmesan cheese

- Preheat oven to 325°.
- Melt butter in large skillet over medium high heat.
- Sauté onions until tender. Remove from heat and stir in milk.
- Layer half of onions, crackers and cheese in casserole dish. Repeat layers and bake for 30 minutes.

Yield: 6 servings

Grilled Vegetables

2	large red onions, peeled and quartered	1	medium yellow bell pepper, seeded and quartered
4	medium zucchini, quartered	½	pound button mushrooms
1	medium red bell pepper, seeded and quartered		

Marinade

⅔	cup olive oil	1	tablespoon minced fresh garlic
⅓	balsamic vinegar		
¼	cup minced shallots	½	teaspoon salt
1	tablespoon chopped fresh basil	¼	teaspoon freshly ground black pepper

- Combine olive oil and remaining marinade ingredients in a bowl, mixing well. Pour into large zip-top plastic bag.
- Add vegetables and chill 3 to 4 hours.
- Preheat grill. Bring vegetables to room temperature while grill heats. Remove vegetables from marinade and grill to desired doneness.

Yield: 6 servings

Grilled vegetables are quick and easy and make bright side dishes with intense flavors. Be sure to keep the grill fire medium hot to avoid scorching or overcooking.

Roasted Vegetables with
Pine Nuts and Goat Cheese

Parliament turned Polowana Island over to the Cusabo Indians in 1711. It was to serve as a reservation as long as the tribe existed. Today Polowana is a private development with 40 homesites on the island.

2	red bell peppers, chopped	¼	cup extra virgin olive oil
2	yellow bell peppers, chopped		Dried thyme to taste
			Dried oregano to taste
1	large eggplant, cut into 2-inch cubes		Dried basil to taste
			Salt to taste
3	summer squash, cut into large pieces		Freshly ground black pepper to taste
2-3	zucchini, cut into large pieces	1	garlic clove, minced
1	large red onion, quartered and separated	1	pound penne pasta, cooked al dente
		¼	cup pine nuts, toasted
2	tablespoons balsamic vinegar	4	ounces goat cheese, crumbled

- Preheat oven to 400°.
- Combine peppers and next 4 ingredients in large bowl and set aside.
- Whisk together vinegar and next 7 ingredients in bowl, mixing well. Pour over vegetables, tossing well to coat.
- Place vegetables in single layer on 2 ungreased baking sheets and roast 15 to 20 minutes.
- Serve over pasta and top with pine nuts and goat cheese.

Yield: 6 to 8 servings

Chunky Potatoes with Pesto and Cheese

4-5 large russet potatoes, cut into ½-inch slices
½ teaspoon salt
½ teaspoon freshly ground black pepper
2 cups half-and-half
3 tablespoons sun-dried tomato pesto

3 tablespoons basil pesto
4 garlic cloves, minced
2 tablespoons minced shallots
1 cup shredded mozzarella cheese
1 cup shredded Jarlsberg cheese

- Preheat oven to 375°.
- Place potatoes in 9x13-inch prepared baking dish. Season with salt and pepper and set aside.
- Combine half-and-half and next 4 ingredients in small bowl, mixing well.
- Pour mixture over potatoes and sprinkle with cheeses.
- Bake for 45 to 50 minutes or until potatoes are tender and cheese is golden brown. Cool 10 minutes before serving.

Yield: 6 to 8 servings

Roasted Potatoes with Herbs

¼ cup olive oil
3 garlic cloves, minced
2 pounds new potatoes
1. tablespoon chopped fresh rosemary
2 teaspoons chopped fresh thyme

Salt to taste
Coarsely ground black pepper to taste
Fresh rosemary sprigs, for garnish

- Preheat oven to 400°.
- Combine olive oil and garlic in small bowl. Cover and set aside 1 hour.
- Place potatoes on lightly greased baking sheet and drizzle with olive oil and garlic. Sprinkle with rosemary and thyme. Season with salt and pepper, tossing well.
- Roast until potatoes are tender and crusty, stirring occasionally (about 40 to 45 minutes).
- Serve hot and garnish with rosemary sprigs.

Yield: 4 servings

A great dish to make ahead that's sure to please your crowd!

~

Buffet Potatoes

8	large potatoes, peeled and diced	½	teaspoon freshly ground black pepper
½	cup butter, divided	1	onion, diced
1	(3-ounce) package cream cheese, softened	12	large mushrooms, sliced
½	cup sour cream		Paprika
¼	cup milk		Minced fresh parsley, for garnish
1½	teaspoons salt		

- Preheat oven to 350°.

- Boil potatoes in salted water until tender (about 15 minutes). Drain and mash.

- Add ¼ cup butter and next 5 ingredients. Blend until smooth.

- Melt remaining ¼ cup butter in heavy skillet; sauté onions and mushrooms until tender (about 10 minutes).

- Layer half of potatoes in large prepared casserole. Top with onion mixture, then remaining potatoes. Sprinkle with paprika.

- Bake for 30 to 35 minutes. Garnish with parsley and serve.

Yield: 10 to 12 servings

TARRAGON POTATOES

3 (15-ounce) cans whole potatoes, drained

½ cup butter, melted

1 cup fresh tarragon, minced

- Preheat oven to 400°.

- Place potatoes in baking dish. Pour butter over potatoes. Sprinkle heavily with tarragon.

- Bake for 45 minutes to 1 hour.

Yield: 6 servings

Herb Sautéed New Potatoes

3	pounds new potatoes, quartered	¾	cup minced green onions
¼	cup unsalted butter	¼	cup minced fresh chives
2	tablespoons olive oil	1	teaspoon dried thyme
			Salt and pepper to taste

- Cook potatoes in large pot of boiling water until tender (about 10 minutes). Drain and cool.

- Heat butter and olive oil in large heavy skillet over medium high heat and sauté potatoes (about 8 to 10 minutes). Add green onions, chives and thyme. Season with salt and pepper.

- Continue cooking until potatoes are golden brown (about 1 to 2 minutes).

Yield: 10 to 12 servings

Sweet Potatoes with Sage Vinaigrette

8	cups peeled and cubed sweet potatoes	
2	tablespoons olive oil	
3	tablespoons champagne vinegar	
1	tablespoon sugar	
2	tablespoons chopped fresh sage	
1	teaspoon salt	

¼	teaspoon freshly ground black pepper
⅓	cup olive oil
2	tablespoons dark sesame oil
1	bunch green onions, sliced diagonally
1	tablespoon sesame seeds
	Fresh sage sprigs, for garnish

- Preheat oven to 450°.

- Line a 15x10-inch jelly-roll pan with foil and spray lightly with cooking spray.

- Toss potatoes with 2 tablespoons olive oil and place on pan.

- Bake until tender (about 30 to 40 minutes).

- Whisk together vinegar and next 4 ingredients. Gradually whisk in oils.

- Toss potatoes gently with green onions, sesame seeds and vinaigrette. Garnish with sage sprigs.

Yield: 6 to 8 servings

Sweet potatoes and yams are not the same thing. The sweet potato is a member of the morning glory family. They were grown in the South and became a staple in Lowcountry cuisine. Yams, popular in the West Indies, are actually tubers.

Sweet Potato Soufflé

4	sweet potatoes, peeled and cooked
4	egg yolks
1	cup sugar
½	cup butter, softened

1	(13-ounce) can evaporated milk
1	teaspoon vanilla
2	teaspoons cinnamon
4	egg whites

- Preheat oven to 350°.

- Mix sweet potatoes and next 6 ingredients with an electric mixer until well blended.

- Beat egg whites until stiff and gently fold into potatoes.

- Pour into a 9x13x2-inch prepared baking dish. Bake for 45 minutes.

Yield: 4 to 6 servings

Many magnificent summer homes, such as the "Cuthbert House", "The Oaks", "Tidalholm" and "The Castle", were built in Beaufort by the Sea Island planters. Collectively these houses, along with the great wealth they represented, made South Carolina's second oldest town—Beaufort—the "most aristocratic" city in the South until the War Between the States.

Summer Tomato Pie

1	tablespoon sugar	½	cup minced yellow bell pepper
1	tablespoon water		
1	teaspoon fresh lemon juice	3	ounces chèvre cheese, crumbled
1	baked pie crust		
2	pounds fresh tomatoes, sliced	½	teaspoon salt
¼	cup minced fresh basil	¼	teaspoon freshly ground black pepper
		1	tablespoon olive oil

- Preheat oven to 375°.

- Combine sugar, water and lemon juice in small saucepan over low heat, stirring until sugar dissolves. Remove from heat and brush onto pie crust.

- Place tomatoes in pie crust in an overlapping pattern.

- Sprinkle with basil, yellow bell pepper and cheese. Season with salt and pepper. Drizzle with olive oil.

- Bake for 25 to 30 minutes.

Yield: 8 servings

Baked Tomatoes with Pesto

3	tomatoes, cored and halved crosswise	½	cup shredded fresh Romano
		2	teaspoons chopped fresh parsley
¼	cup prepared basil pesto		
1	small Vidalia onion, thinly sliced and separated into rings		

- Preheat oven to 350°.

- Hollow out top ¼-inch of tomato halves. Top each tomato with 2 teaspoons pesto and 3 to 4 onion rings.

- Cover and bake for 20 to 25 minutes. Sprinkle with cheese and bake for 5 minutes.

- Garnish with parsley and serve.

Yield: 6 servings

Okra Tomato Pie

2	tablespoons olive oil	1	teaspoon sugar
6	tablespoons chopped onion	1½	teaspoons salt
1	pound okra, sliced	⅛	teaspoon cayenne pepper
1	(1-quart) can tomatoes, drained	8	buttery crackers, crushed
¼	teaspoon curry powder	2½	tablespoons fresh Parmesan cheese

- Preheat oven to 350°.

- Heat oil in large skillet over medium high heat. Sauté onions until tender. Add okra and cook until tender. Stir in tomatoes and next 4 ingredients.

- Pour into 2-quart baking dish. Top with crackers and cheese. Bake for 30 minutes.

Yield: 4 to 6 servings

Bacon drippings may be substituted for olive oil. Frozen okra may be substituted for fresh okra.

This simple dish is a true Southern classic. Okra and tomatoes have been paired together in Lowcountry kitchens for centuries.

Spinach Sauté with Garlic and Tomatoes

2	pounds fresh spinach, stemmed	½	tablespoon unsalted butter
2	tablespoons water	8	ounces cherry or grape tomatoes, quartered
2	tablespoons olive oil		Salt and pepper to taste
3	garlic cloves, minced		

- Wilt spinach in large saucepan with water and set aside.

- Heat olive oil in medium saucepan over medium heat. Add spinach and toss in oil until thoroughly warm (about 4 minutes).

- Add garlic and cook, stirring about 2 minutes. Add butter and tomatoes, stirring until softened (about 2 minutes).

- Season with salt and pepper and serve.

Yield: 8 servings

Dazzle your luncheon guests with this tantalizing tart.

Goat Cheese and Tomato Tart

Crust

1	cup all-purpose flour	¾	cup cold unsalted butter, cut into cubes
¾	cup yellow cornmeal		
1	teaspoon salt	3	tablespoons ice water

- Preheat oven to 375°.

- Pulse together flour, cornmeal and salt in food processor. Add butter and pulse until crumbly. Add ice water and continue pulsing until dough forms.

- Press dough into 3-inch tart pans or 12-cup muffin tin. Roll a rolling pin over the rim of tart pan to trim edges.

- Chill 20 minutes or until firm.

Custard

½	cup chopped fresh basil	2	eggs, beaten
7	ounces mild goat cheese, softened		Salt to taste
			Freshly ground black pepper to taste
6	tablespoons butter, softened	¾	pound cherry or grape tomatoes, halved
¼	cup sour cream		

- Combine basil and next 4 ingredients in large bowl. Season with salt and pepper. Pour into chilled crusts, spreading evenly.

- Arrange tomato halves on top, pressing lightly into custard. Season with salt and pepper.

- Bake on lower rack until custard is set (about 25 minutes). Cool slightly on wire rack and serve warm.

Yield: 12 servings

Fried Green Tomatoes

1	egg	4	large firm green tomatoes,
½	cup milk		cut into ⅛-inch slices
¼	cup all-purpose flour		Cooking oil or shortening
½	cup cornmeal		for frying
			Salt and pepper

- Beat egg and milk together and set aside.
- Combine flour and cornmeal, mixing well.
- Dip each tomato slice in egg mixture, then dredge in cornmeal mixture.
- Heat oil in large skillet over medium heat. Add tomatoes and brown on both sides, turning once.
- Drain and season with salt and pepper.

Yield: 4 to 6 servings

Southerners are well known for their flare for frying, and one of the most popular dishes is Fried Green Tomatoes. To prevent tomatoes from becoming greasy, place them in ice water for 30 minutes before coating with batter.

Squash–Sage Bake

1	pound summer squash, sliced	½	cup shredded Cheddar cheese
2	eggs, beaten		Salt and pepper to taste
½	cup finely chopped onion		Paprika
2	teaspoons chopped fresh sage		

- Preheat oven to 350°.
- Steam squash until tender and drain.
- Combine squash and next 4 ingredients in large bowl. Season with salt and pepper and mix well.
- Pour mixture into prepared casserole and sprinkle with paprika. Bake for 25 minutes or until set.

Yield: 4 to 6 servings

Tabby structures and ruins can be found throughout the Lowcountry. Introduced to the area by the Spanish, oyster shells are burned to obtain lime. The lime is mixed with sand and oyster shells, and then poured into molds to form walls and roofs. The finished building is very sturdy, energy efficient and has a subtle, unique pinkish color.

Feta Spinach Puff

1	sheet frozen puff pastry, thawed and halved	4½	ounces feta cheese, crumbled
1	tablespoon olive oil	1	egg, beaten
1	cup chopped onion		Juice of 1 lemon
3	(10-ounce) packages frozen chopped spinach, thawed and well drained	¼	teaspoon freshly ground black pepper
1	(14-ounce) can artichoke hearts, drained and quartered	⅛	teaspoon ground nutmeg
		1-2	tablespoons melted butter
			Fresh Parmesan cheese

- Preheat oven to 350°.
- Spray an 8x11-inch glass baking dish with cooking spray. Arrange pastry sheet half in bottom of dish.
- Cook onions until translucent in olive oil over medium high heat. Transfer to large bowl; add spinach and next 6 ingredients, stirring well.
- Spoon spinach mixture over pastry in pan. Press gently to make a smooth even layer.
- Top with remaining pastry sheet half. Brush with melted butter.
- Bake for 20 to 30 minutes or until golden brown. Top with cheese 10 minutes before removing from oven.

Yield: 8 servings

Sautéed Spinach

3	tablespoons unsalted butter	1	pound fresh spinach
1	tablespoon olive oil	¼	teaspoon sugar
1	garlic clove, minced	¼	teaspoon salt
			Juice of 1 lemon

- Heat butter and olive oil in skillet over medium high heat. Add garlic and sauté for 30 seconds.
- Stir in spinach, sugar and salt. Cook until spinach wilts, stirring occasionally.
- Toss with lemon juice and serve immediately.

Yield: 4 servings

Dilled Squash

2	tablespoons butter
4	green onions, chopped
2	summer squash, thinly sliced
2	zucchini, thinly sliced
1	garlic clove, minced
2	tablespoons chopped fresh dill
	Salt and pepper to taste

- Melt butter in large skillet over medium high heat. Add onions, squash, zucchini, and garlic. Sauté until crisp tender.

- Toss with dill and season with salt and pepper.

Yield: 4 servings

Yellow squash, both straightneck and crookneck, grow abundantly throughout the South in the summer. Their preparation can be very simple or elaborate making squash a popular side dish.

Zucchini Soufflé

2	pounds zucchini, sliced
¼	cup butter
3	eggs, beaten
½	cup half-and-half
1	teaspoon Worcestershire sauce
1	teaspoon minced onion
2	tablespoons fine Italian breadcrumbs
1	teaspoon salt
½	teaspoon pepper
½	cup fresh Parmesan cheese, divided

- Preheat oven to 350°.

- Boil zucchini in large saucepan over high heat until tender (about 15 minutes). Remove from heat and drain.

- Return to saucepan and add butter, stirring until melted. Set aside.

- Combine eggs and next 6 ingredients, mixing well. Add ¼ cup Parmesan. Stir in zucchini and mix thoroughly.

- Pour into prepared soufflé. Bake for 45 minutes or until firm.

- Top with remaining ¼ cup Parmesan during last 10 minutes of baking.

Yield: 6 servings

Apple Soufflé

½	cup butter, melted	1	cup crushed vanilla wafers
½	cup sugar	1	(15-ounce) can applesauce
2	eggs, beaten	1	teaspoon vanilla
1	cup milk		

- Preheat oven to 350°.
- Cream together butter and sugar. Add eggs, mixing well. Alternately add milk and wafers. Fold in applesauce and vanilla.
- Pour into prepared 2-quart casserole. Bake for 45 minutes to 1 hour.

Yield: 4 to 6 servings

Summer Squash Sauté

2	tablespoons butter	¼	teaspoon fresh lemon juice
½	pound summer squash, cubed	2	pounds cherry tomatoes
			Salt and pepper to taste
1	shallot, minced	½	pound fresh asparagus, trimmed and cut into 1-inch pieces (optional)
1	garlic clove, minced		
1	tablespoon minced fresh basil		

- Melt butter in large skillet. Add squash and next 4 ingredients and asparagus, if using. Sauté over medium heat until squash is crisp tender.
- Add cherry tomatoes and heat thoroughly, stirring frequently (about 1½ to 2 minutes). Season with salt and pepper and serve.

Yield: 6 servings

Holiday Cranberry Casserole

3	cups cored, peeled and chopped apples	½	cup brown sugar
2	cups fresh cranberries	⅓	cup all-purpose flour
¾	cup sugar	1	cup chopped nuts
1½	cups oatmeal	1	cup butter, melted

- Preheat oven to 350°.
- Spread apples and cranberries on the bottom of prepared 3-quart casserole. Sprinkle with sugar.
- Combine oatmeal, brown sugar and flour in small bowl. Sprinkle over fruit.
- Top with nuts and drizzle with butter. Bake for 45 minutes.

Yield: 8 servings

An old-fashioned favorite seen on many Southern sideboards during the holidays.

~

Zippy Zucchini

¼	cup butter	1	teaspoon minced garlic
1¼	pounds zucchini, shredded		Salt and pepper to taste
¼	cup chopped white onion	¼	cup fresh Parmesan cheese

- Melt butter in medium skillet over medium high heat. Add zucchini, onion and garlic. Cook, stirring frequently, about 5 minutes or until tender. (If zucchini is watery, drain excess liquid.)
- Season with salt and pepper to taste. Stir in cheese and cook until cheese melts.

Yield: 4 servings

Zippy Zucchini serving suggestions:
  Use a combination of zucchini and yellow squash.
  Stuff a hollowed tomato and bake at 350° for 20 minutes.

Want to add an extra zip to your fresh vegetables? Try experimenting with herb butters.

1 cup butter, softened

1 tablespoon fresh basil, chopped

1 tablespoon fresh parsley, chopped

1 tablespoon fresh tarragon, chopped

1 tablespoon chopped fresh chives

- Combine ingredients and store in refrigerator until ready to use.

Yield: 1 cup

In 1860 South Carolina produced 3.5 million bushels of rice. "Carolina Gold", as it was called, was considered the best rice in the world and demanded by European and Asian markets. Its flavor is delicate with a creamy, buttery taste that is delicious all by itself. Today Turnbridge Plantation, just outside of Beaufort, produces a pure strain of "Carolina Gold".

Bay Street Wild Rice

2	packages wild rice with flavor packets	1	(7-ounce) can sliced water chestnuts, chopped
4	cups chicken broth	¾	teaspoon dried thyme
3	tablespoons olive oil	¼	teaspoon salt
1	onion, chopped	3-4	tablespoons chopped fresh parsley
1	yellow or red bell pepper, diced		Salt and pepper to taste
1	cup toasted and chopped pecans		

- Cook rice in chicken broth, using 1 flavor packet.

- Heat olive oil in skillet over medium high heat and sauté onion and bell pepper until tender. Reduce heat and add pecans and water chestnuts.

- Add onion mixture to rice. Stir in thyme and remaining ingredients, mixing well, and serve.

Yield: 8 to 10 servings

Rice may be prepared ahead and reheated before serving.

Herbed Couscous

1	cup sliced fresh mushrooms	¼	teaspoon salt
1	tablespoon butter		Black pepper to taste
1	cup water	⅔	cup couscous
1	tablespoon chopped fresh parsley	1	medium tomato, peeled, seeded and chopped
1	tablespoon fresh basil, chopped	4	ounces feta cheese, crumbled
1	tablespoon fresh oregano, chopped		

- Sauté mushrooms in butter in medium saucepan until tender.

- Stir in water and next 5 ingredients. Bring to a boil.

- Stir in couscous. Remove from heat.

- Cover and allow to stand 5 minutes.

- Stir in tomato and feta. Serve immediately.

Yield: 4 servings

Mushroom and Pea Risotto

2	tablespoons butter	1	(8-ounce) package sliced
2	tablespoons olive oil		fresh mushrooms
1	cup Arborio rice,	1	cup frozen green peas
	uncooked	½	cup fresh Parmesan cheese
½	cup chopped onion	¼	teaspoon freshly ground
3	cups chicken broth		black pepper

- Microwave butter and oil in large bowl on high 2 minutes. Stir in rice and onion. Microwave on high 4 minutes, stirring after 3 minutes.

- Stir in chicken broth and microwave on high 10 minutes, stirring at 3-minute intervals.

- Stir in mushrooms and microwave on high 8 minutes, stirring at 3-minute intervals.

- Stir in peas and microwave on high 2 minutes. Cover and allow to stand 5 minutes.

- Sprinkle with Parmesan and pepper before serving.

Yield: 6 to 8 servings

A watchful eye, a little patience and constant stirring—all you need to make perfect risotto every time.

Zesty Rice

1	(15-ounce) can whole kernel corn, drained	2	cups cooked white rice
1	(10-ounce) can whole tomatoes and green chiles, undrained	¼	teaspoon freshly ground black pepper
		1	bunch green onions, chopped
1	(8-ounce) carton sour cream	1	(2¼-ounce) can ripe olives, chopped
1	(8-ounce) jar picante sauce	8	ounces shredded Monterey
1	cup shredded sharp Cheddar cheese		Jack cheese

- Preheat oven to 350°.

- Combine corn and next 8 ingredients in large bowl, mixing well.

- Spoon into prepared 9x13-inch baking dish. Sprinkle with Monterey Jack.

- Bake for 50 minutes.

Yield: 10 to 12 servings

Cornbread Dressing

Always moist and delicious, this dressing can be prepared up to 3 months in advance and frozen for holiday use. Serve with Balsamic Gravy.

2 cups cornmeal
½ cup all-purpose flour
2 teaspoons baking powder
1 teaspoon baking soda
1 teaspoon salt
2 tablespoons chopped fresh sage or 2 teaspoons dried, crushed sage
1 teaspoon sugar
6 eggs, divided
2 cups buttermilk

2 tablespoons bacon drippings or melted butter
½ cup butter
2 bunches green onions, chopped
4 ribs celery, chopped
1 (16-ounce) package herb-seasoned stuffing mix
5 (14-ounce) cans chicken broth

- Preheat oven to 425°.

- Combine cornmeal and next 6 ingredients in large bowl and set aside.

- Beat together 2 eggs and buttermilk in small bowl. Add to cornmeal mixture, stirring until just moistened.

- Heat bacon drippings in 10-inch cast iron skillet or 9-inch round cake pan in oven for 5 minutes.

- Stir hot drippings into batter and pour into hot skillet. Bake until golden (about 25 minutes). Cool and crumble.

- Reduce oven to 350°.

- Melt butter in large skillet over medium heat. Add green onions and celery. Sauté until tender.

- Stir together remaining 4 eggs, cornbread, onion mixture, stuffing mix and chicken broth in large bowl until well blended.

- Spoon into prepared 9x13-inch baking dish and prepared 9-inch square baking dish.

- Bake for 50 minutes to 1 hour or until lightly browned.

Yield: 15 servings

Balsamic Gravy

1	turkey neck and giblets	1½	tablespoons chopped fresh rosemary, divided
5½	cups chicken broth		
1	onion, quartered	1½	tablespoons chopped fresh sage, divided
1	bay leaf		
6	tablespoons unsalted butter	⅓	cup all-purpose flour
2	large onions, halved and thinly sliced	½	cup balsamic vinegar

- Combine turkey, broth, onion and bay leaf in large saucepan and bring to a boil. Reduce heat and simmer until reduced to 3 cups liquid (about 1 hour), skimming occasionally. Remove from heat and strain, discarding solids, and set aside.

- Melt butter in large skillet over medium high heat. Sauté onions about 10 minutes. Add 1 tablespoon rosemary and 1 tablespoon sage. Continue to sauté until onions are golden (about 8 minutes).

- Add flour, stirring 1 minute. Gradually whisk in broth and bring to a boil. Cook until gravy thickens, stirring often (about 3 minutes). Stir in remaining ½ teaspoon rosemary and ½ teaspoon sage.

- Pour juices from turkey pan into large glass measuring cup, spooning off fat. Add juices to gravy.

- Add vinegar to roasting pan, simmering over medium heat. Scrape up browned bits.

- Pour mixture into small saucepan and boil 2 to 3 minutes until reduced to ¼ cup.

- Add to gravy and season with salt and pepper.

Yield: 15 servings

"My favorite meal is rice and gravy. Here is the recipe:

First cook the rice. Then cook the gravy. Mix it together, and you have rice and gravy!"

Macauley Smith,
Grade 3
Beaufort Academy
student

Creamy Four Cheese Macaroni

⅓	cup all-purpose flour	3	ounces processed cheese
2⅔	cups low-fat milk	6	cups cooked elbow
¾	cup shredded Swiss cheese		macaroni
½	cup fresh Parmesan cheese	¼	teaspoon salt
½	cup shredded Cheddar	12	Melba toasts, crushed
	cheese	1	tablespoon butter, melted

- Preheat oven to 375°.

- Place flour in heavy large saucepan over medium heat. Slowly add milk, whisking until well blended and thick.

- Add cheeses, stirring constantly until cheese melts. Remove from heat and stir in macaroni and salt. Transfer into prepared 2-quart casserole and set aside. Mix together toast crumbs and butter. Sprinkle on top of casserole and bake for 30 minutes.

Yield: 8 servings

Penne Pasta with Tomatoes and Cheese

6	tablespoons olive oil, divided	2	cups chicken broth
			Salt and pepper to taste
1½	cups chopped onion	1	pound penne pasta
2	garlic cloves, minced	2½	cups shredded Havarti
3	(28-ounce) cans Italian plum tomatoes, drained		cheese
		⅓	cup sliced black olives
2	teaspoons dried basil	⅓	cup fresh Parmesan cheese
1½	teaspoons crushed red pepper flakes	¼	cup chopped fresh basil, for garnish

- Preheat oven to 375°.

- Heat 3 tablespoons olive oil in heavy Dutch oven over medium high heat. Add onion and garlic and sauté about 5 minutes.

- Add tomatoes, dried basil and red pepper flakes. Pour in broth and bring to a boil. Reduce heat to medium and simmer about 1 hour or until mixture thickens, stirring occasionally. Season with salt and pepper.

- Cook pasta al dente in large pot of salted boiling water. Drain and return to pot.

- Toss pasta with remaining 3 tablespoons olive oil in large bowl. Add sauce, tossing well to blend. Add Havarti cheese.

- Transfer to a 13x9x2-inch prepared baking dish. Sprinkle with olives and Parmesan. Bake for 30 minutes or until thoroughly heated. Garnish with fresh basil.

Yield: 6 servings

DESSERTS

DESSERTS

*Season after season, Lowcountry cooks have lovingly
served and impressed visitors with their tantalizing
desserts. In the spring sideboards feature pies of
strawberries, blackberries or blueberries handpicked in
local berry patches. In the summer tarts, trifles,
cobblers and ice creams are served often in the backyard
as the sun sets and the fireflies emerge.
Apple and pecan pies are celebrations of the fall harvest.
Winter desserts are more indulgent with recipes of
chocolate or preserved fruits served with fine liqueur to
impress holiday guests. We find ourselves in this new
millennium both enjoying a few short cuts and
savoring those treasured recipes from the past which
have endured the "tastes of time."*

Almond–Butter Pound Cake

Pound Cake

3	cups all-purpose flour	1	cup buttermilk
2	cups sugar	1	cup butter, softened
1	teaspoon salt	2	teaspoons almond extract
1	teaspoon baking powder	4	eggs
½	teaspoon baking soda		

- Preheat oven to 325°. Grease and flour Bundt pan very well.

- Mix flour and next 8 ingredients with electric mixer on low speed until moistened. Beat 3 minutes on medium speed and pour into pan.

- Bake for 1 hour to 1 hour, 15 minutes. Prick cake deeply with fork.

Sauce

¾	cup sugar	3	tablespoons water
⅓	cup butter	2	teaspoons almond extract

- Combine sugar, butter and water in small saucepan; heat until butter melts. Remove from heat and stir in almond extract.

- Pour ¾ cup hot sauce over hot cake. Cool in pan about 5 minutes. Invert onto serving plate. Apply remaining sauce over cake with pastry brush.

Yield: 16 servings

"Pound cakes are wonderful gifts to make all year. They can be wrapped easily and tied with seasonal ribbons or garnished with fresh or dried flowers."

Emma Moore Roddey
Beaufort Academy
parent

When life hands you lemons... make lemon pound cake!

Lemon Mint Pound Cake with Strawberries and Cream

Pound Cake

¼	cup sugar	1¾	cups all-purpose flour
¼	cup loosely packed fresh mint leaves	½	cup heavy cream
1	cup butter, softened	2	tablespoons fresh lemon juice
2½	cups confectioners' sugar	2	teaspoons lemon zest
3	eggs		

- Preheat oven to 350°.

- Process sugar and mint leaves in food processor, reserving ¼ cup for Lemon Cream.

- Beat butter on medium speed with an electric mixer until creamy. Add ¼ cup mint mixture and confectioners' sugar slowly, beating 6 to 7 minutes.

- Add eggs one at a time, beating well after each addition. Add flour gradually, alternating with cream. Stir in lemon juice and zest.

- Pour into an 8½x4½-inch greased and floured loaf pan. Bake at 350° for 1 hour.

- Cool cake in pan on wire rack 10 minutes. Remove from pan and cool on wire rack.

Lemon Cream

2	cups heavy cream	2	pints fresh strawberries, hulled and sliced
½	cup confectioners' sugar		Fresh mint sprigs, for garnish
1	(12-ounce) jar lemon curd		
¼	cup mint mixture		

- Beat cream and sugar on medium speed until stiff peaks form. Gently fold in lemon curd. Add mint mixture.

- Serve cake with Lemon Cream and strawberries. Garnish with fresh mint sprigs.

Yield: 8 servings

Fresh Apple Cake

Cake

2	cups sugar	1½	teaspoons baking soda
2	eggs	3	cups flour
1¼	cups cooking oil	3	apples, peeled, cored and diced
1	teaspoon vanilla		
1	teaspoon lemon juice		

- Preheat oven to 325°.
- Grease and flour loaf pan or round cake pan.
- Combine sugar and next 7 ingredients in large bowl, mixing well.
- Bake for 1 hour to 1 hour, 15 minutes. Allow to cool.

10 to 12 servings

BUTTERSCOTCH SAUCE

¾ cup packed brown sugar

1 cup light corn syrup

½ cup butter

1 cup heavy cream

- Boil brown sugar, corn syrup and butter 5 minutes, stirring until sugar is dissolved. Add cream and bring to a boil; remove from heat. Sauce will thicken upon standing.
- Serve a slice of Fresh Apple Cake in a pool of Butterscotch Sauce.

Peach Pound Cake

1	cup butter, softened	¼	teaspoon baking soda
3	cups sugar	2	cups chopped peaches
6	eggs	½	cup sour cream
3	cups all-purpose flour	1	teaspoon vanilla
¼	teaspoon salt	1	teaspoon amaretto

- Preheat oven to 350°.
- Cream butter and sugar. Add eggs one at a time, beating well after each addition, and set aside.
- Sift together flour, salt and baking soda; set aside.
- Combine peaches and sour cream.
- Add flour mixture to butter mixture, alternating with peaches. Add vanilla and amaretto, mixing well.
- Pour into greased and floured 10-inch tube pan. Bake for 1 hour, 15 minutes to 1 hour, 20 minutes.

Yield: 16 servings

Coconut Grove Cake

Cake

4	cups all-purpose flour, sifted	1	cup shortening
5	teaspoons baking powder	2	cups milk
1½	teaspoons salt	1	teaspoon almond extract
6	egg whites	1	teaspoon vanilla
2½	cups sugar, divided	1	cup coconut

- Sift together flour, baking powder and salt. Set aside.

- Beat egg whites until foamy. Add ½ cup sugar and beat until stiff peaks form. Set aside.

- Cream 2 cups sugar and shortening until fluffy. Add flour mixture and milk alternately. Add vanilla and almond extract. Stir in coconut. Fold in egg whites.

- Line bottoms of three (9-inch) cake pans with wax paper. Grease and flour; pour batter into pans.

- Bake at 375° for 20 to 25 minutes. Allow to cool on wire racks.

Zesty Lemon Filling

1	cup sugar	2	tablespoons lemon zest
3	tablespoons cornstarch	½	cup lemon juice
½	teaspoon salt	2	tablespoons butter
1	cup boiling water		

- Combine sugar and next 6 ingredients in saucepan. Bring to a rolling boil, stirring constantly. Reduce heat and boil additional 1 minute.

- Allow to cool completely. Beat with electric mixer on low speed and spread between cake layers.

Seven Minute Icing

2	egg whites, unbeaten	1½	teaspoons light corn syrup
5	tablespoons cold water	1	teaspoon vanilla
¼	teaspoon cream of tartar	½	cup coconut
1½	cups sugar	½	cup chopped nuts

- Combine egg whites and next 4 ingredients in double boiler, beating constantly for 7 minutes. Remove from heat.

- Add vanilla and continue beating to spreading consistency. Fold in coconut and nuts. Spread over top and sides of cake.

Yield: 16 servings

Melinda's Chocolate Cake

Cake

2	cups sugar		½	cup buttermilk
2	cups all-purpose flour		2	eggs
½	cup butter		1	teaspoon vanilla
½	cup shortening		1	teaspoon baking soda
1	cup water		½	teaspoon salt
3½	teaspoons cocoa			

- Combine sugar and flour in large bowl, mixing well, and set aside.

- Combine butter, shortening, water and cocoa in saucepan and bring to a boil. Pour over flour mixture and blend.

- Add buttermilk and next 4 ingredients, mixing well.

- Pour into 9x13-inch prepared baking pan. Bake at 350° for 20 to 25 minutes. Allow to cool.

Frosting

½	cup butter		1	teaspoon vanilla
3½	tablespoons cocoa		1	cup pecans, coarsely
⅓	cup buttermilk			chopped
1	(16-ounce) box confectioners' sugar			

- Boil butter, cocoa and buttermilk in saucepan until it thickens.

- Remove from heat and add remaining ingredients. Spread over cake.

Yield: 24 servings

Land's End Mud Pie

*"'Barefoot and on
the beach' can bring a
fond memory to almost
everyone. 'Barefoot and
in the mud' will also
evoke a smile from most
people. We are lucky at
Land's End to have both
the beach and the mud
in which to wiggle
our toes."*

Erika Dorr Marshall
Beaufort Academy
alumnae and parent

½	cup pecan pieces, toasted and chopped	2	cups semi-sweet chocolate morsels
1	(6-ounce) prepared chocolate cookie pie crust	1⅓	cups heavy cream
		¼	cup butter
17	caramels, unwrapped		Frozen whipped topping
¼	cup evaporated milk		Fresh raspberries, for garnish

- Sprinkle pecans on crust.
- Heat caramel and milk in saucepan on low until smooth. Pour over pecans and set aside
- Heat morsels, cream and butter in saucepan on low until smooth. Pour over caramel.
- Chill 4 hours. Serve with frozen whipped topping and garnish with raspberries.

Yield: 10 servings

Make your own crust. Combine 20 crushed chocolate sandwich cookies with ¼ cup melted butter, mixing well.

Sinful Chocolate Pie

2	deep dish pie shells	1	cup heavy cream
8	ounces unsweetened chocolate	8	eggs, beaten
2	cups butter	2	egg yolks, beaten
5	cups sugar	1	tablespoon vanilla

- Preheat oven to 425°.
- Prick crust with fork and bake 5 minutes.
- Reduce heat to 350°.
- Melt chocolate and butter in large saucepan over low heat.
- Add sugar and cream, stirring until sugar dissolves. Remove from heat.
- Add eggs and egg yolks gradually, stirring until smooth and thick. Add vanilla.
- Pour into pie shell. Bake 20 to 25 minutes, being careful not to overbake.

Yield: 2 pies (16 servings)

Elektra's Caramel Brownie Pie

Crust

½	cup butter, softened	½	cup pecans, chopped and toasted
¼	cup sugar		
¾	cup plus 2 tablespoons all-purpose flour	17	caramels, unwrapped
2	tablespoons cocoa	¼	cup sweetened condensed milk

- Beat butter and sugar until creamy. Add flour and cocoa, beating until well blended. Press into 8-inch round springform pan. Chill 30 minutes.

- Sprinkle pecans on crust.

- Melt caramel and milk in saucepan and heat until smooth. Pour over pecans.

Brownie

2	eggs	1	teaspoon vanilla
½	cup sugar	2	tablespoons butter
¼	cup sweetened condensed milk	2	(1-ounce) squares unsweetened chocolate

- Beat eggs, sugar, milk and vanilla until smooth and set aside.

- Melt butter and chocolate in saucepan on low heat. Stir in egg mixture, mixing well. Pour over caramel layer of crust.

- Bake at 350° for 45 minutes. Cool 10 minutes before removing springform pan.

Yield: 8 servings

Nutty Buddy Pie

1	(8-ounce) package cream cheese, softened	1	(16-ounce) carton frozen whipped topping
⅔	cup crunchy peanut butter	3	graham cracker pie crusts
2	cups confectioners' sugar	1	(16-ounce) can chocolate syrup
1	cup milk	1	cup crushed peanuts

- Combine cream cheese and peanut butter, mixing well. Add sugar and milk. Fold in frozen whipped topping. Pour into pie crusts.

- Top with chocolate syrup and sprinkle with nuts. Chill until served.

Yield: 3 pies (24 servings)

Key Lime Tart

Coconut Crust

1 **cup coconut**	½ **cup graham cracker crumbs**
½ **cup gingersnap crumbs**	¼ **cup butter, melted**

- Combine coconut, crumbs and butter, mixing well. Press mixture firmly into bottom and sides of 9-inch springform pan.

Tart

4 **egg yolks**	⅓ **cup key lime juice**
1 **(14-ounce) can sweetened condensed milk**	**Lime slices, for garnish**
1 **teaspoon lime zest**	**Fresh mint, for garnish**

- Beat yolks with wire whisk until lemon color. Add milk, zest and juice, stirring well.

- Spoon into crust and chill until set. Garnish with lime slices and fresh mint.

Yield: 12 servings

Apple Pie

Pie

½ **cup butter, softened**	12 **Granny Smith apples, peeled and chopped**
½ **cup sugar**	2 **pie shells**
½ **teaspoon cinnamon**	2 **tablespoons water, divided**

- Preheat oven to 350°.

- Cream together butter, sugar and cinnamon; fold in apples. Pour apple mixture evenly into pie shells. Pour 1 tablespoon water on top of each apple dish.

Topping

⅔ **cup butter, softened**	½ **teaspoon cinnamon**
⅔ **cup brown sugar**	¾ **cup flour**

- Cream together butter and brown sugar. Add cinnamon and flour. Mixture will be crumbly. Top apples with mixture.

- Bake for 30 to 45 minutes.

Yield: 16 servings

Raspberry Cream Tart

Crust

8   **graham crackers**   ¼   **cup butter, melted**
¼   **cup firmly packed light
       brown sugar**

- Preheat oven to 375°.

- Process crackers and sugar in food processor until coarsely crumbled. Add butter and process until crumbs are moist.

- Press crumbs firmly into bottom and sides of 9-inch tart pan with removable bottom.

- Bake about 8 to 10 minutes or until crust is firm. Cool completely on wire rack.

Filling

1   **(8-ounce) package cream
       cheese, softened**
⅓   **cup sugar**
½   **cup sour cream**

2   **teaspoons fresh lemon
       juice**
½   **teaspoon vanilla**

- Beat cream cheese and sugar until smooth. Beat in sour cream, lemon juice and vanilla.

- Spread filling over crust. Chill about 5 to 6 hours or until firm.

Topping

1   **pint raspberries**   ¼   **cup seedless raspberry jam**

- Arrange raspberries over filling.

- Whisk jam in small bowl to pouring consistency. Drizzle over raspberries.

- Serve immediately or chill up to 2 hours.

Yield: 8 servings

Lemon Pie with Blueberry Topping

4	eggs	3	tablespoons all-purpose
1	(6-ounce) graham cracker		flour
	crust	½	cup buttermilk
1½	cups sugar, divided	⅓	cup fresh lemon juice
3	tablespoons unsalted	1	(1-pound) bag frozen
	butter, softened		unsweetened
2	teaspoons lemon zest		blueberries
		¾	cup blueberry jam

- Separate 1 egg, placing egg white in small bowl and egg yolk in large bowl. Whisk egg white until foamy and brush inside of crust several times, coating well. Discard remaining egg white.

- Add 1¼ cups sugar, butter and zest to egg yolk. Beat with electric mixer until well blended and smooth.

- Beat in remaining eggs one at time, blending well after each addition. Add flour, buttermilk and lemon juice, mixing well.

- Pour into crust and bake 350° for 45 minutes or until center is set.

- Toss blueberries, jam and remaining ¼ cup sugar gently, mixing well. Top individual slices of pie with blueberry mixture before serving.

Yield: 6 servings

Whether you are young or old, summer blueberry picking is a delightful way to spend early morning and late afternoon hours. Mature bushes provide lower berries for youngsters to reach as well as higher berries for the tallest picker. These thornless bushes also provide a wonderful cover for a game or two of hide-and-seek when the buckets are full.

Amaretto Crème for Fresh Fruit

4	egg yolks, lightly beaten	1	tablespoon amaretto
½	cup sugar	¼	teaspoon vanilla
2	tablespoons all-purpose		Assorted fruit (such as,
	flour		peaches and raspberries)
1	cup milk		

- Combine egg yolks, sugar and flour in medium saucepan over low heat. Add milk gradually, stirring until smooth. Cook 6 to 7 minutes, stirring constantly.

- Remove from heat.
  Stir in amaretto and vanilla.

- Cover and chill. Serve over fruit.

Yield: 1½ cups

Summer Peach Trifle

Orange Custard

2	cups milk	6	egg yolks
2	(1-inch) strips orange peel	⅓	cup sugar

- Combine milk and orange peel in 2-quart saucepan. Cook over low heat until bubbles begin to appear around edge of pan. Remove from heat and set aside.

- Beat yolks and sugar in small bowl with wire whisk until light in color. Whisk in hot milk mixture gradually until smooth; return mixture to saucepan.

- Cook over medium heat, stirring constantly, 5 minutes or until custard coats the back of a metal spoon.

- Place saucepan in bowl of ice water to stop the cooking process and prevent curdling. Stir until custard cools slightly. Remove orange peel and discard.

- Place plastic wrap on surface of custard and chill.

Trifle

1	(3-ounce) package ladyfingers	4	fully ripe peaches, peeled and sliced
½	cup orange juice	1	pint blueberries
2	tablespoons orange flavored liqueur		Frozen whipped topping
	Orange Custard		Mint sprigs, for garnish

- Layer half of ladyfingers in trifle bowl and set aside.

- Combine orange juice and liqueur. Drizzle half of orange juice mixture over ladyfingers.

- Spoon half of Orange Custard evenly over ladyfingers.

- Top with half of peaches and blueberries.

- Repeat layers in same order. Serve with frozen whipped topping and garnish with mint sprigs.

Yield: 6 to 8 servings

Orange Custard may be substituted with one (4.6-ounce) package vanilla pudding prepared according to package directions.

The rich and delicious taste of a trifle is as spectacular as its delicate appearance. Usually served in a large footed glass bowl or compote, its colorful and symmetrical arrangement is a centerpiece in itself!

Chocolate Layered Trifle

1	recipe brownies	1	(16-ounce) carton frozen
¼	cup Kahlúa		whipped topping
2	boxes chocolate mousse		Grated chocolate, for
	pie		garnish
2	cups toffee bits		Cherries, garnish

- Prepare brownies according to package directions. Fork holes in brownies and pour Kahlúa over them. Allow to set overnight. Crumble brownies.

- Prepare mousse according to package directions. (Save crusts for another use.)

- Layer half of brownies, mousse, toffee bits and frozen whipped topping in trifle bowl. Repeat layers in same order. Garnish with grated chocolate and cherries.

Yield: 12 to 14 servings

White Chocolate Coconut Tart

2	teaspoons cornstarch	8	ounces white chocolate
2	tablespoons sugar	¾	cup sweetened coconut
4	egg yolks	¾	cup heavy cream, whipped
2	tablespoons dark rum	1	baked pie shell
¼	cup water	⅓	cup toasted coconut, for
½	cup unsalted butter		garnish
2	tablespoons water		

- Heat cornstarch and sugar in double boiler. Whisk in yolks until smooth.

- Stir in rum and ¼ cup water. Continue cooking 15 to 20 minutes or until thick and smooth, taking care not to boil. Remove from double boiler and stir in butter, mixing well.

- Pour into medium bowl, cover and chill 10 minutes.

- Melt together 2 tablespoons water and white chocolate in clean double boiler. Remove from heat.

- Whisk chocolate into cornstarch mixture and chill about 45 minutes.

- Fold sweetened coconut and cream into chocolate mixture. Pour into baked pie shell and chill 2 hours. Garnish with toasted coconut.

Yield: 8 to 10 servings

Chocolate Truffle Loaf
with Raspberry Sauce

Loaf

2	cups heavy cream, divided	½	cup light corn syrup
3	egg yolks, lightly beaten	½	cup butter
2	(8-ounce) packages semi-sweet baking chocolate	¼	cup confectioners' sugar
		1	teaspoon vanilla

- Line an 8½x4½x2½-inch loaf pan with plastic wrap.

- Combine ½ cup cream with yolks, mixing well, and set aside.

- Melt chocolate, syrup and butter in double boiler over medium heat, stirring constantly. Add egg mixture. Cook 3 minutes, stirring constantly. Cool to room temperature.

- Beat remaining cream, sugar and vanilla until soft peaks form. Fold into chocolate, stirring until no streaks remain.

- Pour into prepared pan and chill overnight. Serve with Raspberry Sauce.

Raspberry Sauce

1	(10-ounce) package frozen raspberries, thawed	1	tablespoon lemon juice
2	tablespoons sugar	1	tablespoon Grand Marnier

- Drain raspberries and reserve juice.

- Combine raspberries, sugar and lemon juice. Puree in blender or food processor until smooth.

- Pour puree through strainer into bowl. Discard seeds and pulp. Add Grand Marnier and enough reserved raspberry juice to puree until desired consistency.

Yield: 12 servings

Molten Chocolate Cake
with Fudge Sauce

Cake

5	ounces bittersweet or semi-sweet chocolate, chopped	3	eggs
		3	egg yolks
10	tablespoons unsalted butter	1½	cups confectioners' sugar
		½	cup all-purpose flour

- Preheat oven to 450°. Grease six (½-cup) custard cups or soufflé dishes.

- Melt chocolate and butter in saucepan over low heat, stirring occasionally. Cook slightly and set aside.

- Whisk eggs and egg yolks in large bowl, blending well. Whisk in sugar, then chocolate mixture and flour. Pour equal amount into dishes. (Batter may be prepared one day ahead, covered and chilled.)

- Bake for 11 minutes or until sides are set but center remains somewhat liquid. Run small knife around cakes to loosen.

- Invert cakes immediately onto serving plates.

Sauce

4½	ounces bittersweet or semi-sweet chocolate, chopped	¼	cup light corn syrup
		¾	teaspoon peppermint extract
2	ounces unsweetened chocolate, chopped	½	pint raspberries, for garnish
⅓	cup hot water		Mint sprigs, for garnish

- Melt chocolates in double boiler on low heat, stirring occasionally. Add water, corn syrup and extract; whisk until smooth. Remove from water and cool slightly.

- Spoon sauce around cake and garnish with raspberries and mint sprigs.

Yield: 6 servings

Sauce may be prepared two days ahead, covered and chilled. Heat in saucepan over low heat, stirring constantly, before serving.

Heath Bar Crunch Cheesecake

Crust

1½	cups graham cracker crumbs	⅛	cup light brown sugar
6	tablespoons unsalted butter, melted	½	teaspoon vanilla extract
		1¼	cups coarsely crushed chocolate toffee

- Preheat oven to 350°.
- Combine crumbs, butter, sugar and vanilla in food processor until moist. Press into bottom and two inches up sides of 9-inch springform pan. Sprinkle toffee on bottom of crust and set aside.

Cake

3	(8-ounce) packages cream cheese, softened	2	tablespoons vanilla extract
1	cup sugar	1	cup sour cream
		4	eggs

- Beat cream cheese, sugar and vanilla in large bowl, mixing well, then beat in sour cream. Add eggs one at a time, mixing well after each addition.
- Pour into crust. Bake at 350° for 1 hour, 5 minutes or until golden on top, cracked around edges and set in center. Transfer cake to wire rack. Cool 10 minutes.

Topping

1½	cups sour cream	Coarsely crushed chocolate toffee
¼	cup sugar	
2	teaspoons vanilla	

- Whisk together sour cream, sugar and vanilla, blending well. Spoon over cake and bake at 350° for 5 minutes.
- Chill immediately, uncovered overnight. Run knife around edges of cake to loosen. Top with crushed toffee.

Yield: 10 servings

Downtown Beaufort's historic waterfront is on the Intracoastal Waterway. A highlight to all who visit is the waterfront park, a beautiful setting for children to enjoy and for parents to relax in a swing and watch the intracoastal boats come and go.

Tidalholm was built in the 1850s by Edgar Fripp, a wealthy landowner, as a summer home. It was the film site for two movies, The Big Chill *and* The Great Santini.

Tidalholm Cheesecake

Crust

1½	**cups graham cracker crumbs**
1	**teaspoon cinnamon**

6 **tablespoons butter, softened**

- Combine crumbs, cinnamon and butter, mixing well. Press crumb mixture into bottom and sides of prepared springform pan.

Cake

3 **(8-ounce) packages cream cheese, softened**
1½ **cups sugar**
5 **eggs, room temperature**
½ **teaspoon vanilla**
½ **pint heavy cream**

1 **(16-ounce) carton sour cream**
2 **tablespoons lemon, lime or almond extract or amaretto**

- Beat cream cheese, adding sugar and mixing well with electric mixer. Add eggs one at a time, mixing well after each addition. Add remaining ingredients, mixing well.

- Bake at 350° for 1 hour. Allow to remain in oven 1 hour with door closed. Allow to set at room temperature 1 hour then chill.

Yield: 8 to 10 servings

Perfect Crème Brûlée

1 **pint heavy cream**
¾ **cup sugar**

5 **eggs**
Brown sugar

- Heat cream and sugar in saucepan until sugar dissolves.

- Pour hot cream mixture over eggs and mix well.

- Strain mixture before pouring into ramekins. Place ramekins in baking pan. Pour about ½ inch of water into pan and bake 20 minutes at 350° in preheated oven..

- Top with brown sugar when set and place under broiler until sugar caramelizes.

Yield: 4 servings

Aunt Betty Ward's Bread Pudding

4	cups milk	2	egg yolks
2	cups bread cubes, crusts removed	1	egg
		⅛	teaspoon salt
1	tablespoon butter	1	teaspoon vanilla
1	cup sugar		

- Heat milk in saucepan; add bread and butter then set aside.
- Combine sugar, yolks and egg; add salt and vanilla, mixing well.
- Combine milk mixture and sugar mixture. Pour into prepared 6x9x2-inch baking dish.
- Place dish in pan of hot water. Bake at 350° for 45 minutes or until set.

Yield: 4 to 6 servings

Use 2 remaining egg whites to make meringue. Spread on bread pudding and brown in oven.

Lemon Mousse Parfaits

1	cup sugar	1	(12-ounce) container blackberries, washed
¾	cup fresh lemon juice		
6	egg yolks	1	(12-ounce) container raspberries, washed
2	eggs		
1	tablespoon lemon zest		Sugar to taste
1	(12-ounce) container strawberries, washed, hulled and halved	2	cups chilled heavy cream, divided
1	(12-ounce) container blueberries, washed		Fresh mint sprigs, for garnish

- Combine 1 cup sugar, lemon juice, yolks, eggs and zest in a double boiler. Whisk until sugar dissolves and mixture thickens.
- Chill until cool, stirring occasionally, and set aside.
- Combine berries and toss with sugar to sweeten. Spoon berries evenly into 8 parfait glasses and set aside.
- Whip cream until soft peaks form. Fold ½ cup cream into lemon mixture. Add 1 cup cream. Spoon lemon mousse evenly over berries.
- Top with a dollop of remaining cream. Garnish with mint sprigs.

Yield: 8 servings

BOURBON SAUCE FOR BREAD PUDDING

½ cup butter

1 cup confectioners' sugar

1 egg yolk, beaten

1 (5-ounce) can evaporated milk

3 teaspoons bourbon

- Combine butter, sugar, egg yolk and milk in double boiler and cook until thickened, stirring frequently.
- Remove from heat and stir in bourbon. Serve over warm bread pudding.

~

You're sure to get rave reviews for this pretty, luscious tasting dessert that can be assembled a day ahead.

Berry Baskets with Fruit

Fresh berries are a delicate way to enhance and vary the level of sweetness in a dessert. If possible, keep freshly picked berries at room temperature until serving time in order to give them that "sun-warmed right off the vine" flavor. Fresh berries should not be washed until ready for use.

Basket

6	tablespoons butter, melted
1	cup plus 1 tablespoon brown sugar
½	cup sliced almonds
9	sheets phyllo dough, thawed
3	cups assorted berries (such as, raspberries, blackberries, strawberries and blueberries)
6	tablespoons honey
3	tablespoons lemon juice

- Preheat oven to 375°.
- Brush muffin cups with butter.
- Combine brown sugar and almonds and set aside.
- Stack phyllo sheets on cutting board and quarter. Press 1 sheet phyllo in bottom of each muffin cup; brush with butter and sprinkle with brown sugar mixture. Repeat process 2 more times, so that each cup has 3 phyllo layers. Bake for 10 minutes.
- Remove from muffin cups and cool.
- Combine berries, honey and lemon juice, tossing gently to coat.
- Fill each phyllo basket with berries and cover with desired topping.

Vanilla Spice Topping

3	teaspoons vanilla
1½	cups sour cream
¾	teaspoon nutmeg

- Combine vanilla, sour cream and nutmeg, mixing well. Chill until ready to serve.

Lime Curd Topping

2	egg yolks
3	eggs
1	cup sugar
½	cup fresh lime juice
1	tablespoon lime zest
½	cup unsalted butter, softened

- Combine yolks and next 4 ingredients in glass saucepan over low heat. Whisk until thickened and coats the back of a spoon, being careful not to boil. Remove from heat and whisk in butter. Chill until ready to serve.

Yield: 12 servings

Beaufort's Best Cookie

1	cup butter, softened	3¼	cups all-purpose flour
2	cups light brown sugar	1	cup oatmeal
1	egg, beaten	1	cup crispy rice cereal
1	teaspoon vanilla	1	cup pecan pieces
1	cup cooking oil	1	cup chocolate mini-morsels

- Cream butter with electric mixer on medium speed. Gradually add sugar, then egg, vanilla and oil, mixing well after each addition. Add flour, mixing well.

- Stir in oatmeal, cereal, pecans and chocolate, blending well.

- Drop by rounded teaspoonfuls on prepared baking sheet. Flatten each cookie with fork dipped in cool water.

- Bake one baking sheet at a time at 325° for 15 minutes.

- Turn cookies onto wax paper to cool.

Yield: 10 dozen

Cookies may be frozen in air-tight container.

"Our family was blessed to be a part of Beaufort Academy from its very beginning, and our memories of those early days are rich. There is nothing as exciting as being pioneers!"

Mrs. Neil Trask, Jr.
Beaufort Academy
parent and friend

Lace Cookies

1	cup instant oatmeal	1½	teaspoons vanilla
1	cup sugar	1	egg, lightly beaten
½	teaspoon salt	½	teaspoon orange juice
3	tablespoons flour	6	ounces chocolate morsels
½	cup butter, softened		

- Line baking sheets with aluminum foil.

- Mix oats and next 4 ingredients by hand and set aside.

- Combine vanilla, egg and juice in small bowl, mixing well. Add to oat mixture, stirring well.

- Drop twelve to fourteen (½ teaspoonfuls) of dough on baking sheet.

- Bake at 350° for 8 to 10 minutes. Allow to cool then peel from foil.

- Melt chocolate morsels in double boiler. Frost bottom of cookie with chocolate then place another cookie on top to make a sandwich.

Yield: 4 dozen

Approximately 30 plantations had frontage on Land's End Road on St. Helena in the mid-1800s. The Chapel of Ease, sometimes called "the Old White Church", was built around 1740 as an extension of St. Helena parish. It provided a place of worship for area planters, who otherwise had to travel into Beaufort for worship services. The beautiful tabby ruins are worth an afternoon visit.

Molasses Cookies

¾	cup cooking oil	2	cups all-purpose flour
1	cup sugar	1	teaspoon cinnamon
¼	cup molasses	½	teaspoon salt
1	egg		Sugar, for garnish
2	teaspoons baking soda		

- Combine oil and remaining ingredients in medium bowl, mixing well.
- Shape dough into walnut-size ball and roll in sugar.
- Bake at 375° for 8 to 10 minutes.

Yield: 3 dozen

Decadent Chocolate Cookies

16	squares semi-sweet baking chocolate, divided	2	eggs
		1	teaspoon vanilla
¾	cup firmly packed brown sugar	½	cup all-purpose flour
		¼	teaspoon baking powder
¼	cup butter, softened	2	cups chopped pecans

- Preheat oven to 350°.
- Grate coarsely 8 chocolate squares.
- Microwave remaining 8 squares on high 1 to 2 minutes, stirring until chocolate melts.
- Add sugar, butter, eggs and vanilla. Stir in flour and baking powder. Add grated chocolate and pecans.
- Drop by rounded teaspoonfuls on ungreased baking sheet.
- Bake for 12 to 13 minutes or until cookies are puffed and set. Cool on baking sheet 1 minute before transferring to wire rack.

Yield: 1½ dozen

White Chocolate Macadamia Nut Cookies

2	cups all-purpose flour		2	eggs
1	teaspoon baking soda		1	teaspoon vanilla
1½	teaspoons salt		¾	cup macadamia nuts, chopped
½	cup butter, softened			
1	cup brown sugar		9	ounces white chocolate morsels
½	cup sugar			

- Combine flour, baking soda and salt in large bowl and set aside.

- Cream butter and sugars until smooth. Add eggs one at a time, mixing well after each addition. Add vanilla, mixing well.

- Add flour mixture slowly to butter mixture with electric mixer on low speed until well blended.

- Stir in nuts and chocolate by hand.

- Drop by rounded teaspoonfuls on prepared baking sheet.

- Bake at 350° for 10 to 12 minutes or until edges are golden brown.

Yield: 2 to 3 dozen

Using a cookie scoop is the ultimate way to drop cookies; however, if you do not own a scoop, try using two spoons— one to scoop the dough and the other to remove dough from the first spoon and drop onto the baking sheet. Both methods will speed your preparation.

Cary Cookies

12	ounces semi-sweet chocolate morsels		1	cup all-purpose flour
¼	cup butter		1	cup chopped pecans
1	(14-ounce) can sweetened condensed milk		1	teaspoon vanilla
			1	tablespoon Kahlúa
			36	pecan halves

- Preheat oven to 350°.

- Melt morsels, butter and condensed milk in microwave.

- Add flour and pecans, stirring well. Add vanilla and Kahlúa.

- Drop by rounded teaspoonfuls on ungreased baking sheet. Top each cookie with pecan half.

- Bake for 9 to 10 minutes. Allow to cool on wire rack.

Yield: 3 dozen

Cookies may be frozen in air-tight container.

Melting Moments

Cookies

1	cup butter	½	cup cornstarch
5½	tablespoons confectioners' sugar	¼	teaspoon almond extract
1¼	cups all-purpose flour	¼	teaspoon orange extract

- Cream butter and sugar with electric mixer.
- Sift in flour and cornstarch and mix well.
- Stir in extracts. Wrap in plastic wrap and chill 1 hour.
- Shape into small balls, being careful not to allow dough to become too warm.
- Place on greased baking sheet 2 inches apart. Flatten to ¼-inch thickness with bottom of a glass.
- Bake at 350° for 8 to 10 minutes, being careful not to brown.
- Spread Sugar Glaze over warm cookies.

Sugar Glaze

1　cup confectioners' sugar
1　tablespoon butter, melted
1　tablespoon lemon juice
1　tablespoon orange juice

- Combine ingredients in medium bowl, mixing well.

Butter Crisps

1   cup sugar
1   cup butter, softened
1   egg yolk
2   teaspoons vanilla

      Pinch of salt
2   cups all-purpose flour
1   egg white
1   cup pecans, chopped

- Cream sugar and butter; beat in yolk.

- Add vanilla, salt and flour, blending until smooth.

- Spread thin layer of dough into prepared 11x15-inch pan.

- Beat egg white until stiff and spread on top of dough.

- Press pecans into dough.

- Bake at 275° for 45 minutes. Cut into squares while hot. Cool in pan.

Yield: 100 cookies

Butter Crisps may be stored and frozen in zip-top plastic bags.

Tea–riffic Truffles

1   (12-ounce) package semi-sweet chocolate morsels
1   tablespoon rum, brandy, Kahlúa or amaretto

1   can dark chocolate ready-to-spread frosting
1-2   cups finely crushed nuts, chocolate sprinkles or unsweetened cocoa

- Melt morsels in saucepan over low heat, stirring constantly. Remove from heat.

- Stir in liquor and frosting, blending well.

- Chill 2 hours or until firm.

- Place nuts, sprinkles or cocoa in pie pan. Shape chocolate into 1-inch balls and roll to coat.

- Serve in foil candy cups.

Yield: 6 dozen

Refrigerate if not served immediately.

EASY AS 1-2-3 COOKIES

1 (18.25-ounce) package yellow cake mix
½ cup cooking oil
2 eggs
1 cup semi-sweet chocolate morsels
½ cup pecans, chopped

- Beat cake mix, oil and eggs in large bowl at medium speed with electric mixer until batter is smooth.

- Stir in morsels and pecans.

- Drop by rounded teaspoonfuls onto ungreased baking sheets.

- Bake at 350° for 8 to 10 minutes.

Yield: 4 dozen

To toast benne seeds, bake in preheated 350° oven until golden brown. You may also roast seeds in a skillet on top of the stove.

Sarah's Benne Cookies

1	(16-ounce) package light brown sugar	½	teaspoon salt
¾	cup butter, softened	¾	cup flour, sifted
1	egg, beaten	1	teaspoon vanilla
½	teaspoon baking powder	1	cup toasted benne seeds

- Preheat oven to 325°.
- Cream brown sugar and butter. Add egg. Stir in baking powder, salt and flour, mixing well. Add vanilla and benne seeds.
- Drop by demitasse spoon onto baking sheet lined with foil.
- Bake for 10 to 15 minutes or until golden brown. (Keep a watchful eye on cookies, as cookies easily burn.)
- Cool completely before removing from baking sheet.

Yield: 6 dozen

Cookies may be stored in an air-tight tin.

Cool Key Lime Squares

½	cup butter, softened	3	tablespoons key lime juice
1	cup all-purpose flour	3	tablespoons all-purpose flour
⅓	cup confectioners' sugar	½	teaspoon baking powder
¼	teaspoon salt	¼	teaspoon salt
2	eggs	1½	teaspoons lime zest
1	cup sugar		

- Cut butter into flour, confectioners' sugar and salt using blender until mixture is crumbly. Press crumbs gently into bottom of 9-inch baking pan.
- Bake at 350° for 15 minutes or until golden brown.
- Combine eggs and remaining ingredients, mixing well 1 to 2 minutes. Pour over crust.
- Bake at 350° for 20 minutes or until center is set. Cool completely before cutting.

Yield: 24 servings

Bite-Size Pecan Pies

1	(18.5-ounce) box yellow cake mix	1⅓	cups dark corn syrup
½	cup butter, softened	1	teaspoon vanilla
1	egg	3	eggs, beaten
⅔	cup firmly packed brown sugar	1	cup pecans, coarsely chopped

- Set aside ⅔ cup cake mix.
- Combine remaining cake mix, butter and 1 egg. Stir with fork until coarse crumbs form. Press crumbs gently into bottom of greased 12x9-inch baking pan.
- Bake at 350° for 15 minutes until golden brown.
- Combine ⅔ cup cake mix, brown sugar, corn syrup, vanilla and beaten eggs with electric mixer on medium speed 2 minutes. Pour over crust and sprinkle with pecans.
- Bake for 35 minutes or until center is set. Cool completely before cutting into 1-inch squares.

Yield: 48 servings

Chocolate Almond Crunch

1	cup butter	2	cups finely chopped almonds, toasted and divided
1⅓	cups sugar		
1	tablespoon light corn syrup	2	cups semi-sweet chocolate morsels, melted
½	teaspoon almond extract		
3	tablespoons water		

- Melt butter in large saucepan. Add sugar, corn syrup, extract and water, cooking over medium heat until candy reaches 300°. (Use candy thermometer to measure temperature.) Add one cup almonds.
- Pour and spread into prepared baking sheet. Allow to cool.
- Spread melted chocolate evenly atop candy.
- Sprinkle remaining almonds over chocolate.
- Cool completely before removing and breaking into pieces.

Yield: 1½ pounds

THE PECAN

Crisp like the fall days during their harvest,

Crunchy like hundreds of curled brown leaves

On the ground beneath my feet.

Walking along the seemingly empty orchard,

A lumpy burlap sack slung heavily on my shoulder,

And the taste of a delicious papershell pecan on my lips.

~ Anonymous

Auntie M's Brownies

1	cup butter	4	eggs
4	tablespoons cocoa	2	teaspoons vanilla
3	cups sugar	1	cup nuts, chopped
2	cups self-rising flour		

- Melt butter in large saucepan. Remove from heat and stir in remaining ingredients. Pour into prepared 9x13-inch baking pan.
- Bake at 350° for 35 to 40 minutes. Cool at least 30 minutes before cutting into squares.

Yield: 24 servings

Brownies may be served with a scoop of vanilla ice cream and topped with raspberry sauce for a formal occasion.

"This recipe was requested so often by the Beaufort Academy Class of 1997, that the recipe was dedicated to them and printed in their Senior annual."

Sharon Sanders
Beaufort Academy
parent

~

Aunt Martha B's Christmas Fudge

1	(24-ounce) package semi-sweet chocolate morsels	1	(13-ounce) can evaporated milk
1½	cups butter	3	tablespoons vanilla
4	cups sugar	2	cups crushed pecans

- Line 17x11-inch jelly-roll pan with wax paper.
- Place morsels and butter in medium glass mixing bowl and set aside.
- Bring sugar and milk to a boil. Continue to boil 6 minutes, stirring constantly and reducing heat to prevent boiling over. Pour over morsels and butter.
- Add vanilla and beat to thick consistency 5 to 10 minutes.
- Add nuts and pour into jelly-roll pan.
- Refrigerate overnight. Cut into small squares. Store in refrigerator.

Yield: 15 dozen

"Night on the Town", sponsored by Mainstreet Beaufort, USA, falls on the first Friday in December and kicks off a month of festive downtown shopping and free parking! On Sunday the Christmas Parade delivers Santa and Mrs. Claus atop Beaufort's 1955 American La France Fire Engine to everyone's delight.

Lighthouse Bars

Crust

½	cup butter
5	tablespoons cocoa
¼	cup sugar
1	egg, beaten
½	teaspoon vanilla
2	cups graham cracker crumbs

- Melt butter in saucepan; add cocoa and sugar, stirring frequently. Add egg and vanilla, continuing to stir. Add crumbs and mix well.

- Press mixture into bottom of prepared 9x9-inch baking pan and chill.

Filling

1¼	cups confectioners' sugar
½	cup butter, softened
3	tablespoons custard dessert mix

- Beat sugar, butter and custard powder together to form a smooth dough.

- Spread over crust and chill.

Topping

3	semi-sweet chocolate squares
2	tablespoons butter
	Few drops of vanilla

- Melt chocolate, butter and vanilla in saucepan. Pour over filling, working quickly to get a smooth, even layer.

- Cover and chill until set. Cut into bars and keep refrigerated.

Yield: 24 servings

Custard dessert mix is found in the gelatin and pudding section of the grocery.

The first lighthouse built on Hunting Island in 1859 was destroyed by Federal troops in the War Between the States. The second lighthouse was built in 1875. It has since been moved to its present location due to erosion. Today visitors are welcome to visit and climb the spiral staircase to the observation deck and enjoy the view.

**THICK AND RICH
HOT FUDGE SAUCE**

4 (1-ounce) squares
semi-sweet chocolate

2 tablespoons butter

1 (14-ounce) can
sweetened condensed
milk

1 teaspoon vanilla

Dash of salt

• Melt chocolate and
butter in saucepan over
low heat. Stir in
remaining ingredients.

• Cook, stirring
constantly, about
5 minutes or until
mixture thickens.

Yield: 1⅔ cups

**Sauce may be
refrigerated then
reheated over low heat,
stirring constantly.**

Peppermint Ice Cream

6	eggs	Few drops of peppermint
3	cups sugar	extract
4	cups heavy cream	Few drops of red food
3	cups milk	coloring

• Process eggs and sugar in food processor until thick and frothy.

• Transfer to large bowl and fold in cream and milk. Add peppermint extract and food coloring.

• Churn until frozen.

Yield: 1 gallon or 20 servings

Serve with Thick and Rich Hot Fudge Sauce.

Lemon Ice Cream

3	lemons	1½	cups sugar
2	cups milk		Pinch of salt
2	cups half-and-half	1	teaspoon vanilla

• Grate rind of 1 lemon and juice all lemons.

• Combine zest, juice and remaining ingredients and freeze according to freezer instructions.

Yield: 2 quarts

Peach Ice Cream

9	fresh peeled and pitted peaches, mashed	½	pint heavy cream, whipped
3	cups sugar	1	pint half-and-half
			Sprinkle of salt

• Combine peaches and remaining ingredients and freeze according to freezer instructions.

Yield: 2 quarts

Cinnamon Ice Cream

14   egg yolks
1½   cups sugar
½   teaspoon salt
3½   cups half-and-half
3   cups heavy cream

¼   cup apple brandy
1½   teaspoons vanilla
2   teaspoons cinnamon
     Dash of nutmeg

- Beat egg yolks, sugar and salt with mixer until light and fluffy; set aside.

- Heat half-and-half in double boiler, being careful not to boil. Add egg yolk mixture to double boiler, stirring constantly until custard coats back of spoon. Do not boil. Remove from heat and set aside.

- Stir apple brandy, vanilla, cinnamon and nutmeg into cream and mix thoroughly. Add to custard and mix well.

- Pour through fine mesh strainer before freezing.

- Freeze according to ice cream maker instructions

Yield: ½ gallon

Delicious served with Apple Pie.

"For over nineteen years, my special place was Beaufort Academy. Not only were my children educated there, but I was also employed in the office. I watched this community of children, parents and staff grow in status, wisdom and character."

Norma Duncan
Beaufort Academy
parent and friend

Mocha Icing

½   cup butter, softened
1   teaspoon instant coffee
     (dissolved in 1 teaspoon
     hot water)
6   tablespoons cocoa
7   tablespoons evaporated
     milk

1   (16-ounce) box
     confectioners' sugar
¼   cup chopped pecans or
     walnuts (optional)

- Blend butter and next 4 ingredients until fluffy. Fold in nuts.

Yield: frosts a 3-layer cake

A quick tip for a mom on the run—this Mocha Icing on your favorite commercially prepared pound cake will dazzle your guests.

*Time and Tide
wait for no one.*

Strawberry Ice Cream Glaze

4	tablespoons balsamic vinegar	1	dozen strawberries, hulled and quartered
4	tablespoons packed light brown sugar		Vanilla ice cream

- Heat vinegar and sugar in small saucepan over medium heat, stirring until sugar is dissolved.
- Simmer about 1 minute. Remove from heat and add strawberries, tossing to coat.
- Serve strawberries over ice cream.

Yield: 4 servings

Hard Sauce

½	cup butter, softened	Brandy or bourbon to taste (optional)
1½	cups brown sugar	
1	teaspoon vanilla	

- Beat butter and sugar together with fork. Add vanilla, mixing well. Add brandy or bourbon if desired.
- Store at room temperature.

Yield: about 1½ cups sauce

Serve with apple pie or over ice cream.

The *Full Moon, High Tide* Committee would like to express our appreciation to the families and friends of Beaufort Academy who shared their recipes with us. The Cookbook Committee received more than 1,500 recipes for consideration and these were triple tested for accuracy. We regret that we were unable to include all recipes submitted due to similarity or availability of space.

Achurch, Laura
Aimar, Ginger L.
Aitken, Pat
Akins, Jeff
Alderman, Dana
Anderson, Julia
Ashley, Marie
Ayers, Elizabeth
Babalis, Judy
Baker, Laura
Barnard, Fran
Baysden, Cindy
Bellamy, Bette
Booth, Erin
Boulware, Beth
Bowen, Julie
Brown, Linda
Brown, Nancy
Brown, Alise Tuttle
Brown, Emaline K.
Campsen, Lalla Lee
Cavendish, Susan
Cecil, Bettye
Clark, Genine
Collins, Cindy
Cook, Cameron
Cook, Chandler

Cook, Gloria
Copps, Mrs. James F.
Corley, Joy
Counts, Sandra Harley
Creely, Joyce
Crockett, Naomi
Crossman, Alison V.
Cummins, Barbara S.
Cummins, Jody
Dalton, Bill
Danielson, Mary Ward
Danielson, Ward
Danielson, Janette
Dardes, Elizabeth
Davis, Lore' Dorr
Deane, Harlene
Deaton, Janet
Della-Volle, Susan
Dennis, Nancy
Domby, Sally
Dorr, Cecile Holloway
Dukes, Marvin H.
Duncan, Norma P.
DuRant, Peggy
Dyson, Sarah
Edmonds, Karen M.
Edwards, Stephanie

Emerson, Mrs. George Waldo
Evans, Doadie
Evans, Jennifer V.
Eversole, Anne W.
Feeser, Jeni Cecil
Ferry, Nancy
Frazer, Carolie
Frierson, Margaret
Gambla, June
Garrett, Marguerite
Gately, Mrs. Stock
Gerwig, Kelli Landes
Gibson, Shera Lynne
Gibson, Wendy
Givens, Nicole
Grace, Beth
Grace, Katherine S.
Gray, Kelly
Haffey, Kay
Hand, Patsy
Harris, Kathy
Hartzog, Evelyn
Hatcher, Caroline
Hayes, Sara
Hines, Kate
Hirleman, Cheryl
Hodges, Kathy

Horsley, Jean M.

Howell, Sissy

Hurt, Gray

Jahn, Holly Healy

Jennings, David

Johnson, Sandy

Kern, Sarah

Kilgore, A.J.

Kilgore, Kathy

Konoza, Holly Jean

Koppernaes, Robin

Kraft, Amy

Laffitte, Mary

Laffitte, Darryl R.

Lampright, Bruce

Larson, Grace

Lewis, Mary Jo

Mack, Connie

Manos, Jane

Manos, Peter

Mark, Robyn

Marshall, Erika

Marshall, Sally Stephenson

McClaine, Jim

McDonough, Karen

McElveen, Sharon Aimar

McElwee, Mrs. Joe

Middleton, Mary E.

Mix, Vicki

Mix, Lin

Morrissey, Carol

Mozley, Janet

Myrick, Sandra Aimar

O'Connell, Sean

O'Farrell, Fleetwood

Oliphant, Margaret

O'Neill, Nikki

O'Neill, Liz

Olsson, Kimberly

Olsson, Alyce

Parks, Wanda

Pate, Debbie

Patterson, Pat

Post, Sally

Reichel, Ty

Rentz, Jo Ella

Rentz, Christina C.

Rentz, Rhoda G.

Rhodin, Maura Connelly

Roddey, Emma Moore

Rountree, Paige Lewis

Runyan, Beth

Rutter, Woody

Sanders, Sharon

Sanders, Fran

Sheiley, Carol

Shuford, Sue

Smith, Archer Lee

Smith, Ken

Smith, Patricia

Snow, Ada

Spearman, Starr

Spears, Lillian

Speights, Judy

Stanley, Sharon

Stockell, Charles

Tatum, Mary

Taylor, Jimmy

Tedder, Anne

Thompson, Suzanne Klatt

Threatt, Cathy

Tompkins, Sallie

Towle, Middy

Trask, Margaret Scheper

Trask, Kim Edmonds

Trask, Julie R.

Trask, Donna B.

Trask, Laura

Trask, Priscilla Aimar

Trask, Sally

Trask, Becky

Treneff, Amy

Trogdon, Susan

Trumps, Blanche

Trumps, Christi

Tucker, Trea

Turcotte, Sandra

Vadyak, Kimberly

Vinoski, Marsha

Walsh, Priscilla

Waskiewicz, Betty Logan

Webb, Martha Lynn

Webb, Charles

Webb, Leith

Westcob, Alan

Westcob, Charlotte

Whitaker, Beverly

White, Cinta

Wise, Carol

Wise, Tara

Wise, Edward

Wood, Marcia

Wreden, Bonita

Wunder, Donna

Young, Dyan

Index

G

FULL MOON, HIGH TIDE

Tastes and Traditions of the Lowcountry

Post Office Box 70131
Beaufort, SC 29902
Phone 1-843-470-0078
Fax 1-843-470-0079

Please send me _____ copies of FULL MOON, HIGH TIDE   @ $22.95 each _____

Postage and handling   @ $ 3.00 each _____

TOTAL $ _____

Name _____

Address _____

City _____ State _____ Zip _____

*Make checks payable to: **BA/Full Moon, High Tide***

Or, please charge to my   (circle one)   Visa   MasterCard

Card Number _____ Expiration Date _____

Signature of Authorization _____

- -

FULL MOON, HIGH TIDE

Tastes and Traditions of the Lowcountry

Post Office Box 70131
Beaufort, SC 29902
Phone 1-843-470-0078
Fax 1-843-470-0079

Please send me _____ copies of FULL MOON, HIGH TIDE   @ $22.95 each _____

Postage and handling   @ $ 3.00 each _____

TOTAL $ _____

Name _____

Address _____

City _____ State _____ Zip _____

*Make checks payable to: **BA/Full Moon, High Tide***

Or, please charge to my   (circle one)   Visa   MasterCard

Card Number _____ Expiration Date _____

Signature of Authorization _____